TYPE VII U-boats

TYPE VII U-boats

ROBERT C. STERN

◀ It was usual for an officer of the flotilla staff to address the crew on the deck aft of the tower before the crew was released from duty to go ashore. The sprays of flowers or leaves decorating the tower were a typical touch. After a month or more at sea, the crew appreciated anything fresh that didn't smell of U-boat. (ECPA)

BROCKHAMPTON PRESS
LONDON

This is for Beth, not only smart and beautiful, but extraordinarily patient as well.

This edition published 1998 by Brockhampton Press,
an imprint of The Caxton Publishing Group
Reprint 2002

ISBN 1 86019 8554

Arms and Armour Press
An Imprint of the Cassell Group
Wellington House, 125 Strand, London WC2R 0BB

First published in 1991

British Library Cataloguing in Publication Data: a catalogue record for this book is available from the British Library.

Designed and edited by DAG Publications Ltd. Designed by David Gibbons; edited by Michael Boxall; layout by Anthony A. Evans; typeset by Ronset Typesetters Ltd, Darwen, Lancashire; Camerawork by M&E Reproductions, North Fambridge, Essex;
Printed at Oriental Press, Dubai, U.A.E.

Notes

The following shorthand is used to save space in the footnotes:

Conduct of the War at Sea	Conduct
Kriegstagebuch des BdU	KTB
The Sea Wolves	SW
U-Boat Commander	CO
Interview – Willi Brinkmann	WB
Interview – Eberhard von Ketelhodt	EvK
Interview – Werner Hirschmann	WH
The Tenth Fleet	10th
Technical Mission Report – Snorkel	TR-S
Il Radar: la guerra sui mare	Arena
Naval Radars	NavRad
Ten Years and Twenty Days	10 Years
U-Boat War in the Atlantic	Atl

Photograph Credits

The photographs used in this book came from a variety of sources. For the most part these are official sources. Much of the official German photographic material from the Second World War was held at the US National Archives immediately after the war and much of it was copied before it was returned. This has been my primary source. Other photographs came from the private collections of U-boat survivors or others who have a personal interest in U-boats. When the credit 'via X' is used without further credit, it indicates that the photograph came from X's personal collection and I have no idea what the original source was. In those cases where there's no credit at all, it is purely the fault of my sometimes imperfect record keeping. The explanation of the abbreviations I have used in the photo credits follow:

Ahme	Jochen Ahme
Albrecht	Johan Albrecht
Baker	Arthur D. Baker III
ECPA	Etablissement Cinématographique et Photographique des Armées, Fort d'Ivry, Ivry-sur-Seine, France.
GW	Germania Werft, Kiel.
MacPherson	Ken MacPherson
NARA	US National Archives & Records Adm., Washington, DC.
Rumpf	Ed Rumpf
Schmidt	Ernst Schmidt
SFL	US Submarine Force Library, Groton, CT.
USAF	US Air Force, Defense Audio-Visual Agency, Washington, DC.
USN	US Navy, Naval Photographic Center, Washington, DC.
v. Ketelhodt	Eberhard von Ketelhodt

Contents

Preface

The Type VII U-boat was the quintessential U-boat, the one that comes to mind whenever the subject of the Battle of the Atlantic in the Second World War is raised. Its capabilities determined the dimensions of that critical battle; its weaknesses and the ability of the Allies to exploit those weaknesses led in good part to the ultimate defeat of Germany. Incredibly, its greatest successes occurred when there were very few Type VIIs available for action. The 'Happy Times' ('Fette Jahre') that began in mid-1940 came when there were often no more than ten Type VIIs available for operations at any one time. Later, when ten times that number or more were operational, the successes would be relatively fewer and farther between.

Like any story of rise and fall, the story of the Type VII U-boat is a fascinating one, full of drama and laced throughout with tales of extraordinary action. It is a complex story, with multiple themes and subthemes and side plots that could be followed in almost any direction. We chose here very carefully among those plots and themes to tell just one part of this U-boat's story.

This is not an operational history of the Type VII U-boat, though parts of some typical operations will be described to illustrate a point. It is equally not a design history, though many aspects of the evolution of the design will be outlined. Rather this book attempts to present a detailed technical description of the Type VII as a weapons system.

The concept of a weapons system is a modern one, having evolved only in the last few decades in response to the increasing complexity of current weaponry. Nevertheless, the Type VII U-boat very much fits the modern definition. A weapons system is a combination of discrete subsystems that, working together, allow the delivery of a weapon against a target at a chosen time and place. This book looks at the Type VII U-boat from just such a perspective. Like all modern weapons systems, the Type VII U-boat had certain characteristic elements (propulsion, guidance, sensors, weapons, etc.) which permitted it to perform its mission: the sinking of enemy shipping. Those individual elements will be described in detail and the way in which they worked together as a system to allow the carrying out of that mission will be shown. Whenever possible, descriptions of technical details are accompanied by narrative sections taken from recollections of U-boat crew survivors, which illustrate how the systems worked.

Being a technical history, this book will describe in detail the technological war fought by and against the Type VII U-boats. This technical thrust and parry, fought as much by scientists and engineers as by warriors, had a drama all its own. It was composed not only of what was actually done or not done, but equally of what was believed and not believed. Each side tried desperately to gain the crucial technical advantage that could tip the scales of war in its favour. In this struggle they employed any means to determine the true capabilities of the opposing side and any deception to hide their own. And, based on their beliefs, they planned new weapons or sensors that pushed beyond the enemy's presumed capabilities. As the war turned against Germany, this led to experimentation with systems that were often years ahead of their time. As each system in the boat is described in the following text, the relevant aspects of these technical strokes and counterstrokes will be detailed.

Acknowledgements

The material used to put this book together has been accumulated over the years, much of it through hours spent in archives in Washington, DC; New London, Connecticut; Ottawa, Canada; and Koblenz, West Germany. Much of the remainder has been acquired through the kind offices of many friends and associates who shared my consuming interest in U-boats. I don't know where to start on this acknowledgement of debt, but certainly could find no better starting-point than to thank Ken MacPherson of Toronto, Canada, for opening up his extensive photo collection to me, for introducing me to many of his acquaintances among the U-boat survivor community and for sharing his awesome knowledge of this subject. Among the U-boat survivors I have had the pleasure to meet or correspond with, I should like to thank several for patiently answering my numerous questions. This list includes Eberhard von Ketelhodt (CO, *U712*), Willi Brinkmann (IWO, *U534*), Ernst Schmidt (IWO, *U821*), Werner Hirschmann (LI, *U190*), Wolfgang Hirschfeld (Funker, *U109*), Johan Albrecht and Gerhard Beck.

Additionally, I should like to thank several others, including Ed Rumpf, Arthur D. Baker III, Bruce Culver, Dana Bell and Bob Cressman. I have quite possibly left off a name or two that should be on this list. Allow me to apologize in advance to any I have neglected to mention.

The many who have contributed directly or indirectly to this effort have all helped to make it a more complete work. Any errors that may be found here, however, are solely the responsibility of the author.

Introduction

With the defeat of Imperial Germany in 1918, the first great U-boat offensive came to an end. The First World War had been caused by a myriad of factors, not the least of which was a rivalry in naval construction between Germany and Great Britain. The young Imperial German Navy, under the guiding hand of von Tirpitz and supported by an ambitious Crown, had the impudence to challenge the long-standing naval supremacy of the British by attempting to build a fleet of modern battleships and battlecruisers. In the end, however, the monies spent by Germany on her massive capital ships proved to have been wasted. The effective commercial blockade established by the Royal Navy was never seriously threatened by Imperial Germany's battle fleet. Instead of the magnificent dreadnoughts, Germany's most potent naval weapon turned out to be the submarine.

The Germany Navy had been among the last to show interest in the first primitive submersibles that began to appear soon after the start of the twentieth century. In 1908, when Germany had just two experimental U-boats, France and Great Britain each had more than 60 submarines. By the time war broke out in 1914, Germany still had only twenty operational boats, though most of these were comparatively large, fast sea-going craft.

The course of that war is well known and need not be recounted here. Suffice it to say that the U-boats of the Imperial German Navy played havoc with the merchant shipping upon which England, as an island nation, so heavily depended. German U-boats sank more than 18,000,000 tons of merchant shipping, threatening to cut England's supply lines and starve that nation into surrender. In February 1917, Germany's U-boats were finally freed from all political restrictions and allowed to sink merchant shipping without warning. The immediate rise in sinkings to 600,000 tons a month forced the Royal Navy to respond to the threat. The devastation continued until a pair of tactical and technical innovations combined effectively to counter the U-boat offensive. The British had started the war with no adequate anti-submarine weapon, but eventually hit upon the depth-charge (called Wasserbombe, or wabo, by the Germans) which was first deployed in July 1916. But the depth-charge was useful as a weapon only if the warship carrying it were near the attacking U-boat, and the British system of independently sailing merchant shipping scattered the Royal Navy's anti-submarine forces to such an extent that armed escorts encountered U-boats only by chance. It was only the May 1917 decision to institute a convoy system that made the depth-charge an effective weapon. Now, the U-boats had to come to the escorts, rather than the other way round. Additionally, since U-boats hunted alone in individual zones of operations, the clustering of merchant shipping into convoys meant that most U-boats could now pass an entire patrol without seeing a target unless by chance they intercepted a convoy. The cumulative result of these changes was a sharp drop in merchant shipping losses and an appreciable increase in U-boat sinkings. By autumn 1917, the U-boat offensive had been contained.

By the end of the war, the defeat of the U-boats had been so decisive that many naval experts thought that the submarine had been discredited as an effective weapon of war. Add to this the immediate post-war development of ASDIC (Sonar) echo location devices and one can understand how that conclusion could be reached by reasonable men. In the 1930s, with war looming once more, the Royal Navy held a series of exercises to test the thesis that submarines were no longer a serious threat to Britain's survival. Again and again, they proved to their own satisfaction that individual submarines, hunting alone, would be no more effective than they had been at the end of the war. Unfortunately, this led to a complacency that, if anything, put Britain at even greater risk than before and helps account, in part, for the initial successes of U-boats during the Second World War. Apparently the British failed to consider that perhaps the rules of the

▲ The *sine qua non* of much of the photography in this book, the *Kriegsberichter* (war correspondent), at the left in this photograph. These enlisted reporters doubled as photographers, carrying their trusty Zeiss 35mm cameras to the docks and, occasionally, on patrols. At sea photography was

more likely the work of someone like the fellow at the right, a U-boatman who was skilled enough with a camera to be allowed to record the proceedings. (NARA)

game might be changed by the other side; that the Germans wouldn't blindly repeat the mistakes of the previous war.

The story of the initial success and ultimate failure of the Type VII U-boat during the Second World War has many similarities to the rise and fall of the fortunes of the German U-boat during the first war. In both cases the U-boats achieved their great success against an enemy who was materially and psychologically unprepared to combat the threat they presented, and, in both cases, they were ultimately defeated by a combination of tactical and material innovations that completely altered the basis of that initial success.

Note: Reference is made throughout this text to a person known as BdU. The reference is to the position of *Befehlshaber der Uboote*, literally Commander-in-Chief (CinC) Submarines. This position was created on 1 October 1939 and was occupied from the start by Konteradmiral Karl Dönitz, the leader of the U-boat arm from the time of its public announcement in 1935. The position brought together the tactical command of U-boats in the Atlantic and planning responsibility for the growth and development of the U-boat fleet. When Dönitz was named to the position of C-in-C Kriegsmarine in 1943, his long-time assistant, Admiral von Friedeburg, replaced him as BdU. Von Friedeburg was replaced in turn by Admiral Godt in the closing days of the war.

Part One: Design Genesis

If sheer numbers are any criterion for success, the Type VII U-boat was easily the most successful submarine design of its day. As with all successful designs, its configuration wasn't arrived at by chance. Its parameters and characteristics owe equal debt to a series of design antecedents and to a set of operational requirements that defined a boat of just this size and shape and no other.

Direct Antecedents

The lineage of the Type VII U-boat runs all the way back to the first German U-boat, *U1*, of 1906. But the direct inheritance came from a trio of small and medium-sized U-boat types built or projected during the second half of the First World War. The first of these types was the UBIII series of sea-going submarines that was initiated with the launching of *UB48* in 1917. The UBs were conceived as coastal boats, intended to operate in the confined waters of the North Sea and Baltic. The first series, the UBIs of 1915, were indeed small boats with a surface displacement of 127 tons, two small-diameter (45cm) torpedo tubes and a range commensurate with their small size. Their design was in reaction to the increasing size and, even more seriously, the increasing building time of the 'mainstream' U-boats under development. The Germans needed many more U-boats than could be provided by building only full-sized boats, and they were willing to accept considerable reduction in capability to get more boats as quickly as possible. The resulting UBIs proved to be handy boats that quickly built up a good record, but they were simply too small. After only seventeen had been built, they were succeeded on the builders' slips by the UBII series, twice as big at 263 tons surface displacement, slightly beamier and a bit faster, all making for better handling. They mounted a pair of full-size (50cm) torpedo tubes, giving them more of a punch.

The UBIIIs represented a complete redefinition of the concept. Nominally still classed as coastal boats, they were in fact sea-going boats, very nearly as capable as the mainstream Mittel-U-

▼ *UB23*, a UBII boat, seen at Corunna, Spain, where she was interned after being damaged in a depth-charge attack, August 1917. The UBII was the interim design in the UB series of smaller, easier-to-build U-boats evolved in response to the increasing size of the main line of U-boat development. (USN)

boats, differing primarily in having a shorter operating range due to their somewhat smaller size. They were, however, significantly bigger than the earlier UB series, displacing 516 tons and armed with five torpedo tubes (four in the bow and one in the stern). They were designed not only to fight in the bordering seas but in the open ocean around the British Isles.

They were immediately successful, representing an almost ideal compromise between the big, powerful and long-ranged *U-Kreuzer* and the diminutive and handy, but short-legged and weakly armed, coastal boats of the earlier UB series. The initial examples of the type were so popular that repeats and later improvements of the initial *UB48* class were ordered in large quantities. Particulars of the *UB48* class are given in the following table:

Class:	*UB48* (UBIII)
Displacement	516/651 tons (surfaced/ submerged)
Length	55.3m
Beam	5.8m
Draft	3.7m
Machinery	1,100bhp/788hp (2-shaft diesel/ electric)
Speed	13.6/8 kts (surfaced/submerged)
Range (nm/kt)	8500/6 surfaced; 55/4 submerged
Armament	5×50cm TT (5 reloads); 1×8.8cm gun
Crew	34

The UBIIIs did have their critics. By trying to pack so much capability into as small a package as possible, the Germans had created a U-boat that was very complicated to build and notoriously difficult to handle.[1] Also, like most of the earlier U-boat designs, the UBIIIs carried their fuel oil in tanks external to their pressure hull. Wartime experience had shown that these external tanks were susceptible to damage by depth-charging. An attack that was not accurate enough to endanger the U-boat's pressure hull might still rupture a fuel oil tank. Once a U-boat's position was given away by oil leakage, its chances of survival were slim.

In the autumn of 1917, a proposal was put forward for a U-boat intended primarily for operations in the North Sea. These boats were to be much simpler to build and operate than the UBIIIs, and they were to have their fuel tanks and main diving tanks within the pressure hull. This design, designated UF, called for a boat of about 350 tons. The response to the new design was enthusiastic. Due to the simplicity of its construction, orders were placed with small yards that had had little or no prior U-boat construction experience. By June 1918, orders for 92 UFs had been placed. Already, thought was being given to the logical successor to the UF, as its small size and short range would limit its operational usefulness. What was wanted was a UF-type boat that had greater range. An enlarged UF of about 570 tons was proposed, designated UG. This would have the same characteristics of design simplicity and internal fuel tanks as the UF in an enlarged hull. It would incorporate the same power components as a UBIII, supercharged to give greater power.

The general opinion was that the UG design represented the ideal medium-sized U-boat and that it should be proceeded with at once. Only the first fifteen UFs, for which materials had already been ordered, were to be completed. All the others would be replaced on the stocks by UGs, of which 101 were to be ordered for delivery

▼A surrendered UBIII boat, probably *UB88*, is seen at the end of the war in New York harbour. This boat was placed on display at several East Coast harbours after the war before being disposed of as a target. (USN)

in 1920. Needless to say, the collapse of Imperial Germany in November 1918 precluded the fulfillment of these plans. No UFs were completed, and no UGs were even laid down. It was now for the victorious Allies to determine the future of German U-boat development.

The Treaty of Versailles forbade Germany from possessing any of the major new weapons types that had emerged during the war. They were specifically denied military aircraft, tanks and submarines. Yet the reconstituted Reichsmarine was not willing, any more than were the other branches of the Weimar Republic's armed forces, to sit idly by while other nations perfected these new weapons. As early as 1920, an Inspectorate for Torpedoes and Mines was established in Kiel. At first this organization did little more than gather together all KTBs, trials plans and any other documentation relevant to U-boat development and use that it could find. In particular, it gathered material for a planned analytical history of U-boat operations in the recent war, with particular emphasis on ASW techniques. It also kept up-to-date files on the whereabouts of surviving U-boat officers and designers, in anticipation of the day when their talents would again be needed. Private shipyards, with behind-the-scenes encouragement from the Reichsmarine, did their part in trying to keep this talent pool intact. Although forbidden even to build submarines for other countries, they were not restricted from contracting out their design teams to foreign shipyards.

The Reichsmarine decided to get still more intimately involved in the process when, in 1921, the Argentinian Navy obtained the services of *KK a.D.* Karl Bartenbach, commander of the Flanders Flotilla during the war, to help them create a submarine branch. The plans he developed for Argentina involved the construction of a fleet of ten submarines based on German models from the recent war. When he approached the Reichsmarine with his need for design and construction assistance, they responded, in July 1922, by arranging the financing of a clandestine Submarine Development Bureau. The front for this organization was a naval engineering firm (*Ingenieurskaantor voor Scheepsbouw* – IvS) established at 's Gravenhage (The Hague) in the Netherlands. The intent of this organization was to design and oversee the construction of the submarines for Argentina and other nations, building on the best designs of 1918. As a side-effect, it would train a new generation of designers and engineers in anticipation of the day when Germany would again openly build U-boats.[2]

IvS produced a series of designs from 1922 until 1932, when the Germans began again to design U-boats for themselves. The plan developed for Argentina was for a 570-ton boat based on the UBIII design. In the event, the client lost interest and this design was never proceeded with. The first IvS design to be built was generated at the request of the new Turkish Navy, which, in its seemingly eternal rivalry with Greece, wanted a submarine force. It too was based directly on the UBIII design. A pair of hulls to this design were laid down in 1926. Initial testing of the first began in April 1927 and continued into June with an IvS-supplied crew under a German CO and LI. They were accepted by the Turks with the names *Birindci Inönü* and *Ikindci Inönü*, literally 'Number 1' and 'Number 2'.

This pattern, of IvS building submarines to evolutionary versions of war-time designs in foreign yards, and of the trials of those submarines being supervised by 'retired' German naval officers, was to be repeated several more times. While not the same as having U-boats of their own, it was as close as the Reichsmarine could get. For Finland, IvS generated a design for a derivative of the war-time UCIII minelayer design. The Finns contracted for three of these boats in 1926. The three submarines were commissioned into the Finnish Navy as *Vetehinen*, *Vesihiisi* and *Iku-Tursu* in 1931.

In 1927, IvS was requested by the Reichsmarine to develop a submarine to updated UG plans. It was agreed with the Spanish Government that a UG-based submarine would be built for Spain, with all construction monies advanced by the Reichsmarine. The hull was to be built in sections in Holland and only assembled in Spain. This plan was derailed by the Spanish Navy, which intervened with a number of requests for modifications to the UG design to give higher surface speed and longer range. In order to accommodate these requirements, the design evolved into a boat significantly larger than the UG and without internal fuel storage. In this form, it very much resembled an enlarged UBIII rather than a UG. Assembly of the boat, designated *E1* by the Spanish yard, was begun in February 1929 and completed on 22 October 1930. It was put through acceptance trials by a German crew, for more than a year and then the Spanish declined to purchase the boat due to internal political upheaval, and it was retained by the Reichsmarine as a testbed until 1935 when it was purchased by the Turkish Navy at a considerable discount and commissioned into their navy as *Gur.*

Two more boats were designed and built under the auspices of IvS, both for Finland. These were the diminutive *Sauko* and the slightly larger *Vesikko.* The former was so small, at just 114 tons surface displacement, that the Reichsmarine had little interest in it. The latter was a 250-ton boat closely modelled on the UF design and was seen by the Reichmarine as the prototype for a small, rapidly built boat that would be a valuable training tool when U-boats were again to be built for Germany. *Vesikko* was launched in May 1933 and was used as a training boat by the Germans, not being commissioned into the Finnish Navy until January 1936!

New U-boats for Germany

Preparations for renewed U-boat construction in Germany began with the establishment of a U-boat Plans Office of the Reichsmarine as early as 1927. It was this office that had pushed for the building of a UG-based boat that led to E1. The office, under a variety of names, funnelled money to IvS, arranged for the trials crews for the boats IvS built and secretly planned for the day when Germany would again build U-boats. By 1932 these plans had evolved to the point of determining the need for three U-boat types, a small coastal boat for operations in the Baltic and North Seas, a medium-sized sea-going boat for operations in the North Atlantic and a medium-sized, sea-going minelayer for operations in the Mediterranean. Practical considerations demanded that these boats be built to IvS designs: *Vesikko, E1/Gur* and *Vetehinen*. Emphasis was to be on the first two types.

As plans were being formulated for the construction of the first U-boats, funds were allocated in early 1933 to build a U-boat base at Kiel-Wik and to train the first 100 U-boatmen under the cover of the *Ubootsabwehrschule* (Anti-Submarine Warfare School) starting in October of that year. Building of the first pair of *Vesikko*-type boats (designated MVBII boats – MVB stood for *Motorenversuchsboot* – motor research boat) was planned to begin in the autumn of 1933. Funding for long-lead-time parts, such as diesels and torpedo tubes, for the first two boats was authorized in March of that year and by the autumn, that funding had grown to cover four more MVBIIs and two large *E1/Gur*-type boats (designated MVBI).

Political reality prevented construction of the first boats from starting until 1935. Hitler had just consolidated his hold on power as head of the German state and he wanted to tread carefully lest he find himself in trouble with the Versailles Powers, particularly Britain. Nevertheless, the clandestine preparations continued. Parts for the eight boats now ordered were completed in Germany, shipped to IvS in Holland and then reshipped back to Germany. The material for the six MVBIIs were stored at Deutche Werke, Kiel, where three large construction sheds were built. By August 1934 complete material for all six boats was in storage. Parts for the two MVBIs were being gathered at Kiel as well, although construction was to be done by AG Weser, Bremen.

While this was going on, questions were raised about the next U-boat types to build. A minelaying U-boat of approximately 880 tons was proposed as the MVBIII. Other proposals called for a large resupply and repair U-boat, a large U-boat to carry a pair of small motor torpedo-boats, a large steam-powered U-boat and a large boat powered by the Walter closed-cycle propulsion system. These proposals carried various designations while they were under consideration, but they met a common fate when the terms of the proposed Anglo-German Naval Agreement were revealed. This agreement acknowledged the invalidity of the Versailles restrictions on German armaments and allowed the Germans to build their naval strength up to set percentages of Royal Navy tonnage. Specifically, it allowed the Reichsmarine (which during this period changed its name to Kriegsmarine) to build U-boats up to 35 per cent of the British total, or approximately 18,500 tons. With eight MVBIIs and two MVBIs just waiting for assembly and parts for six more slightly enlarged MVBIIs on order, just 14,000 tons were left for any foreseeable U-boat development.

The problem now was deciding how best to use that limited tonnage. The decision to scrap the various proposed large boats and the dedicated minelayer was easy; there just wasn't the tonnage to waste. The demands of economics and the requirement to train large numbers of U-boat personnel decreed that a further dozen MVBIIs should be ordered. But there remained the need for a more capable boat together with the small MVBIIs. With the remaining 11,000 tons, the Germans could build fourteen more MVBIs or 22 of a boat in the 500-ton range. The attraction of a larger number of somewhat smaller boats of sea-going range over a smaller number of larger boats was irresistible. Casting around for a design to build, the Kriegsmarine thought again of the never-built UG proposal of 1918. Following the same process that led to the development of the UG proposal from the UF design, the planners quickly extrapolated the MVBII design (a direct descendant of the UF) to 500 tons. On 16 January 1935, Germania Werft received an order for six U-boats of the new design, designated MVBVII. The MVB prefix was dropped in March 1935, when Germany officially renounced the military provisions of the Treaty of Versailles.

1. The loss of control that led to the abandonment of *UB68*, commanded by OL z.S. Dönitz (see Appendix B) was far from a unique instance.
2. IvS also designed other warship types besides submarines. For example, in 1939 they prepared the drawings for a battlecruiser project being contemplated by the Dutch Navy.

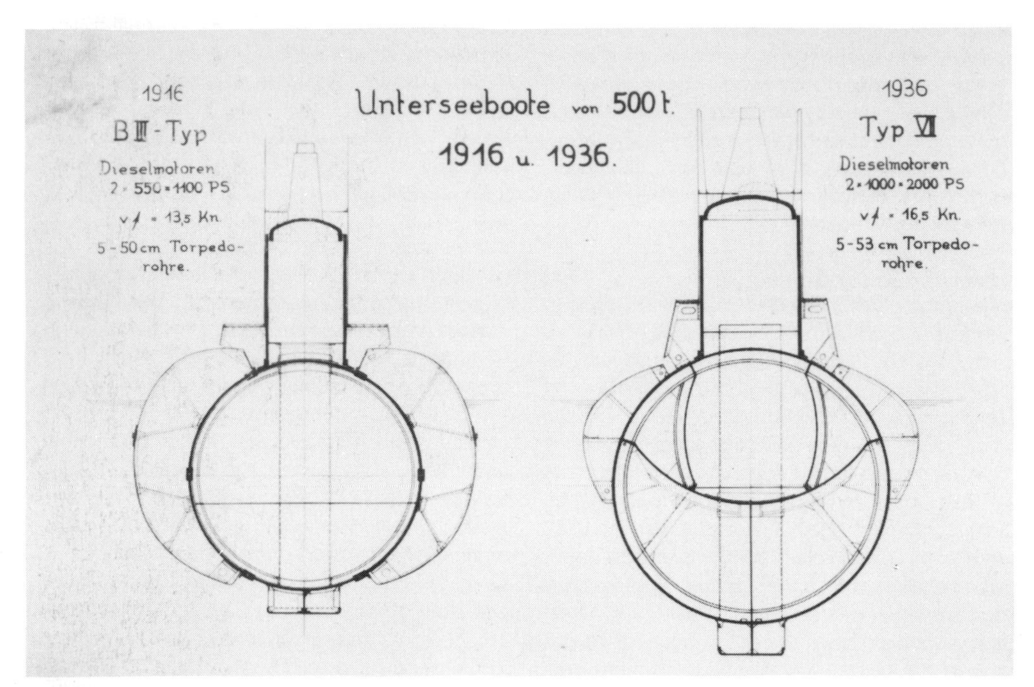

◀ A drawing comparing the midships cross-sections of the comparable 500-ton boats of 1916 and 1936. The Type VII had a significantly larger diameter of pressure hull than the UBIII, which it used, in part, for the internal storage of diesel fuel, hence the semi-circular internal bulkhead separating the control room above from the fuel bunker and ballast tank below. Large cells for fresh water and hydraulic fluid flanked the control room in the Type VII. With so much internal storage of fluids, the saddle tanks could be much smaller in size. (via Baker)

Evolution of the Type VII

The six MVBVIIs, soon to be renamed Type VII and then Type VIIA, were the first of more than 700 of this type to be built. During the course of its developmental history, stretching well into 1944, Type VII U-boats were built, or were intended to be built, in six distinct sub-types, with a few sub-sub-types thrown in for good measure.

Type VIIA

The first batch of Type VII U-boats set the general dimensions and characteristics of the type. Like the Type II design from which it was developed, the initial Type VII sub-type was a single hull boat (meaning the pressure hull could be, and in parts was, the outer hull of the boat) that stored all oil fuel inside the pressure hull. Additionally, much of the space below the decking of the control room section and between the watertight bulkheads that sealed the forward and after ends of the control room was given over to a ballast tank. This was also very similar to the arrangement in the Type IIs. However, since the Type VIIs were considerably bigger than the Type IIs, this single central ballast tank, together with bow and stern tanks outside the pressure hull, wasn't large enough to provide either sufficient reserve buoyancy when blown to keep the deck casing above water or sufficient ballast when flooded to give rapid diving capability. The Type VIIA therefore had saddle tanks added to both sides of the hull with room for two more large ballast tanks on each side. These provided the necessary buoyancy and ballast and gave the class its characteristic bulged appearance.

Above the pressure hull was built a substantial deck casing including slender tapering bow and stern sections that streamlined the forward and after ends of the pressure hull. Between the hull and the deck casing ran the plumbing, wiring and ducting necessary to ventilate the boat, receive fuel and tap into external electrical sources. From the centre of the deck casing rose the external tower structure which encased the conning tower, a vertical extension of the pressure hull. Armament was five torpedo tubes, an 8.8cm gun and a 2cm Flak weapon.

The exact particulars of the Type VIIA were:

Class:	*U27* (Type VIIA)
Displacement	626/745 tons (surfaced/ submerged)
Length	64.5m
Beam	5.8m
Draft	4.4m
Machinery	2,320bhp/750hp (2-shaft diesel/ electric)
Speed	16/8 kts (surfaced/submerged)
Range (nm/kt)	4,300/12 surfaced; 90/4 submerged
Armament	5×53.3cm TT (6 reloads); 1×8.8cm; 1×2cm guns
Crew	44

The initial order for six Type VIIAs from Krupp's Germania Werft (GW) was pared down to four on 28 January 1935. At the same time, AG Weser

ʔight and below: A pair of the earliest Type VII U-boats, *U27* and *U34*. Both are seen early in their careers, still sporting the large white hull numbers painted on their towers. There were minor differences in appearance between the boats built by the two manufacturers of the A sub-type. *U27* was the first of the type, built by AG Weser. Although it had the lowest hull number of any Type VII, it was in fact the second to be launched. *U34* was the second in the series of four Type VIIAs to be built by Germania Werft and the fourth of the type to be launched. Note the difference in the pattern of free-flooding holes in the deckcasing of the boats built by the two yards. (USN)

was awarded a contract to build six. The ten boats were given U-numbers starting with *U27*. Permission to begin assembly work on all U-boats was finally given on 8 February 1935. The first of the sub-type to be launched was *U33* at GW on 11 June 1936. AG Weser's *U27* followed thirteen days later. All ten had been launched by February of the next year.

Type VIIB

The two Type IAs (MVBIs) and the first Type VII (*U33*) came into service within months of each other in the summer of 1937. As there remained strong proponents of both types within the Kriegsmarine, it seemed only logical that the two types should be compared in head-to-head tests. *U33* came out the clear winner. The only points that went to the Type IA were underwater turning radius (due to the IA's twin rudder compared to the VIIA's single rudder), torpedo storage, surface speed and range. On every other point, the Type VII was adjudged the victor. Most telling were the comments concerning the relative ease of handling underwater of the Type VII compared to its bigger rival.

The Type VII was the obvious choice. Nevertheless, the original Type VII plans were reworked in an attempt to develop a variant that was better than the Type IA in all aspects. The effort very nearly succeeded. The redesigned Type VII had a smaller underwater turning radius, improved range, higher speed and greater torpedo storage

than the VIIA. The turning radius was improved by resorting to the same expedient used by the Type IA, twin rudders. By placing a rudder behind each screw, and in the process nearly doubling the rudder area, the underwater turning radius of the new Type VII was vastly improved. As an added benefit, this new arrangement allowed the rear torpedo tube, which had been mounted externally on the Type VIIA, to be brought within the pressure hull in the new boat, firing out between the rudders. Torpedo storage was improved by storing a reload for the stern torpedo tube within the hull under the deck of the motor room and by adding a pair of external torpedo stowage tubes, one each forward and aft, between the pressure hull and the deck casing. Speed was increased by boosting power by 20 per cent through the use of superchargers on the MAN diesels. Range was increased the simplest way, by increasing fuel bunkerage. The boat was lengthened by two metres, which increased the size of the internal fuel tanks by a small percentage, but not enough. To obtain the desired increase of nearly 40 cubic metres of fuel bunkerage, it was necessary to store a significant amount of oil fuel in the saddle tanks. A large self-compensating fuel tank (*Regelbunker*) was added between the ballast tanks on both sides. The term self-compensating refers to the fact that the tanks were open to the sea at the bottom, so that as fuel was drawn from the top of the tank, it was replaced by sea water entering from below. Because fuel oil is lighter than water, it floated above the water in the tank. This arrangement made room for the needed fuel but added a serious complication. When the boat was surfaced, these new tanks would add significant weight at considerable distance from the longitudinal centre of rotation of the boat. Simple physics indicated that in any weather, they would make the boat roll terribly. In order to combat this tendency, room was made in the saddle tanks for a pair of compensating tanks (*Regelzelle*). These were tanks that were built much like standard ballast tanks, with valves at the top and bottom and air ducts from inside the boat, though they were used quite differently. In rough weather, they were to be partially flooded and then sealed so as to dampen any increased roll caused by the added fuel tanks.[1] In order to find room in the saddle tanks for the added fuel and compensating tanks without seriously reducing reserve buoyancy, it was necessary to increase the size of the saddle tanks. They were therefore made both longer and fuller in cross-section. This, together with the increased length of the boat, increased the actual displacement by some 120 tons.[2]

The first seven of these new Type VIIs were ordered from GW as *U45 – U51*, on 21 November 1936. The resulting boat, designated Type VIIB, had the following particulars:

Class:	*U45* (Type VIIB)
Displacement	753/857 tons (surfaced/ submerged)
Length	66.5m
Beam	6.2m
Draft	4.7m
Machinery	2,800bhp/750hp (2-shaft diesel/ electric)
Speed	17.2/8 kts (surfaced/submerged)
Range (nm/kt)	6,500/12 surfaced; 90/4 submerged
Armament	5×53.3cm TT (9 reloads); 1×8.8 cm; 1×2cm guns
Crew	44

◀ The VIIB differed in a number of significant ways from the VIIA. One of the most important was the adoption of a double rudder. This not only improved manoeuvrability, but allowed the previously external after torpedo tube to be lowered so that its inner end was now internal to the pressure hull. It now fired out from between the rudders. This view, looking up the starboard side of a nearly completed boat in one of Germania Werft's construction sheds, shows the saddle tanks along the boat's side, the circular pressure hull below that, the deckcasing above the tanks and blending into the deadwood aft which contained the after dive tank. (via Baker)

▲ ***U101*, a Type VIIB boat, seen just before the outbreak of war. It is rare in retaining a netcutter at the bow. Few early boats carried them and these were all removed before the war. One of the few distinguishing marks between the Bs and the following Cs, which they closely resembled externally, is the external air trunking up the side of the tower. Experience with Type VIIAs and Bs showed that the air intakes for the diesels, which had been located at the side of the tower below the 2cm gun platform, was too small and prone to flooding in high seas. Therefore enlarged air trunks were added up the outside of the tower to the level of the tower edge.**

Early in 1937 the British and the Germans went back into negotiation over the Naval Agreement. Germany demanded, and received, from the British concessions that brought her percentages more into line with those granted to the French and Japanese in the London Naval Treaty of 1936. In anticipation of increased legal U-boat tonnage, orders were placed with GW for two additional Type VIIBs on 15 May 1937, with two more being ordered on 16 July. The next day, the revised Anglo-German Naval Agreement was signed, allowing Germany 45 per cent of the Royal Navy's total submarine tonnage, or approximately 31,500 tons. As a consequence, from December 1937 to June 1938, three more batches of four Type VIIBs were ordered from GW and from a pair of smaller yards that were new to U-boat work, Bremer Vulkan Vegesack and Flenderwerft Lübeck.[3]

Type VIIC

The order for the first eight Type VIICs actually preceded the orders for the last VIIBs by a few days. Unlike the change from the A to B models of the Type VII, the change from B to C wasn't the result of any perceived inadequacy of the preceding sub-type. The Type VIIB was exactly the boat that FdU Karl Dönitz and almost the entire U-boat force desired. It had very nearly identical characteristics as the Type I on a smaller displacement, which gave faster diving times and better manoeuvrability. (There remained in the Kriegsmarine's leadership a faction that still wanted bigger, faster, longer-ranging boats. In parallel with the development of the Type VII, the Kriegsmarine built successive marks of the Type IX, a Type I derivative with improved speed, range and armament. Type VIIs and Type IXs were built in a rough ratio of two to one until the outbreak of war.)[4]

The change to the Type VIIC was motived not by any dissatisfaction with the Type VIIB, but by the planned availability of a new, and seemingly important, sensor technology. The S-Gerät (*Such Gerät* – search device), an active sonar intended to allow U-boats to detect minefields or targets, was considered ready for installation in the next U-boats that were ordered. The Type VIIB design lacked the space for the installation of the S-Gerät's electronics, so its design was modified by adding a full frame section, 60cm in length, into the centre of the control room. A number of benefits accrued as a side-effect of the increased length. Above the control room, the cramped conning tower was increased in length by 30cm and in width by 6cm. Below the control room, the after internal fuel tank (between the internal ballast tank and the after bulkhead of the central

▲ **An unusually configured late-war boat. By the time the fully extended *Wintergarten* and armoured boxes (*Kohlenkasten*) had been added to the tower of a Type VII U-boat, the deck gun would generally be removed to compensate the added weight. The white circle on the tower side is a temporary tactical sign typical of the type carried by boats assigned to the Baltic training flotillas. (SFL)**

watertight compartment) was increased in length by 60cm, giving a volume increase of 5.4 cubic metres. Externally, the saddle tanks now had room for a new small buoyancy tank (*Untertriebszelle*) on each side which, when blown, provided a bit of additional buoyancy but which, in comabt, could be partially flooded to allow faster dives.

At the same time that these structural changes were being made, the opportunity was taken to include some minor upgrades to the Type VII's mechanical systems. The new variant included an oil filtration system designed to prolong the life of the diesel lubricating oil and thus increase the range possible from a fixed amount of lubricant. One of the two electrical compressors, used to fill the compressed air tanks that fired torpedoes and blew ballast tanks, was replaced by a Junkers diesel-powered compressor. This was designed to reduce the demands on the electrical system. Finally, the First World War vintage electrical control system used in earlier Type VII variants, which featured knife switches, was replaced by a modern knob switch system manufactured by AEG.

The initial batch of eight Type VIICs (*U93 – U100*) was ordered from GW on 30 May 1938. The particulars of these boats were:

Class:	*U93* (Type VIIC)
Displacement	761/865 tons (surfaced/ submerged)
Length	67.1m
Beam	6.2m
Draft	4.8m
Machinery	2,800bhp/750hp (2-shaft diesel/ electric)
Speed	17.0/7.6 kts (surfaced/submerged)
Range (nm/kt)	6,500/12 surfaced; 80/4 submerged
Armament	5×53.3cm TT (9 reloads); 1×8.8cm; 1×2cm guns
Crew	44

On 30 December 1938, the British bowed to persistent pressure from the Germans and agreed to yet another revision of the Anglo-German

▲ A typical mid-war Type VIIC soon after launch from Germania Werft's yard in Kiel. The vertical bulge up the side of the tower was the housing for the telescoping long-range radio mast which was a standard fitting to most boats by 1941. At launch, Type VII U-boats were largely complete with little additional fitting out to be done before delivery. One notable missing item is the deck gun, which has yet to be fitted. (GW via MacPherson)

Naval Agreement. The revised agreement allowed the Kriegsmarine to build U-boats up to 100 per cent of the Royal Navy's total of approximately 70,000 tons. In the first few days of January 1939, orders were placed for thirteen more Type VIICs from the same three yards that were building Type VIIBs. These were the last Type VIIs ordered before the outbreak of war on 3 September 1939. Thereafter orders came in a flood. Before the end of the year, orders for 131 additional Type VIICs had been distributed among thirteen shipyards.

The changes from the VIIB resulted in a boat that was marginally slower, because its increased size was unmatched by increased power. For the same reason, the slight increase in fuel storage brought no increase in surface range. Because electrical storage wasn't increased, the greater displacement led to a decrease in submerged range. And the S-Gerät, the sole reason for the VIIC being created in the first place, proved to be far from ready for installation in U-boats, so the first several batches of Type VIICs were completed without that active sonar device. Nevertheless, the Type VIIC became the standard U-boat type of the Kriegsmarine.

Not surprisingly, as the war progressed, combat experience led to a series of incremental changes in the type. Periodically, thought was given to 'rationalizing' these changes into official sub-types of the Type VIIC. One of these was produced in small numbers and two more were planned but never actually built.

Type VIIC/41

The entry of America into the war following the Japanese attack on Pearl Harbor opened up a whole new hunting ground where for a few brief months the clock was turned back and U-boats hunted freely among disorganized and unprotected shipping. This success didn't blind BdU to the fact that prior to Pearl Harbor, the level of defensive pressure on the main North Atlantic convoy routes had been steadily increasing. Thought had to be given to improving the basic U-boat type of this war, the Type VIIC. A series of studies and reports dating from the summer of 1941 pointed to increased surface speed (up to 22kts) as the most needed offensive improvement, and deeper diving capability (to 300 metres) as the most needed defensive aid.

The immediate result was the Type VIIC/41. The aim of this design was to make those changes to the design that could be achieved without major structural redesign. To the greatest extent possible, the production lines shouldn't be disrupted. The resulting redesign made no effort to alter the powerplant of the basic VIIC except to save weight. Weight saving among the existing power and electrical setups was achieved by rationalization and replacement of equipment by newer, more compact designs so as to save a total of 11.5 tons of hull weight. Ten tons of this saved weight was used to increase the basic thickness of the pressure hull from 18.5mm to 21mm. This increased the approved normal depth rating of the hull from 150 to 180 meters and the calculated failure depth (frequently exceeded by U-boats during depth-charging) from 250 to 300 metres. At the same time, the forecastle was widened and the bow extended by 13cm in an attempt to increase seaworthiness and decrease water resistance. This was the so-called Atlantic Bow (*Atlantiksteven*). These changes gave the Type VIIC/41 the following particulars:

Class:	(Type VIIC/41)
Displacement	759/860 tons (surfaced/ submerged)
Length	67.2m
Beam	6.2m
Draft	4.8m
Machinery	2,800bhp/750hp (2-shaft diesel/ electric)
Speed	17.0/7.6 kts (surfaced/submerged)
Range (nm/kt)	6,500/12 surfaced; 80/4 submerged
Armament	5×53.3cm TT (9 reloads); 1×8.8cm, 1×2cm guns
Crew	44

The first orders for Type VIIC/41s were placed on 14 October 1941. These weren't new contracts, simply instructions to all yards already building Type VIICs that all boats for which materials had not yet been ordered were to be built to this standard. Such was the lead time for the ordering of hull plates and other equipment that the first of the VIIC/41s didn't appear until mid-1943. Additionally, a series of new contracts specifically for this sub-type were awarded to yards that had already started work on all contracted Type VIIs.

Type VIIC/42

Having taken the design to its limits without fundamental change, the planning process began to look at the kind of changes that would be required seriously to improve the surface speed and diving depth. To achieve a higher speed, more power had to be obtained from the diesels. The Type VIIs from the B sub-type on used a single-stage supercharger or turbocharger to boost the basic output of the diesels to 1,400bhp. Adding a second stage of boost and increasing rpms increased this to 2,200bhp. The additional equipment added 80cm to the planned length of the engine room. The increased power, however, was calculated to add just 1.6 knots to the top speed.

In order to boost range, the saddle tanks were to have been widened 35cm. The pressure hull itself was to have been increased in diameter by 30cm. This was done in part to provide more internal fuel bunkerage and in part to increase buoyancy to make up for a 68-ton increase in hull weight. This increased weight went mainly into thickening the pressure hull to 28mm and switching from standard ship steel to an armour grade steel. This thicker pressure hull gave a calculated normal test depth of 300 metres and a failure depth of 500 metres. The particulars of this sub-type were:

Class:	(Type VIIC/42)
Displacement	999/1,099 tons (surfaced/ submerged)
Length	68.7m
Beam	6.7m
Draft	5.1m
Machinery	4,400bhp/750hp (2-shaft diesel/ electric)
Speed	18.6/7.6 kts (surfaced/submerged)
Range (nm/kt)	10,000/12 surfaced; 80/4 submerged
Armament	5×53.3cm TT (9 reloads); 8×2cm guns
Crew	45

The first orders for Type VIIC/42s were placed on 16 July 1942 with GW. This was part of a series that had already been ordered as VIICs and was in the process of being reordered as VIIC/41s. This order was premature by almost six months as the final dimensions of the design were far from finalized. Most of this time was spent discussing a long llist of features that one group or another wanted to add to the new design. Among the items ultimately incorporated into the VIIC/42 design were a third air compressor to give faster refilling of larger compressed air tanks, more and better bilge pumps capable of pumping out water at greater depth, a heating and air-conditioning/dehumidifier system for all compartments, a freezer and refrigerator for food as well as a large dehumidified potato storage locker and an arc welding unit for emergency repairs. At one point, in November 1942, two rival designs had been put together, differing from each other by five metres in length and 20 cm in beam. The fact that the larger design would have been too big for the U-boat slips at most yards tipped the scales in favour of the smaller project.

Although some 174 Type VIIC/42s were eventually ordered, none was completed during the war. By mid-1943 the rules had changed irreversibly in the North Atlantic. A number of technological factors (radar, HF/DF, etc.) now allowed Allied defenders to find surfaced U-boats at any time and in any weather. The Type VII, in any of its forms, was incapable of truly effective offensive operations under these circumstances. As powerful new types were projected, they replaced the Type VII as BdU's U-boat of choice. To make room for these new boats in the yards and to gear up for their mass production, all existing orders for Type VIIs not yet actually laid down were cancelled by a telegram dated 30 September 1943 sent to all yards.[5] Any boats actually laid down, however, were to be completed. This effectively ended work on the Type VIIC/42.[6] Since none had been laid down, all that were on order were cancelled. It had the same effect on those VIIC/41s which hadn't yet been laid down. These were cancelled at the same time. One yard only, the tiny Flensburger Schiffbau, which wasn't included in the Type XXI programme, was permitted to continue laying down Type VIIs. *U1308*, a Type VIIC/41, was laid down there on 28 January 1944 and then that yard too was ordered to start no more Type VIIs.[7]

Type VIIC/43

One more sub-type of the VIIC was projected as an even more capable follow-on to the VIIC/42. It was to have been identical with the Type VIIC/42 in all respects except for torpedo armament. Given the increasing difficulty of getting into a good

▲ *N23*, a late-model Type VIIC in Russian service after the war. This could be one of the five boats ceded to the Russians after the surrender, or one of the unknown number, at least three, C/41s finished from parts at Danzig.

◀ *U977* **seen at La Plata, Argentina, after having made its extraordinary underwater journey from the coast of Norway after learning of the surrender of Germany. The trip included a stretch of 66 days of continuous snorkelling without surfacing. (via Albrecht)**

firing position near a convoy, and the length of time required to reload torpedoes, it was proposed to increase the number of torpedo tubes and thus the number of torpedoes ready to fire when a good opportunity presented itself. The plan was to double the number of torpedo tubes by increasing the array at the bow to six (two vertical columns of three) and at the stern to four (two columns of two). The structural changes that this would require were localized in the bow and stern sections of the pressure hull and outer hull and actually wouldn't have meant a total redesign of the VIIC/42. Nevertheless, the urgency of the need for the deeper diving C/41 and C/42 sub-types was such that on 11 May 1943 it was decided not to pursue this variant.

Type VIID

The submarine-laid mine had been an important weapon during the First World War, and plans had been mooted throughout the pre-war period for the construction of dedicated minelaying U-boats like the UE classes of the First World War. The development of the TM series of torpedo tube mines took away some of the pressure to develop specialized minelayers. Nevertheless, the desire still existed for U-boats capable of carrying the larger SM series mines. (The TMA had a warhead of 215kg, while the SMA's warhead was 350kg.) Even the development of successors to the TMA with significantly larger warheads didn't deter the development of the Type X series of long-range minelayers. For mine work closer to home, the need was felt for a variant of the Type VII specialized for minelaying. As a result, six Type VIID minelayers, *U213 – U218*, were ordered from GW on 16 February 1940.

The Type VIID was derived directly from the Type VIIC, with which it shared all basic mechanical components and most hull structures. The mine-laying capability was added by the simplest of expedients. An additional hull section of 9.8 metres length was added just aft of the control room which gave room for five vertical mineshafts, each of which held three SMA mines. The added room inside the pressure hull that was not taken up by the mineshafts was occupied primarily by narrow vertical mine trim tanks which were flooded to compensate for the weight of released mines. Room was also found for two more bunks and a pair of large refrigerated lockers for food storage, unheard-of luxuries in the more cramped VIICs. The additional length also increased the volume of the saddle tanks, allowing a fuel tank, a ballast tank and a compensating tank to be added on each side. The particulars of the sub-type were as follows:

Class:	*U213* (Type VIID)
Displacement	965/1,080 tons (surfaced/ submerged)
Length	76.9m
Beam	6.4m
Draft	5.0m
Machinery	2,800bhp/750hp (2-shaft diesel/ electric)
Speed	16.0/7.3 kts (surfaced/submerged)
Range (nm/kt)	8,100/12 surfaced; 69/4 submerged
Armament	5×53.3cm TT (9 reloads); 1×8.8cm, 1×2cm guns
Crew	44

The addition of the minelaying capability by the expedient of adding a midships hull section had the advantage of leaving the offensive armament of the original Type VIIC intact. Thus, the six Type VIIDs had the same torpedo and gun armament as their design predecessor. This was fortunate because, as the VIIDs came into service in the spring and summer of 1942, the use of SMA mines was forbbiden by SKL, and in their initial war patrols, the VIIDs were employed as standard Type VIIs with somewhat greater range.[8] The retention the Type VIIC's power plant, the narrow hull form (only 2cm wider than a VIIC) and the added water resistance of the mineshaft housing meant that the VIID paid for its greater range with reduced performance and manoeuvrability and increased diving time.

Type VIIE

This sub-type was a design project only, intended as a testbed for the lightweight Deutz V-12 two-stroke diesels. Delay and eventual abandonment of the diesel's development caused the VIIE to be

dropped. Except for the surface power plant, the VIIE was to have been similar to the VIIC. The intent was to put the weight saved in the diesels into a thicker pressure hull, allowing deeper dives.

Type VIIF

The gradual decimation of the surface resupply network during the summer of 1941 led BdU to consider a modification of the Type VIIC similar to the Type VIID with the express intention of developing an easily manufactured supply U-boat.[9] As U-boats ventured farther and farther afield, the time spent on passage ate up an increasing percentage of a patrol's duration. Since the supply of torpedoes was most often the limiting factor of a patrol, it was obvious that the ability to supply operational boats with additional torpedoes when their stocks were depleted would vastly increase their offensive power. The Type VIIF torpedo resupply U-boat was rapidly designed, using the already proven expedient of adding a 10.5 metre section aft of the control room. Most of this added section, the aftermost 7.8 metres of it, provided room for a stock of 24 extra torpedoes, stored in four layers of six torpedoes. An additional aft-facing torpedo hatch gave access to the storage area. The remainder of the added length was used to provide the same extra luxuries enjoyed by the Type VIID, a pair of extra bunks and a pair of large refrigerated food lockers. The extra bunks were even more necessary in a VIIF because the crew was increased by two men to supply added muscle for torpedo transfer. As was the case with the VIID, the added length made room for additional oil bunkerage in the saddle tanks.

With the Type VIID model to follow, the plans for the new variant were rapidly developed. On 22 August 1941, orders for four of the new type were placed with GW. Hull numbers U1059 – U1062 were assigned. The particulars of the Type VIIF were:

Class:	*U1059* (Type VIIF)
Displacement	1,084/1,181 tons (surfaced/submerged)
Length	77.6m
Beam	7.3m
Draft	4.9m
Machinery	2,800bhp/750hp (2-shaft diesel/electric)
Speed	16.9/7.9 kts (surfaced/submerged)
Range (nm/kt)	9,500/12 surfaced; 75/4 submerged
Armament	5×53.3cm TT (9 reloads); 1×8.8cm, 1×2cm guns
Crew	46

Construction of the new boats was slow, the first of the VIIFs not being ready until mid-1943. The mission for which they had been constructed was,

▲ A view of one of the six Type VIIDs, probably *U213*, seen at Brest in 1942, returning from a patrol. The raised deckcasing aft of the tower covering the tops of the five vertical mineshafts provided a handy place for the crew to assemble. Like the rest of the class, this boat was used as a conventional U-boat on her first missions because the SMA mines she was intended to carry had not been released for operational use.

▲ The same U-boat seen minutes later, tying up alongside a Type VIIC across the harbour from the concrete U-boats pens at Brest. Note the size difference between the C and D variants. The speculation that this is *U213*, the first Type VIID, is based on the presence of the 7. Uflot insignia, the Bull of Scapa Flow, on the tower. *U213* was the only D to serve with 7. Uflot. She was transferred after her first patrol to 9. Uflot at Brest and all the remaining Ds were assigned there from the beginning of their operational careers.

by then, no longer realistic. Allied airpower made the slow surface transfer of torpedoes completely impossible in the North Atlantic. Nevertheless, they were still very useful boats. Like the Type VIIDs, they retained their full armament. Unlike the VIID, they were given a fuller hull form (a full 1.1 metres wider than a VIIC) which gave them essentially the performance of the smaller VIIC. They were put to work on transport missions, running supplies to isolated outposts in Norway and elsewhere. Their long range made them attractive as the shortage of strategic raw materials made itself felt. One of the four (*U1062*) was actually used as a torpedo transport, making a successful run to Penang, arriving there on 19 April 1944 with a desperately needed supply of torpedoes for the *Monsun* boats operating from there.[10]

1. This was due to the fact that during a roll, the trapped air would add buoyancy to the side rolled underwater, while the weight of the trapped water on the high side would tend to cause that side to stop rolling.
2. Due to the arcane way in which submarine standard displacements were figured for the London Naval Treaty, the displacement of the Type VIIB increased only twelve tons as far as the Anglo-German Naval Agreement was concerned. Standard displacement was defined as the displacement of a complete ship, fully manned and with full loads of ammunition and stores but without fuel or boiler feed water. For submarines this was further defined as excluding the weight of any water in floodable compartments, lubricating oil or fresh water. Thus the massive increase in volume represented by the much enlarged saddle tanks of the Type VIIB contributed almost nothing to the standard displacement.
3. One additional Type VIIB joined the Kriegsmarine as *U83*. This was a boat being built at Flenderwerft under export contract, which was taken over on 8 August 1938.
4. At that time, of the 57 U-boats in service, eighteen were Type VIIs and seven were Type IXs.
5. This order included all boats not in the 'Elektroboot' programme and meant the cancellation of all orders for Type IX and Type XVII as well.
6. An unknown number of U-boats were completed by the Russians after the end of the war in dockyards captured by the Red Army at Danzig (now Gdansk in Poland). Although these boats hadn't been laid down, the major hull and mechanical components had been assembled at the respective yards and simply abandoned there when the stop-work order of 30 September 1943 was received. At least three Type VIIC/41s (*U1174, U1176* and *U1177*) are known to have been so completed at the Danziger Werft. An unknown number of Type VIIC/42s from the series *U2301 – U2318* are suspected of having been completed at the Schichau yard in Danzig. If so, these would have been the only examples of the type completed.
7. *U1308* was not only the last Type VII to be laid down, she was also the last to be commissioned into the Kriegsmarine, in January 1945.
8. KTB, 1 March 1942. *U213*'s first operation was off the Hebrides, patrolling against a suspected Allied invasion of Norway.
9. Purpose-built supply boats, the Type XIV *Milchkühe*, were ordered as early as May 1940. These were primarily tankers, as opposed to torpedo resupply boats. The Type XIV carried only four torpedoes in deck tubes.
10. KTB, 22 March 1944.
    KTB, 19 April 1944.

Why more than 700?

More than 700 Type VII U-boats were built by Germany before and during the Second World War. The exact number is difficult to determine because there is no agreement on what represents a countable U-boat. Many more Type VII U-boats were planned than were actually ordered, many more ordered than were started and many more started than were completed. Should the count be of all that were ordered? All that were started? All that were actually completed? All that were ready for combat?

Part of the problem is that it's hard to determine when work actually starts on a boat. Is it when the first long-lead-time components (such as diesels) are ordered, or is it when assembly of those components begins? While the start of new Type VIIs officially came to an end in 1943, one yard didn't complete the last of its authorized boats until January 1945. And then there were the boats finished by the Russians after the end of the war. Other boats were damaged by Allied bombing during the building process and construction of them was abandoned. Should any of these be counted?

Despite this confusion, reasonable counts are possible.[1] The best estimate is that a total of 1,452 Type VII U-boats were built, ordered or projected. This number includes all Type VIIs for which orders were placed with building yards and U-numbers were actually assigned. Of these, 411 were cancelled before any materials were actually ordered by the building yard, which means that material such as steel for hull plates and machinery for 1,041 Type VIIs was ordered. A total of 324 Type VIIs for which materials had been ordered were cancelled in the stop-work order of 30 September 1943, meaning that 717 were actually laid down on a building slip at a yard. Once a Type VII was laid down, it was generally completed. The stop-work order applied only to boats on which assembly work had not already begun. The only cause of discrepancy between the figure of boats laid down and boats completed was the case of boats being destroyed by Allied air attack during the assembly process. This occurred in six cases. Thus 709 Type VII U-boats were actually delivered to the Kriegsmarine. Of these, 665 were VIICs or VIIC/41s.

Irrespective of which of these numbers is considered to be the actual count of Type VII U-boats, the important point is that it is a very large number of any one type of submarine to build.[2] Such a great number of Type VIIs couldn't have been built without the solid backing of the leadership of the U-boat arm and of SKL. Particularly, it would never have happened without the enthusiastic support of Karl Dönitz. So the question of why more than 700 Type VII U-boats were built is really the question: why was Dönitz so enthusiastic a supporter of this basic design? The answer lies in the plans, and the theoretical bases for those plans, evolved by Dönitz during the inter-war years.

Dönitz's theories were embodied in his daring *Rüdeltaktik* (pack tactics). These new tactics were based on Dönitz's experiences during the First World War and directly addressed the causes of the German defeat in that war. As Dönitz saw it, the defeat of the U-boats was caused by two factors: (1) the inability of U-boats to find targets after the Allies had instituted the convoy system in May 1917, and (2) the inability of single submerged U-boats successfully to penetrate the escort screen and attack a convoy should it be lucky enough to encounter one. *Rüdeltaktik* was designed to solve both of these problems.

The idea of co-ordinated pack attacks didn't originate with Dönitz. It earliest mention was in a plan authored by Kommodore Bauer, head of Germany's U-boat arm in 1917. Bauer proposed the fitting of several large *U-Kreuzer* with radio equipment powerful enough to reach home and with direction-finding equipment and cryptanalysts to help it find convoys. Once the *U-Kreuzer* had found a convoy, it would communicate the finding back to Germany. U-boat Headquarters would then direct other boats to the convoy's location. Unfortunately, the idea was

▼ An extremely rare view of a Type VIIF at launch from Germania Werft, Kiel. Note the extreme length of the boat and the extra free-flooding holes added along the side to try to aid diving time. The wooden scaffolding constructed above the boat was put in place during building to hide her from RAF reconnaissance overflights and was a common feature as the war went on. (GW via MacPherson)

ahead of its time. The radio equipment of the day was insufficiently powerful and reliable for the job. The one official experiment with the idea, tried in June 1917, failed when the U-boat involved was unable to contact Germany. Dönitz himself tried an unofficial pack attack in September 1918 in co-operation with the commander of *UB48*. That boat and Dönitz's *UB68* attempted a co-ordinated attack on a convoy off the coast of Italy on the night of the new moon.

These ideas and experiences were the inspiration for Dönitz's thought during the years before his appointment as head of Germany's new U-boat arm. By the time he assumed that position in 1935, he had the *Rüdeltaktik* well thought out. The basis for this new tactic was the operation of U-boats in organized groups. Operation of these groups would be controlled from a central point, either by an at sea pack leader or, even better, by Dönitz himself from a land-based operations centre, where all the resources of intelligence services could be brought to bear.

The U-boats in the pack would be formed into sweep lines across the suspected path of convoys. As soon as any boat sighted a convoy, it would become a shadower, not attacking, but reporting the convoy's position to the control point. The tactical commander would calculate the course of the advancing convoy and direct the remaining boats to converge on the target. Only the second, and subsequent, boats on the scene would be allowed to attack.

Once the attack had commenced, the local tactics would differ markedly from past practise. Where previously the primary attack mode had been a submerged attack in daylight, Dönitz substituted the surfaced night attack. Taking advantage of the U-boat's small size, he felt that it would be possible to manoeuvre close to convoys and among the escorts with little chance of detection in the dark of night. In part this change had been brought about by the invention of ASDIC since the end of the First World War. This underwater sound location system was the one major new factor in the U-boat equation which hadn't been present in the previous war. But even more important in the decision to favour surfaced night attacks was the simple fact that a submerged U-boat was slow and virtually blind. The old tactic of sighting a target, rushing ahead of it on the surface, submerging in its path and waiting for it to pass across the torpedo tubes worked in only a small percentage of cases. Even in cases when the target was making no evasive course changes, the range of vision from a periscope was so limited that a mistake of only 100 metres in predicting the enemy's course was often enough to miss the target. Only after the attack would Dönitz's boats submerge and then only to evade the escorts' counter-attack.

The boat that could implement this new doctrine had to have certain characteristics that combined some of the best qualities of the large *Mittel* U-boats and the small UB boats of 1914–18. The boat had to be large enough to operate effectively in the North Atlantic ap-

◀ **Type VII U-boats were tiny specks on the ocean and rarely met another U-boat, even when part of the same wolf pack (*Rüdel*), except when deliberately making a rendezvous with a resupply boat. The war correspondent Buchheim, in his novel *The Boat*, described one of those rare accidental encounters. In real life, Buchheim witnessed the chance meeting of *U96*, which he joined for two patrols, and *U572* during heavy weather.**

proaches to the British Isles. This meant having the range, speed and armament characteristic of large boats. But they had to be highly manoeuvrable and fast diving like the smaller boats. The closest any boat of the First World War era had come to this ideal was the UBIII design which Dönitz knew well. The Type VII design that emerged was much to Dönitz's liking, much more so than the larger Type IX which was favoured by many at SKL. In fact the Type VII proved to be more robust than its larger counterpart and survived much better the rigours of the North Atlantic convoy battles. For example, in April 1943, Type VIIs outnumbered Type IXs in the North Atlantic by three to one, yet suffered casualties at a much lower rate. Seven of the larger boats were lost compared to only four Type VIIs. Of these, five of the Type IXs were sunk during convoy attacks, as opposed to two Type VIIs.[3] Above all the boat had to be easy to build because Dönitz knew he needed these boats in unprecedented numbers.[4] 'It must be emphasized repeatedly that the enemy today can no longer be found and successfully attacked by small numbers of boats.'[5] These numbers were required because the battle that would be fought in any renewal of U-boat war was very clearly defined in Dönitz's mind. A renewed battle of the Atlantic would be a *Tonnageschlacht* (tonnage battle).

'England was in every respect dependent on sea-borne supply for food and import of raw materials, as well as for development of every type of military power. The single task of the German Navy was, therefore, to interrupt or cut these sea communications. It was clear that this object could never be obtained by building a fleet to fight the English Fleet and in this way win the sea communications. The only remaining method was to attack sea communications quickly. For this purpose only the U-boat could be considered, as only this weapon could penetrate into the main areas of English sea communications in spite of English sea supremacy on the surface.'[6]

'The "tonnage war" is the main task for submarines, probably the decisive contribution of submarines to winning the war.'[7]

The mathematics were clean, precise and merciless. Britain would starve if her lifeline of food and raw materials were cut. That could be accomplished only by sinking merchant shipping faster than it could be replaced, so that each month fewer and fewer vital shiploads would arrive in the United Kingdom. A quick calculation that took the estimated annual production of the shipyards and divided that figure by 12 gave the minimal monthly sinkings required for stalemate. Given the

▶ **Early in the war, U-boats would often torpedo their targets from the surface and have a chance to witness the sinking. A lookout on the gun platform watches the death throes of a tanker that has been broken in two by the U-boat's attack.**

▶ **Seen from the surface, the effects of a U-boat's attack on a convoy were psychologically as well as physically devastating. Here, a pair of American troop transports from the 'Torch' convoys are torpedoed off the coast of Morocco, 13 November 1942. Their location is identified only by the smoke of their explosion. The remaining transports in a convoy can only keep moving while escorts, such as the destroyer to the left, converge on the suspected location of the attacker. (USN via Rumpf)**

excess tonnage with which Britain entered the war, the fact that not all neutral tonnage would be scared off by the U-boat blockade, the fact that the large Belgian, Dutch, Norwegian and French merchant fleets fell almost intact into British hands in the spring of 1940 and the fact that Germany wanted victory and not just a stalemate, Dönitz calculated that a significantly higher tonnage figure was required. His calculations in 1940 were that a monthly figure of 700,000 GRT sunk would strangle Britain within two years.

One other factor would help determine his chances of success. That was the willingness of the political and military leadership of the nation to commit those boats that were available to this battle and to this battle only. A recurrent theme throughout the early parts of the war would be Dönitz's resistance to SKL plans to divert U-boats to other activities than the sinking of merchant shipping and to other theatres than the North Atlantic.

> 'BdU is clearly convinced that the weight of the U-boat war must be carried out in the Atlantic, that only war against tonnage will be effective in the overall war and that any deviation from these fundamental concepts will only lead to damage of the total war effort.'[8]

Given the theory of *Tonnageschlacht* and the practise of *Rüdeltaktik*, Dönitz believed that if he had sufficient boats with which to fight and clear strategic commitment to the *Tonnageschlacht*, he had the means by which to gain victory. *Rüdeltaktik* was tried out in a full-scale experiment just before the outbreak of war.[9] In the last major naval exercise before the war, held in the spring of 1939, the Germans assembled a convoy of fleet auxiliaries and escorts, and repeatedly carried out pack attacks against it as it moved between Cape St. Vincent and Ushant. Dönitz declared the experiment a success. Once war had started, however, the low number of available U-boats prevented the adoption of *Rüdeltaktik* as a normal practice. Nevertheless, Dönitz managed to assemble three U-boats into a pack to attack the traffic on the Gibraltar convoy route beginning on 17 October 1939. He tried leaving tactical command in the hands of a local commander, KL Hartmann of *U37*, who was given charge of the other two boats, *U46* and *U48*. The three boats formed a sweep line across the suspected convoy route and began the search for targets. *U48* encountered a convoy and shadowed it, reporting its position on a regular basis. Hartmann ordered *U46* to join in the attack, but remained out of the battle himself. The two boats that did attack

◀ **If the crew of the sinking merchantman were lucky, their vessel sank slowly and they were close enough to shore to reach safety or the convoy's escorts or salvage vessels would pick them up. This oiler, SS *Gulftrade*, sunk by *U588* on 10 March 1942, was hit close off the Barnegat Light on the New Jersey shore and the crew's chances of survival were good. Many others weren't this lucky. (USAF)**

accounted for four ships from the convoy before it came under shore-based aircraft cover.

> 'The attack as a whole proved a success and showed that cooperation between U-boats is a practical proposition, in spite of the small number of only three boats.'[10]

Based on this success, Dönitz tried out the tactic again in mid-February 1940, again with Hartmann in *U37*, now commanding a pack of four other boats.[11] Dönitz was critical of one aspect of these experiments. He didn't like having an on-site commander. He felt that he couldn't afford to reserve one of his few boats to just a command role, but if the local commander's boat participated in the attack, it would probably be much less effective in command. The solution he adopted, when *Rüdel* attacks began in earnest in June 1940, was to retain tactical command in his hands at his operational headquarters. When Gruppe Prien was formed from six boats on the 12th of that month, it received its orders directly from BdU. The boats that made up the pack, with only one exception, were Type VIIs.[12]

1. These counts are based on the best reconciliation of all sources available to the author and agree exactly with none of them. The disagreements range from which hull numbers were to be which VIIC sub-type down to how many boats were actually completed. The results of that effort are shown in the table in Appendix C.
2. The next largest class of submarines built was the American *Gato/Balao* class, of which 204 were ordered and 194 built.
3. Atl, vol. 2, p. 106.
4. KTB, 21 August 1939. At the beginning of the war, Dönitz had 43 U-boats at his disposal. He considered this to be an unsatisfactory number. 'In order to occupy the positions [assigned around England], which are not many, without a break with the minimum of boats, I would need a further 43 boats and an additional 43 boats which, as experience shows, would be in dock undergoing overhaul. Thus, for a war of some length, 130 U-boats should be necessary. Even then I would have no reserves, so that I could send out 3 or 4 boats from home against a worthwhile transport reported by the intelligence service. Also there are not enough boats for the Atlantic and none for remote sea areas. Therefore, the minimum requirement to be aimed at is 300 U-boats.'
5. KTB, 10 October 1941.
6. Conduct, p 3.
7. KTB, 31 December 1942.
8. KTB, 15 November 1942.
9. It should be emphasized that Dönitz wasn't privy to the inner workings of the Nazi Government and had no advance warning that war would break out in September 1939. Not that he was the least bit reluctant to fight England again, but he had been repeatedly assured that war with England wouldn't begin until 1945 at the earliest. In 1939 he had far too few U-boats to win and he knew it.
10. KTB, 18 October 1939.
11. KTB, 15 February 1940.
12. KTB, 12 June 1940. Gruppe Prien was formed of *U47, U32, U28, U25, U30* and *U51*. Of these, *U25* was a Type I, the rest were Type VIIAs and Bs. They were formed into a sweep line of five boats with a trailer on the projected course of advance of the target convoy, HX48.

Below right: The pressure hull sections of a Type VII U-boat, eight in number, were built up of rolled sheet steel plates welded over a set of ribs placed 75cm apart. Each sheet of steel was rolled to the correct curvature before delivery to the yard. There they were assembled in a procedure which started by laying the first sheet in an appropriately curved jig, welding the ribs to this sheet and then, in turn, welding the remaining sheets to the ribs and the sheets already in place. The pressure hull was almost entirely arc welded. Since this was best done in an environment of controlled temperature and humidity, the early Type VIIs were assembled inside sheds. (via Baker)

Part Two: Physical Characteristics of the System

This section will present the physical description of a typical Type VII U-boat, with the understanding that there was no such thing. Despite the fact that more than 700 Type VII U-boats were built, there never was anything like the mass production of these boats in a manner similar to the mass production of aircraft or tanks. Type VIIs were never built as Henry Kaiser built Liberty Ships in the USA or that Merker built the later Type XXIs or XXIIIs in Germany. There were always differences not only between sub-types but within those sub-types as the design continued to evolve. Additionally, there were subtle differences also between the boats built by different yards. (Sixteen different yards built Type VIIs though some, like Oderwerke Stettin and Vulkan Stettin completed only one or two.)

The following subsections will describe the primary physical systems (hull, propulsion, crew, feeding and sanitation) of a mid-war Type VIIC U-boat .

Hull

The Type VII U-boat was a single hull design,[1] meaning that its pressure hull was also its outer watertight hull. Around this, forward and aft, was a thin, non-watertight structure which provided streamlining and room for ballast tanks. On each side were long, bulbous saddle tanks that provided room for additional ballast tanks and, in all but the A model, fuel bunkerage. Along the top of the boat ran a flat-topped deckcasing which provided a flat stable surface for any work that had to be done on deck. The space between the deckcasing and the pressure hull was used for torpedo storage, air trunks, ready ammunition stowage and, later in the war, for the stowage of inflatable life rafts. The tower was also a multi-layer structure. Inside was the watertight conning tower from which torpedoes were aimed and fired when the boat was submerged. Surrounding it was the external tower structure, which provided a protected site for the lookouts and a Flak platform. The air trunks that fed air to the diesels ran up the after part of the external tower structure.

Pressure Hull

The life of a U-boat took place inside the pressure hull. All activities that had to go on whether the boat was surfaced or submerged were located

Type VIIB (1940), outboard profile and plan

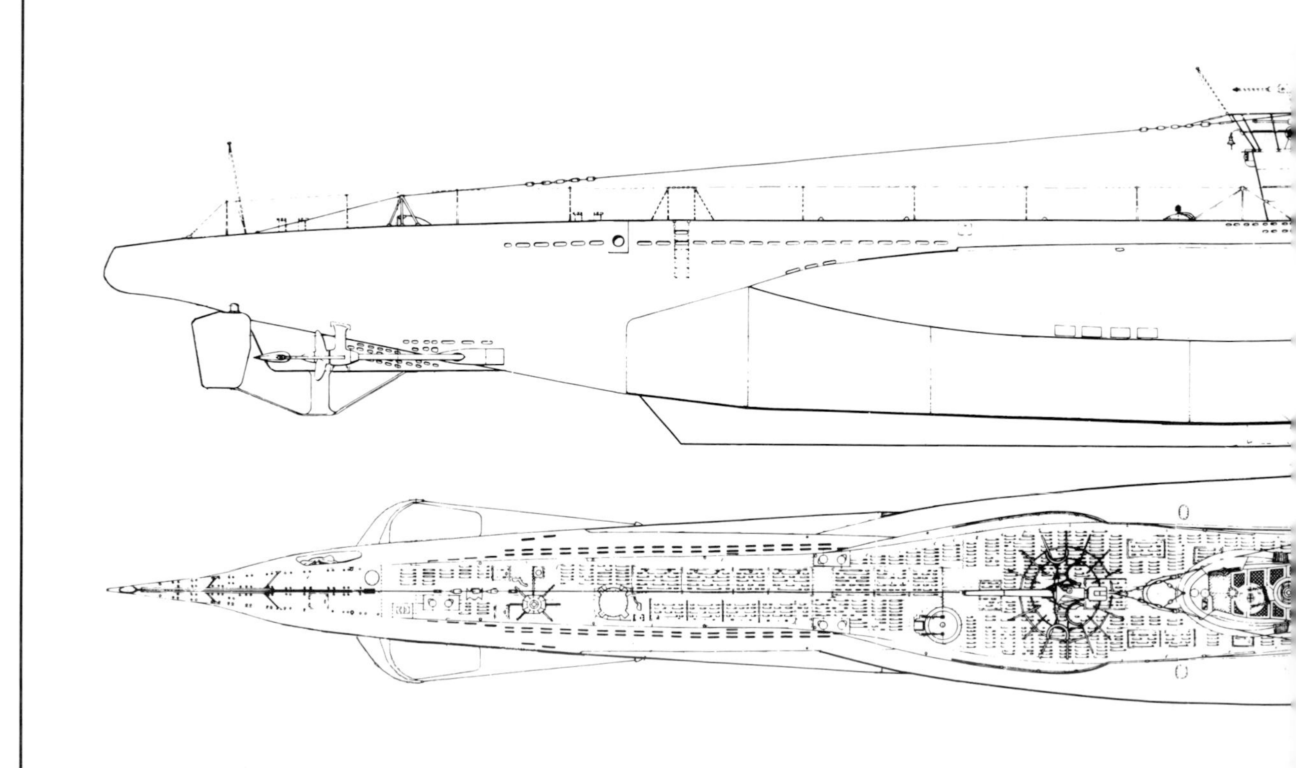

◀ **The extreme bow and stern sections of the pressure hull had cast steel caps already pierced by the holes for the torpedo tubes. The section at the far left in this view is the bow section, with two of the four large holes visible. Next to the right is a stern section. (via Baker)**

within its confines. On a Type VIIC, the pressure hull was a structure of circular cross-section, 4.7 metres in diameter at its widest. It was constructed of rolled galvanized sheet steel ranging in thickness from 1.6cm at the bow and stern to 1.85cm at the pressure hull's widest point, the control room. The effect of gradually thickening the hull steel as the diameter of the hull sections increased was to give a hull with consistent strength throughout its length. The pressure hull was further thickened at its only naturally weak spot, the point where the conning tower was connected to the main hull, to a thickness of 2.2cm.

For only about 20 per cent of the length of the pressure hull was the hull truly cylindrical. Of the eight sections that made up the hull of a Type VII U-boat, only the two central sections, the control room and the petty officers' room immediately aft were cylindrical. The remaining sections were truncated cones. The six central sections of the pressure hull were constructed by welding the rolled sheet steel that made up the skin of the pressure hull to a set of circular ribs spaced at regular 60cm intervals. The only exceptions were the very ends of the hull which were each prefabricated of three rolled and stamped pieces, two half conic sections and a spherical section end cap. This end cap was pierced by holes for the torpedo tubes and the various pipes associated with the tubes.

For assembly, all eight sections were moved to the slip by crane, where they were welded together end-to-end and the conning tower added. At this point, the pressure hull was complete except for a large hole aft of the tower. Through this hole were lowered the various components and devices that made up the interior of the boat, from the smallest nut and bolt to the massive motors and diesels that powered the boat. This activity was precisely scheduled so that the bow and stern were filled in first and the centre sections later. The diesels were the last major internal component to be installed. After they were in place the remaining hull plates were welded into place and the hull was watertight.

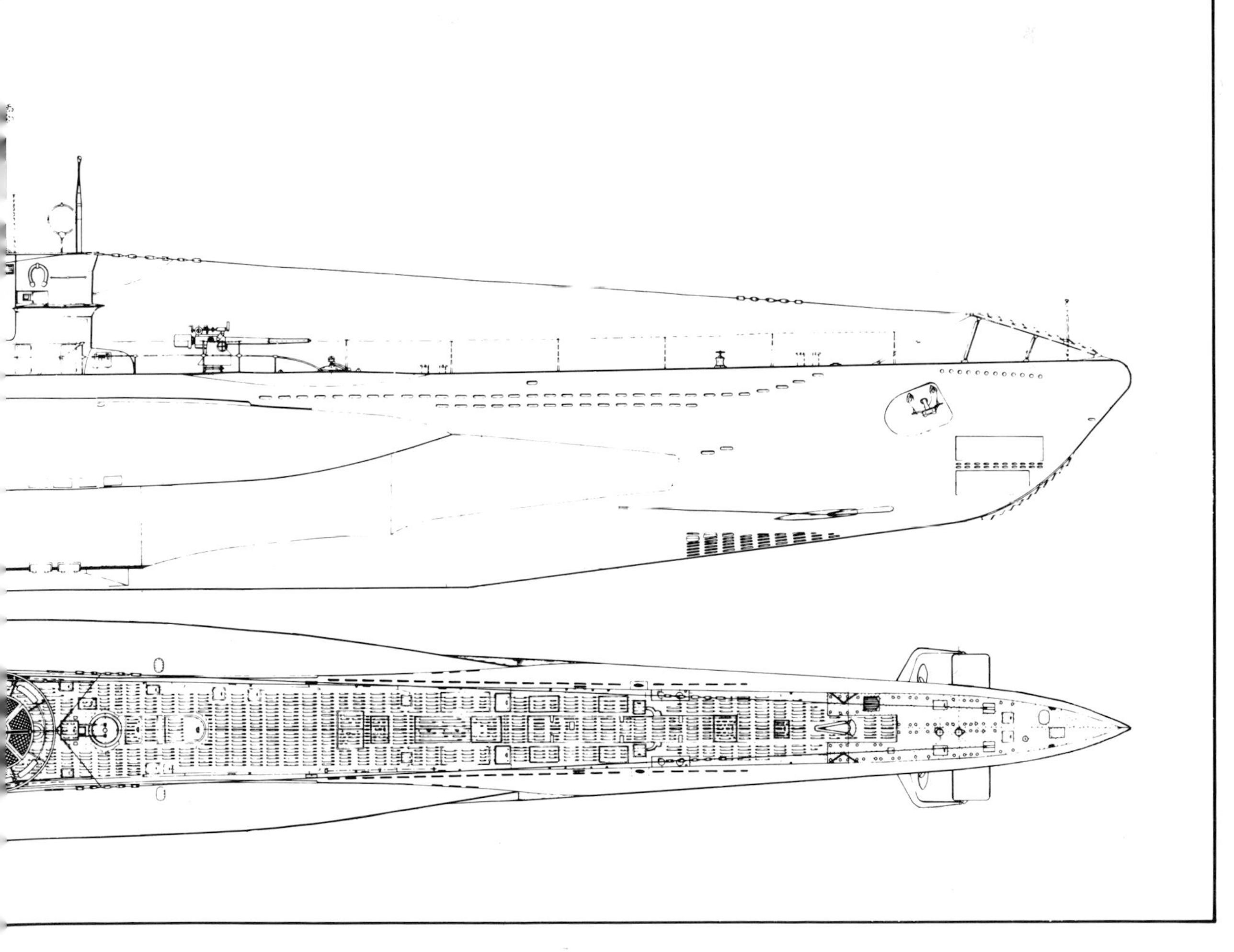

◀ The control room section (Section 5) had transverse watertight bulkheads built into each end and dive and fuel tanks located below a curved longitudinal bulkhead. This view shows the end of Section 5, rightside up, with its concave transverse bulkhead, not yet pierced by the circular hatchway, and the end of the main internal dive tank below the longitudinal bulkhead. (via Baker)

◀ As the pace of production increased, the need for space to assemble sections of Type VIIs exceeded the available shed space at shipyards and production moved outside. At this yard, multiple lines of partially completed sections, in various stages of assembly, are seen, surrounded by the parts that are used to assemble them. A pair of control room bulkheads can be seen at the bottom of this view. At the right can be seen a pair of the thinner bulkheads, pierced by the tall, narrow hatchways, used to separate other compartments. (via Baker)

◀ Once sections were completed, they were set aside until needed to assemble a boat's pressure hull. Here, a row of completed sections, finished on the outside but virtually bare inside, await final assembly. Note the holes in the outer skin of the nearest section. A U-boat's pressure hull was pierced by innumerable holes for the pipes that pumped air, water and oil into or out of the boat. (via Baker)

Within the circular pressure hull, a horizontal deck was built separating the main level at which the crew worked and slept and a lower level that was primarily devoted to storage or bunkerage. The level of this deck varied from compartment to compartment. In the centre sections, the deck was at the mid-point of the circular section, but forward and aft the deck was lower. In the forward section, the deck was lower in order to give access to all four torpedo tubes. Aft, in the engine room, the decking was set lower to allow full access to the diesels, whose height nearly filled the available space inside the pressure hull.

From forward to aft, the layout of the inside of a Type VII U-boat was:

Forward Torpedo Room (*Bugtorpedoraum*). The bow of the boat was given over to the forward torpedo room, which was dom-inated by the torpedo tubes and the equipment needed to move and store torpedoes. The inner ends of the four forward torpedo tubes projected almost four metres into this compartment. They were arranged in two vertical banks of two, the upper tube of each bank slightly outboard of the lower. Outboard of each tube, between the tube and the pressure hull, was a two-metre-long compressed-air cylinder, which stored the air needed to launch a torpedo from that tube.

Aft of the torpedo tubes, as the diameter of the hull increased, room became available for storage of spare torpedoes and the equipment needed to handle them. Beneath the removable deck plates, storage room existed for four torpedoes. At full load, two additional torpedoes were generally stored in the forward torpedo room, hanging from the overhead, one on each side. The torpedo hatch set into the overhead at the after end of this compartment allowed torpedoes to be loaded nose first into the torpedo hoist. The sleeping accommodation for the crew was almost an afterthought in this arrangement. Two rows of three bunks were laid out on each side of the compartment. These folded out of the way to provide room to handle or stow torpedoes. Three wooden tables could be erected when it was time to eat meals. These were stowed under the lower bunks when not in use. The reserve compressed air cylinders used to recharge the launch cylinders between shots were also located under the lower bunks. The crew kept the few personal belongings they were allowed on shelves fitted between the hull frames outboard of the folding bunks.

Below the torpedo storage, the hull was divided horizontally by a curved bulkhead below which were located the forward trim tank and the two forward torpedo tanks used to counterbalance the weight of fired torpedoes. Between the forward torpedo room and the forward accommodation section next aft was a thin bulkhead and a hatchway, which could be closed to give some privacy to the CPOs.

Forward Accommodation (*Oberfeldwebelraum, Offizierraum, Horchraum* and *Funkraum*). The next section aft was more spacious, because here the hull was almost full diameter and the crewmen who lived here held higher rank. The forward head was located on the port side aft of the dividing bulkhead. Opposite, to starboard, was a small food locker. Next aft came the small space to accommodate the four CPOs. Their area was only long enough to fit their bunks, two each side. The passageway there was offset somewhat to port so that a permanently erected drop-leaf table for eating and other work could be fitted to the starboard side. Three small cabinets (two port and one starboard), as well as shelves between the hull frames, provided storage for the CPOs' kit. Another thin bulkhead and hatch separated the CPOs from the officers, whose accommodation came next aft.

The officers' area was the most spacious on-board, though hardly plush by the standards of most other nations' submarines. Like the CPOs' area, this space was only as long as the bunks, which were also arranged two on a side. Since normally only three officers lived in this space, the upper bunk on the port side was normally lashed up. A permanent mess and work table on the port side allowed this space to double as the boat's wardroom. Four large wardrobes were provided for the officers because the space between the hull frames, used in other parts of the boat for storage, was used here for a drinking-water tank.

Aft of the wardroom, on the port side, was the Commanding Officer's compartment, the only private space in the boat. Even here, the privacy was minimal since only a heavy felt curtain separated the CO's room from the wardroom. This lack of privacy was intentional. The CO needed to be able to hear what was going on in the rest of the boat. The most important activities of the boat were all located within earshot of the CO's quarters. The control room was just aft and the sound and radio rooms were just across the passageway. The sound room, just aft of the watch officers' bunks, and the radio shack, next aft, were the ears of the boat. There the *Funkers* or telegraphists listened to the sounds of the world around them, near and far, with banks of hydrophonic and electronic equipment. These devices became more and more sophisticated as the war progressed, and as U-boats spent more and more time submerged, these compartments became increasingly the primary source of information about the boat's surroundings. The forward circuit-breaker cabinet was located aft of the CO's compartment on the port side. This section of the boat was separated from the control

◄ Yard workers put the finishing touches to an early Type VII that is nearly ready for launch. Note the net cutter that was found on only a few early boats. Another Type VII approaches completion in the background. To the left is another in the early stages of final assembly. The torpedo tubes have yet to be fitted in their holes in the bowcap of the pressure hull. That needs to be done before the external bow can be added to the boat. The frames for the port saddle tanks can just be made

Type VIIB, inboard profile and deck plan

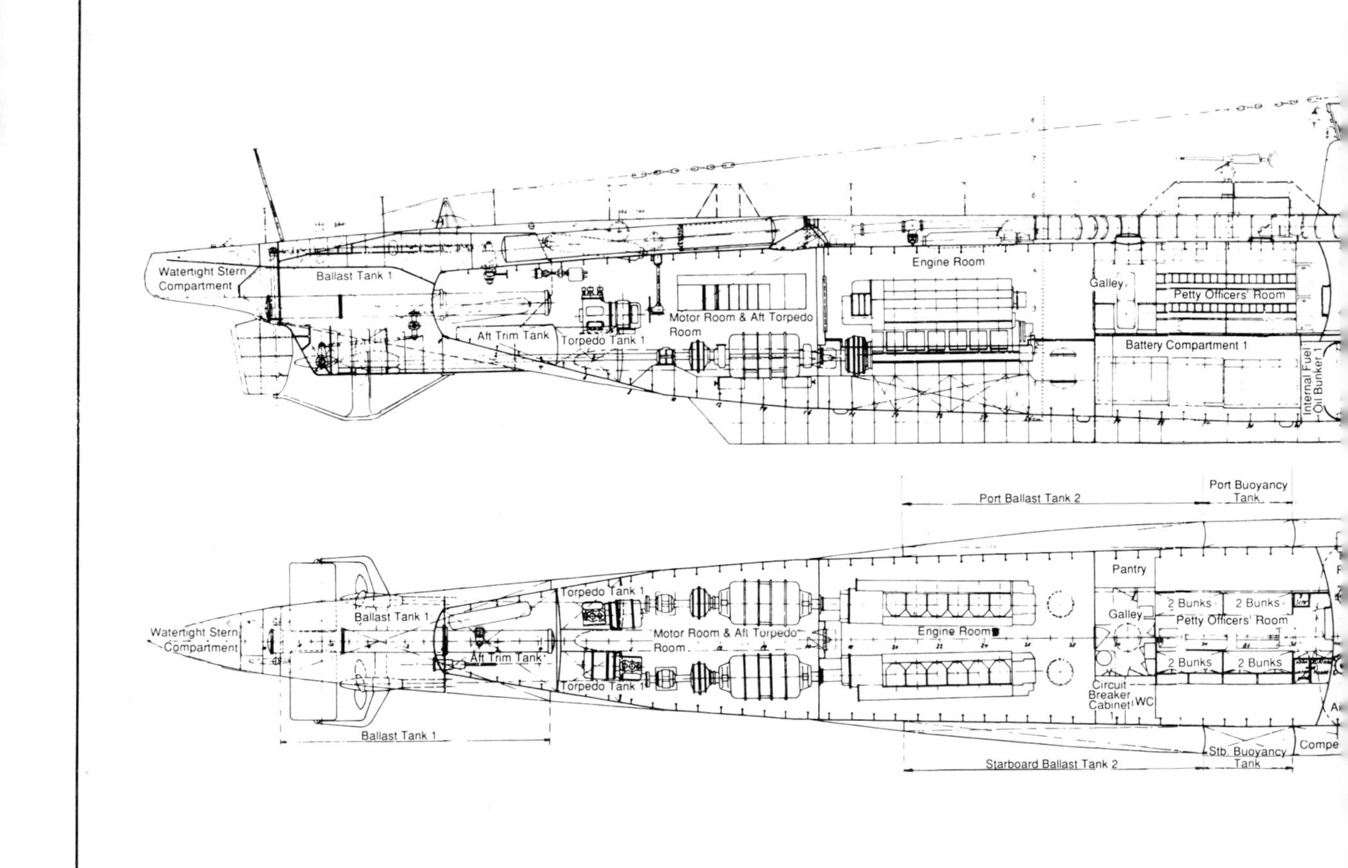

out along the side of the hull.

▶ An early Type VII, probably a B, is ready for launching, probably at Germania Werft, as a crowd of onlookers watches the ceremony. The parts necessary to build the next one are already accumulating to the left and right in this view. (via Baker)

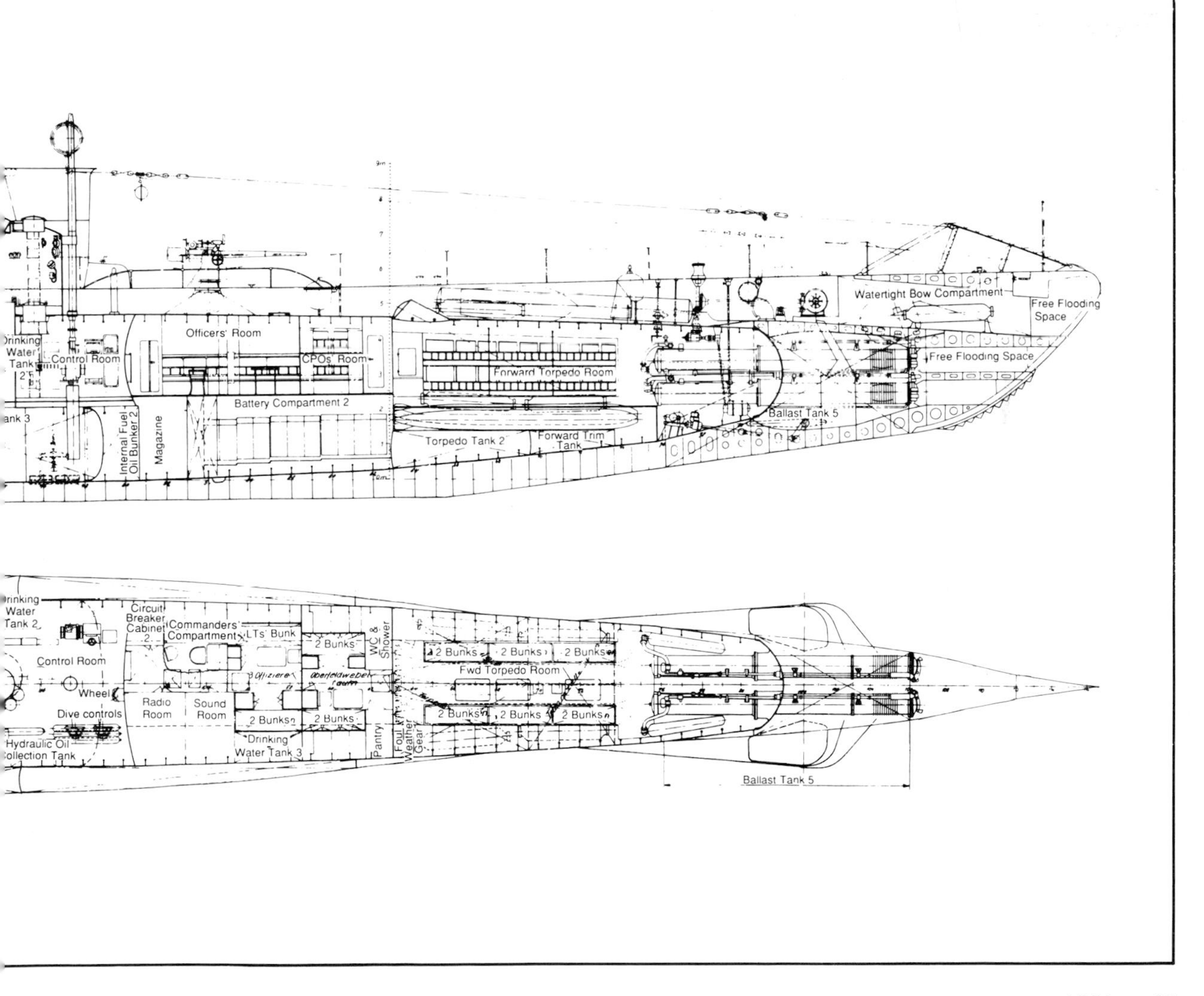

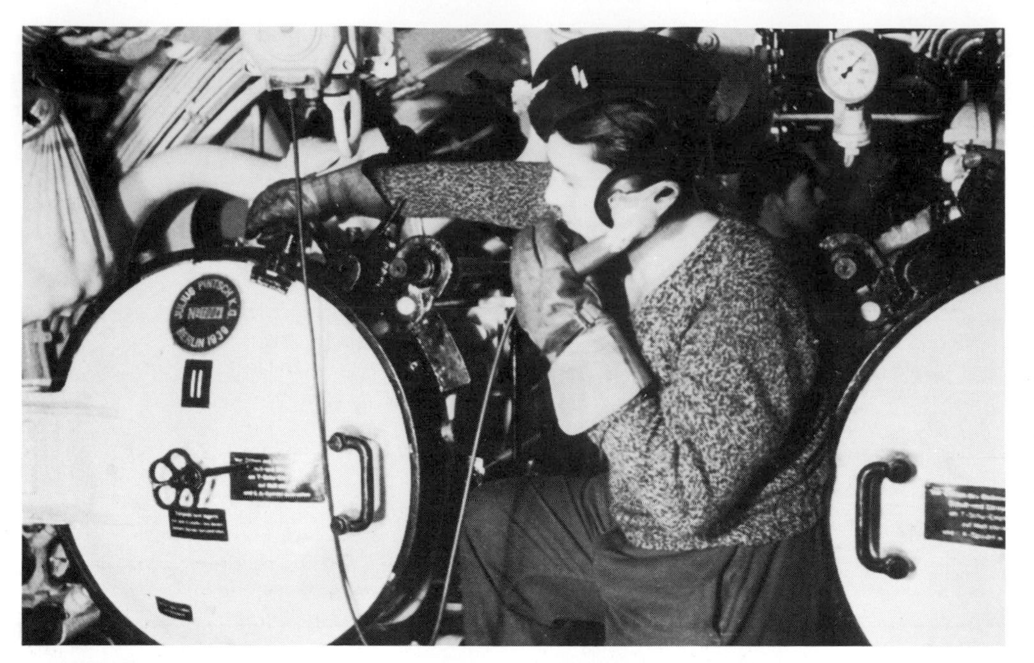

◄ The *Mechaniker* checks the settings on tube No. 2 in the forward torpedo room of a U-boat. The setting up and firing of torpedoes was normally done automatically by the action of the attack computer and torpedo control board in the control room and conning tower, but back up controls were provided in the bow in case the automatic systems failed. (Actually, this view shows the forward torpedo room of a Type IXB, *U65*, not a Type VII, but the appearance of this compartment in a IX was nearly identical with that in a VII.)

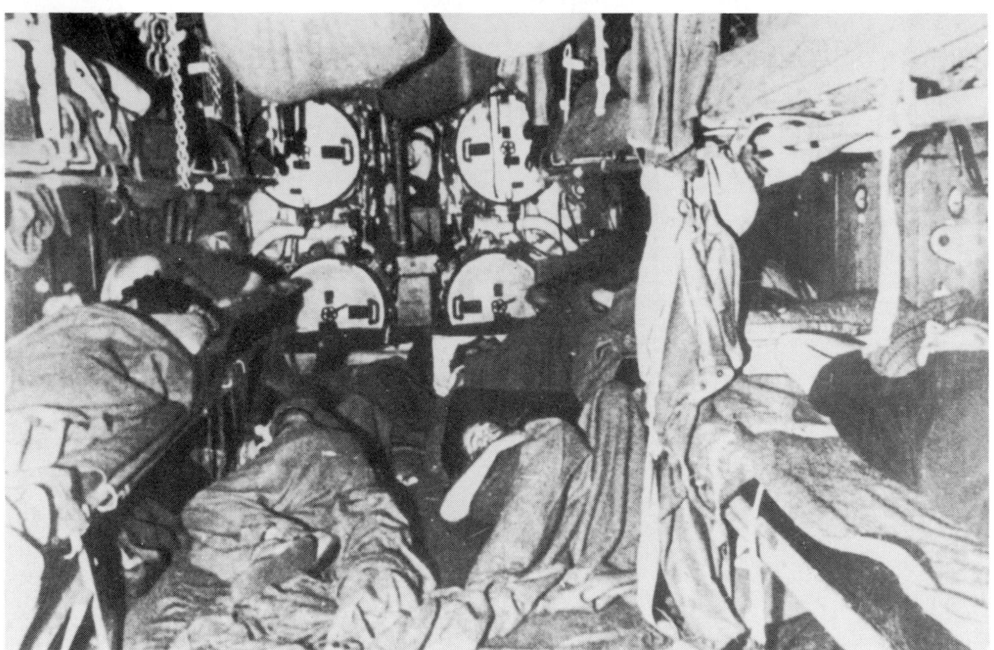

◄ Even when there weren't torpedoes taking up half the bunk space, there were still occasions when there weren't enough bunks in the forward torpedo room for crewmen who needed sleep. Then the latecomers simply grabbed a blanket and made themselves as comfortable as possible on the deck. (SFL)

room by a watertight bulkhead. Passage through the bulkhead was by a circular watertight hatch offset to port.

The area below the deck plating, in this section, was almost as large as the living and working spaces above it. Most of the forward section below deck was taken up by the forward battery compartment. Aft of this was the magazine, where ammunition for the deck and Flak guns were stored. Outboard of these compartments on both sides was a forward extension of the large forward fuel oil tank, which connected through the watertight bulkhead to the main body of that tank.

Control Room (*Zentral*). The command of a Type VII U-boat, at least when it was submerged, was done from the control room. Here were located the controls that guided the boat on the surface and submerged, the valves that controlled the flooding or venting of tanks and most of the mechanical devices that actually drove those controls. The centre of the room was dominated by the shafts for the two periscopes, the larger sky periscope and the attack periscope further aft. The

► Despite the cramped conditions and lack of materials, Christmas was celebrated by the Lords (U-Boat ratings) with as much festivity as the circumstances allowed. A small artificial tree has been smuggled onboard, a few bottles of wine have been opened, an accordion is being played and the forward torpedo room, at least temporarily, becomes a festive place.

main helm position was at the forward end of the compartment, just starboard of the watertight hatch. Along the starboard side of the control room were located the two planesmen's positions that controlled the vertical movement of the boat. The navigator's chart table was located just behind them. The after end of the starboard side of the control room was taken up by the auxiliary bilge pump. The port side was completely given over to machinery: the periscope motor, the banks of valve handles controlling the flooding or venting of the boat's ballast tanks and the main bilge pump. The valve handles were painted red or green to indicate the location of the tank they controlled. A small drinking-water tank was located on the port side and a similarly sized hydraulic oil tank on the starboard.

A downward-curved horizontal bulkhead separated the control room proper from the lower part of the circular hull section. This space, crescent moon in shape, was given over to the large internal tanks that were so characteristic of this design. This tank space was further subdivided into three parts by two vertical partitions. Forward and aft were the main fuel oil bunkers. The large main ballast tank was located in the middle.

Conning Tower (*Turm*). In the control room overhead, between the two periscopes, was a watertight hatch and a ladder giving access to the conning tower. This tiny compartment, projecting above the circular pressure hull for a height of only slightly more than two metres, contained the equipment needed to aim the boat's torpedoes. This included the attack computer, a compass repeater and the attack periscope. In the overhead of the conning tower was the watertight hatchway leading to the bridge.

After Accommodation and Galley (*Unteroffizierraum* and *Küche*). The after end of the control room, like its forward end, was sealed by a watertight bulkhead pierced by a circular hatch. Immediately aft of the bulkhead, on the starboard side, was a tiny refrigerated compartment, aft of which were stacks of small storage lockers for the petty officers. Next aft came the petty officers' bunks, two rows of two on each side. Outboard of the bunks, the after internal fuel oil bunker extended upward, taking up the space between the bunks and the pressure hull. The after end of this section was given over to the galley. This tiny area had a sink and wash space on the starboard side forward, and a two-burner electric stove aft. Outboard on the starboard side was the after pantry. The after head, most often used as additional food storage, and the after circuit-breaker cabinet took up the port side of the galley space.

The after battery compartment was located below the decking of this section. Outboard of the battery compartment, the diesel oil bunker continued aft to the thin bulkhead separating this section from the engine room.

Engine Room (*Dieselmotorenraum*). The two big diesels that provided the surface propulsion for a Type VII U-boat were located side by side in the engine room. Their bulk was such that they occupied nearly all the space within this compartment. Space in this section that wasn't taken up by the engines themselves was occupied by their substantial foundations, which had to be strong enough to keep the engines in alignment throughout the vicissitudes of U-boat combat.[2] The narrow central passageway gave access to the engines' valves and cylinders. Small compressed air and carbon dioxide tanks were located

Type VIIC, 1940

Diesel-engine room

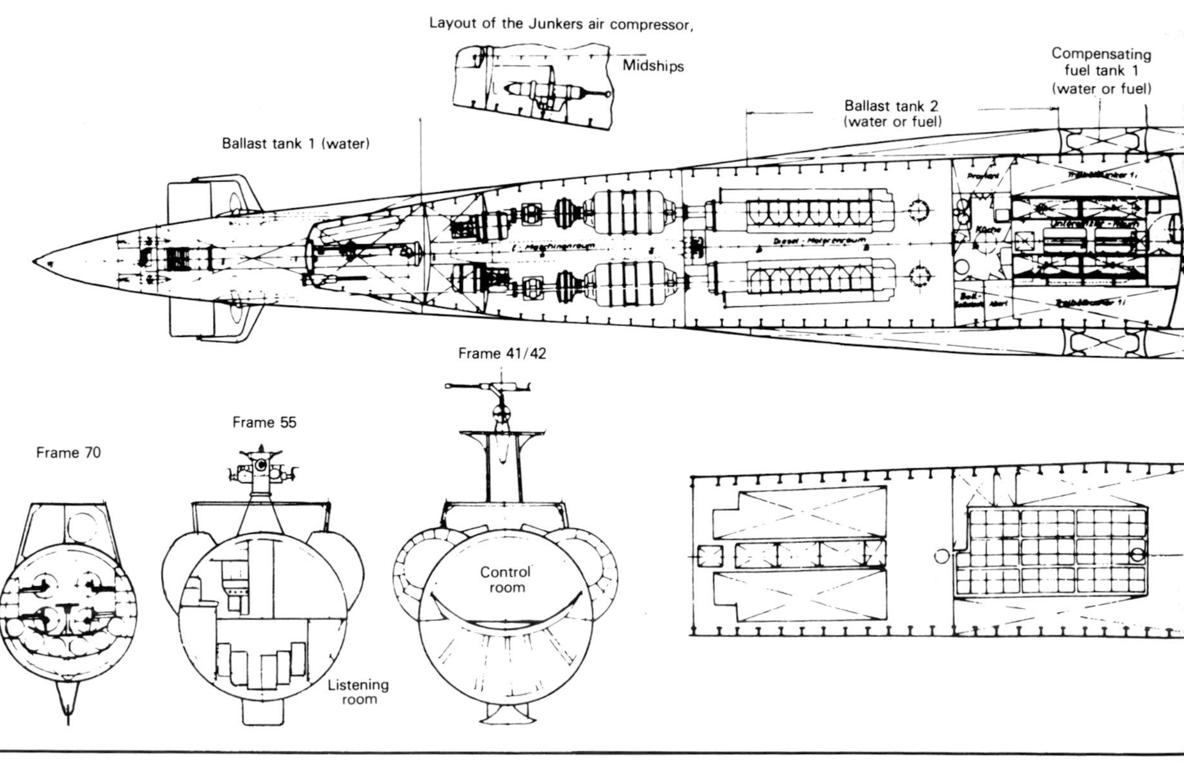

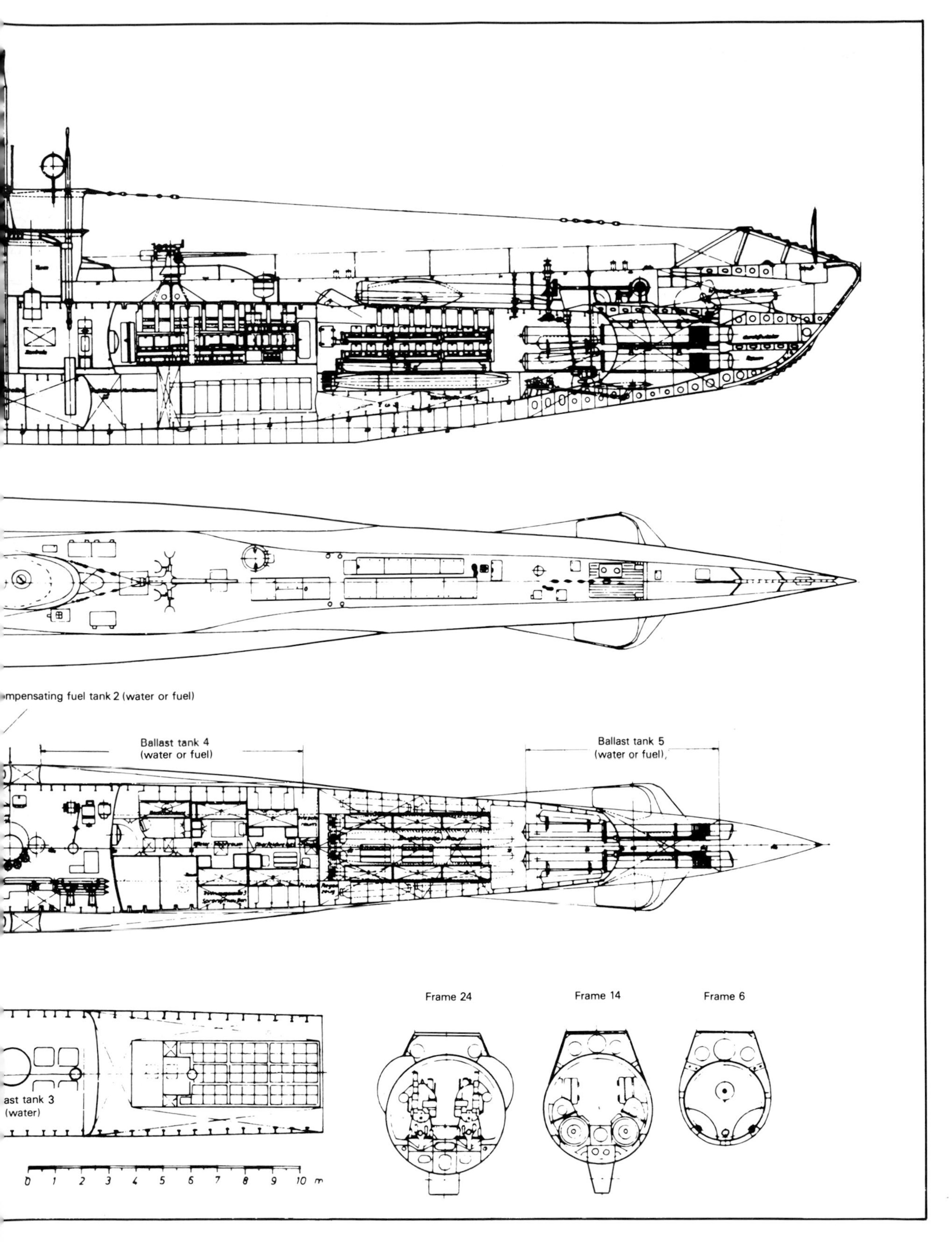
mpensating fuel tank 2 (water or fuel)
Ballast tank 4
(water or fuel)
Ballast tank 5
(water or fuel),
Frame 24
Frame 14
Frame 6
ast tank 3
(water)
0 1 2 3 4 5 6 7 8 9 10 m

outboard of the engines, the former used to start the engines, the latter to fight fires. A thin bulkhead with a hatchway separated this compartment from the aftermost.

Motor Room and After Torpedo Room (*E-Maschinenraum* and *Hecktorpedoraum*). The last two compartments filled the narrow after end of the boat. The two electric motors were aligned on the drive shafts from the diesel engines. The motors were tiny in comparison with the diesels, taking up very little space in these compartments. Geared to the starboard motor, and mounted above it, was the compressor for the small refrigerated compartment. The control panels that monitored the boat's electrical power system were located above the motors.

The two large air compressors were located aft of the motors, the electrical compressor on the port side, the smaller, diesel-driven Junkers compressor on the starboard. The auxiliary helm was located here as well, the large wheel swung up out of the way when not in use. Aft of this was the single after torpedo tube and its associated compressed air tanks. The space below the decking between the motors provided stowage for the single reload for the after torpedo tube. The hoist for this torpedo was centered on the overhead. The after torpedo loading hatch pierced the overhead just aft of the bulkhead dividing this compartment from the engine room. It was angled so that a torpedo loaded nose first would be pointing aft. The after torpedo tank and trim tank were located below the decking aft of the torpedo stowage.

▲ A U-boat inspector steps through the watertight hatchway connecting the forward accommodation section of a Type VII U-boat to the control room. Before a U-boat was accepted by the Kriegsmarine, it was put through a series of rigorous tests under the supervision of EGRU (*Erprobungsgruppe für Uboote*).

Saddle Tanks

In enlarging the Type II design to become the Type VII, it was found that the ballast tanks in the pressure hull and external hull were inadequate for rapid diving and surfacing of the boat. So the Type VIIA was given a long saddle tank on each side, along the waterline, running for slightly more than half the length of the boat. In the A variant, the saddle tanks were divided into two ballast tanks on each side, one forward and one aft.

In each later model of the Type VII, the saddle tanks were increased in size. The B model had a fuel tank and a compensating tank added on each side of the boat between the ballast tanks. The C model added another small tank to the array, this time a small extra buoyancy tank. The D model, due to its greater length, was able to multiply the bunkers of each type within the saddle tanks. From forward to aft, they were: a ballast tank, a buoyancy tank, a compensating tank, a self-compensating fuel tank, two more ballast tanks, another buoyancy tank and a fuel tank. The Type VIIF, because it had less room inside the pressure hull for internal storage of fuel, increased the size of the saddle tanks still further. From forward to aft, its saddle tanks contained: a fuel tank, a ballast tank, a buoyancy tank, a compensating tank, a self-compensating fuel tank, another ballast tank and another fuel tank.

External Hull

Streamlining the boat and providing room for the myriad of tanks and trunks, the deck-casing and forward and aft external hull made up a second, outer skin covering much of the outside of a Type VII U-boat. Most of the area between the pressure hull and the external hull was free-flooding, being open to the sea, but, there were compartments and tanks outside the pressure hull that were watertight or where the access of water was controlled to ballast or trim the boat.

▲ The starboard side of the control room, looking forward. The two planesmen are seated, hands on the large wheels that controlled the dive planes, staring intently at the 'bubbles', the fluid levels that told them the angle on the boat. The large circular gauge to the right was the depth gauge, marked off in 10 metre increments down to 200 metres.

The external hull covered the entire bow and stern sections of the boat and extended along the top of the boat. The pressure hull was the outer skin of the boat only in the lower half of the midships sections of the boat. Because the tall, narrow shape of the external bow had to blend into the circular cross-section of the pressure hull, the edge between the external hull and the pressure hull forward was complex, the covering of the pressure hull by the external hull extending farther aft at the top and bottom of the boat and less in the middle. From forward to aft, the external hull was composed as follows:

Bow Section. The extreme bow of a Type VII was a free-flooding area. It contained the channels for the torpedo tubes, the mechanisms for opening and closing the external and outer torpedo tube doors, and the anchor hoist. The space between and around the torpedo tubes was taken up by the bow ballast tank. The recess into which the anchor was drawn by the hoist was on the starboard side, level with the forward ends of the torpedo tubes. The external torpedo tube doors were hinged at their forward end and opened inward to allow torpedoes to be fired. When closed, they streamlined the bow over the torpedo tube channels.

The foreplanes were located low on each side of the external bow. These were protected by a guard which projected from the hull forward of the planes and curved around their forward edge. These protected the planes from damage from flotsam or ice and also provided an outboard end to the pivot around which they were rotated. The holes for the GHG (*Gruppenhorchgerät* – fixed hydrophone array) were located on each side in a semi-circle around the foreplanes. The open end of the semi-circle faced downward. One pair of the circular diaphragms of the UT (*Unterwasser Telegraphie* – underwater sound telegraph) on each side was sited directly above the GHG installation. The other pair was about 50cm aft.

Forward Deckcasing. The foredeck of a Type VII U-boat was an extension of the external bow, leading back to the tower. Basically a flat-decked, thin steel structure, its upper surface, except at the extreme bow, was made of hardwood planks, primarily because a metal surface would ice up much more quickly in freezing weather. Numerous segments of the deck planking were either hinged or entirely removable to permit access to hatchways or storage areas below. The wooden planks were spaced approximately 1cm apart to allow rapid drainage of water during rough weather and easy escape of air during a dive. The lower edge of the deckcasing on each side was marked by a long line of large free-flooding holes to further facilitate the entry and exit of water. Where the deckcasing met the saddle tanks, a narrow gap was left for the same reason.

The space forward between the deckcasing and the pressure hull was used primarily for storage. The motors and gearing for hauling in the anchor was located at the bow. Aft of this, on all models except the A, was the forward torpedo storage tube, offset to port of the centreline. Later in the war this was omitted on some boats.[3] Some late war boats were fitted with a set of four watertight canisters for inflatable life rafts on the starboard side of the torpedo storage tube, a concession to the altered circumstances in which the Type VII was now operating. Next aft came the hinged access door to the forward torpedo hatch, which projected nearly all the way up to the deck planks. The space between the torpedo hatch and the tower was used differently in early and later boats. Up until mid-war, this section housed a watertight container for ready ammunition for the 8.8cm deck gun and the supports for the gun itself. Between them was the access to the forward battery hatch. Unlike the other hatches in the pressure hull, this one was intended to be opened only in dockyard, for the purpose of replacing battery cells. It therefore bolted shut rather than being sealed by a hinged hatch door. The access space was normally used as an open storage area for docking gear such as lines and fenders. Later in the war, starting in 1943, the deck gun and its associated ready storage container were removed to conserve weight. Later still, the port side of this space was used as stowage for the snorkel when lowered.

The upper surface of the deckcasing had a number of standard features. Forward of the anchor gear, there was a pair of retractable bollards. These were manually extended only when needed to moor the boat. Most early boats were equipped with a rotating hydrophone array, known as the KDB (*Kristalldrehbasis Gerät* – rotating crystal apparatus), just aft of the foremost bollards. Next aft was a capstan, also retractable, needed only if the electrical anchor hoist should fail.[4] If the four life-raft canisters were fitted, they came next, as did the removable deck sections

Type VIIC (1944), inboard profile and outboard deck plan

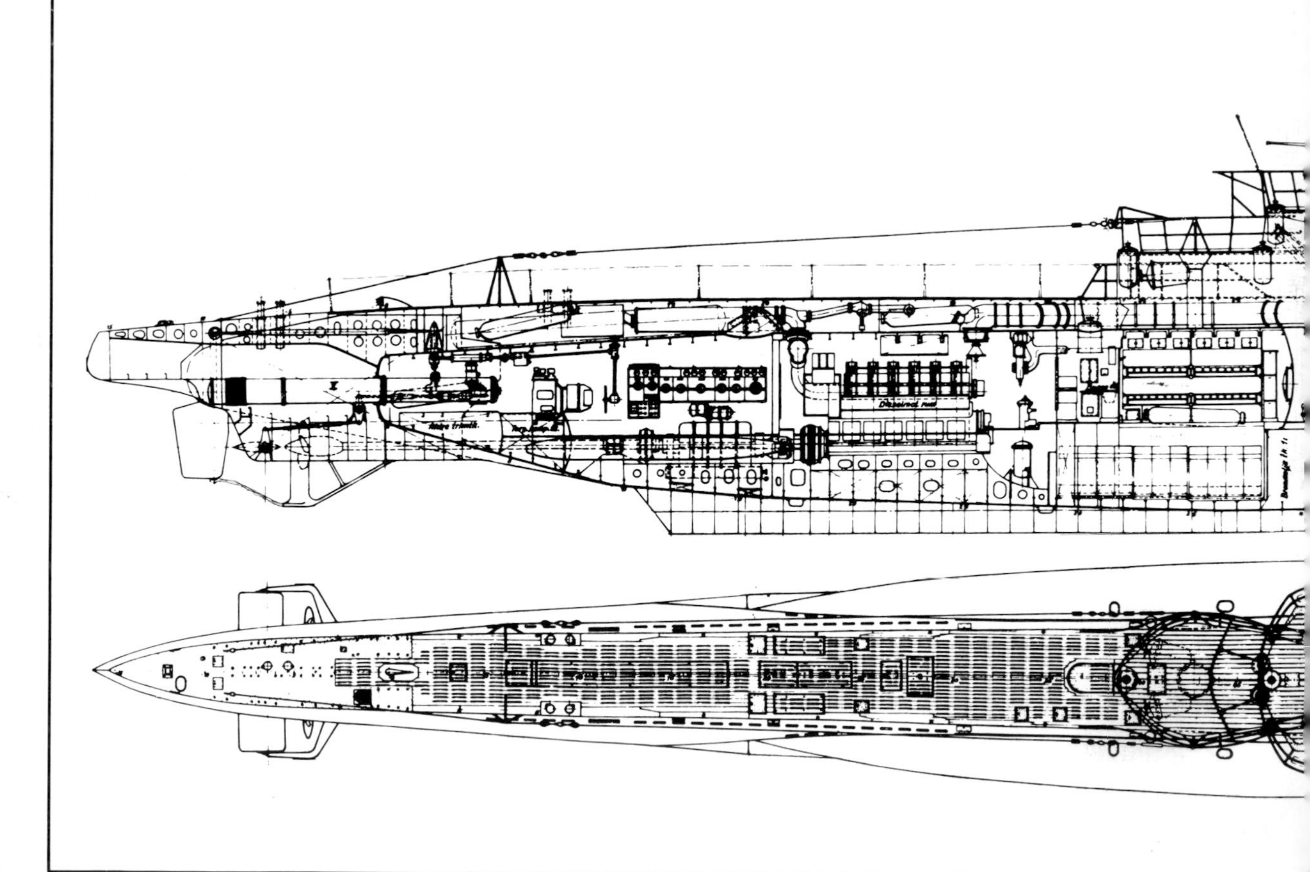

covering the torpedo storage tube. Another pair of retractable bollards was fitted, one on each side aft of these. The remaining deck area between this and the tower was taken up with the gun and its ready storage container or later with the trough for the snorkel.

Tower. The external tower structure of Type VII U-boats evolved continually from the day that the first A model was launched until the end of the war. In its original form, the tower of the first VIIAs was a simple structure, a flat-decked, tear-drop shaped enclosure around the pressure hull conning tower. The forward part of that structure was built up with vertical sides for about 1.5 metres above the bridge deck to give some weather protection to the lookouts who were posted there. Aft of the built up bridge was a small open area, enclosed only by a railing. In its earliest form, this area had no specific purpose and was used only for smoking. The aft-facing Flak gun was mounted on the rear deck just aft of the tower. This was soon seen to be a poor site for a Flak gun, taking too long to man because of its distance from the tower hatch. Before the war, the open area aft of the bridge was enlarged and the 2cm Flak gun was resited there.

A tube protecting the sky periscope was built into the inside of the forward edge of the bridge. Built up structures down the centreline of the enclosed bridge area covered the shaft for the attack periscope and provided support for the UZO (*Uberwasserzieloptik* - surface attack optics) and the binnacle, and provided attachment points for a signal light and other necessary gear. A slot for retraction of the D/F (direction-finding) loop (*Funkpielrahmen*) was provided on the starboard side of the bridge.

On the outside, this early form of the tower was quite plain. The forward horizontal edge of the bridge was curved outward just slightly to give some deflection of wind and spray. Navigation lights were set in recesses in each side of the tower. Also, an attachment was provided on each side for a horseshoe life-preserver on the outside

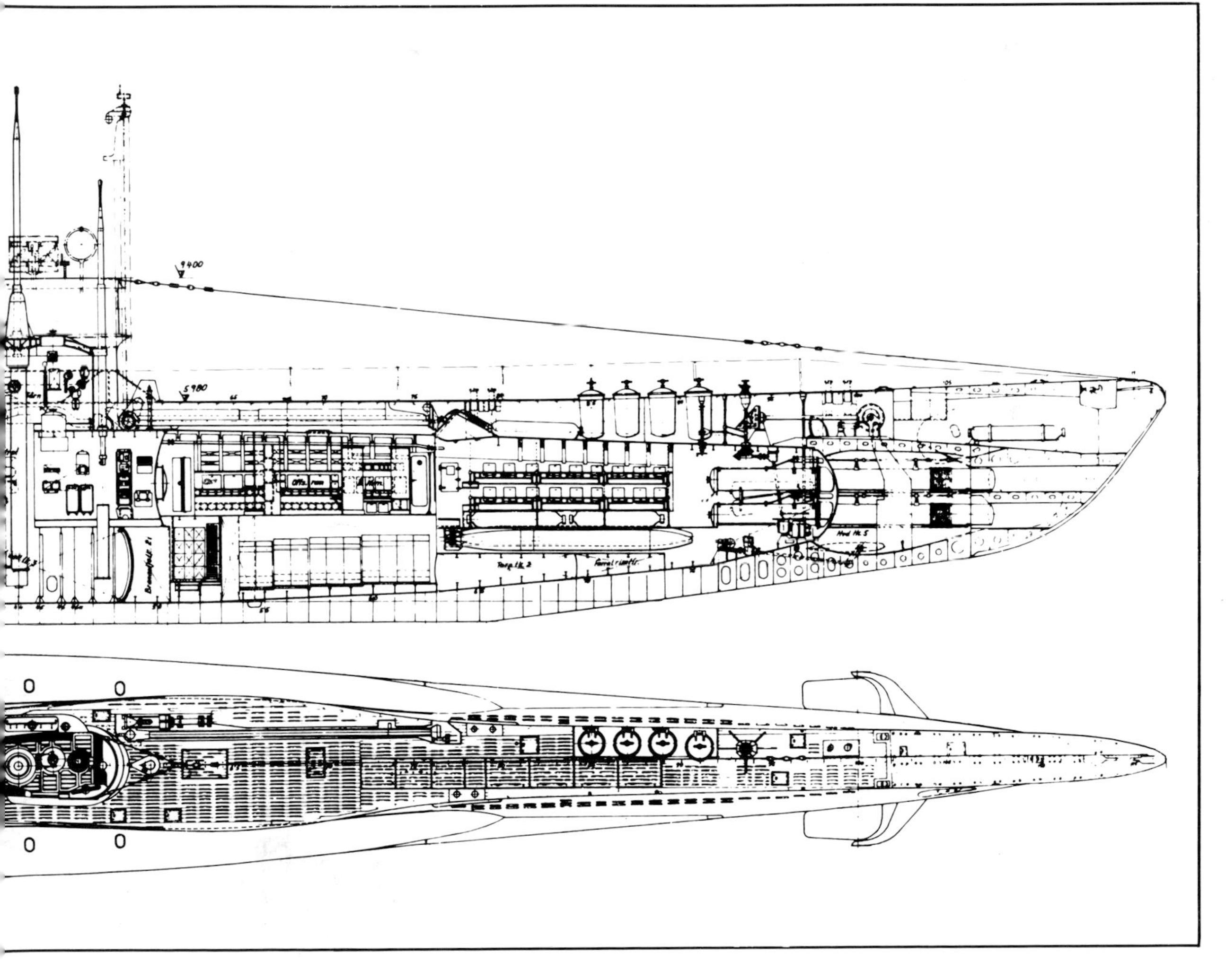

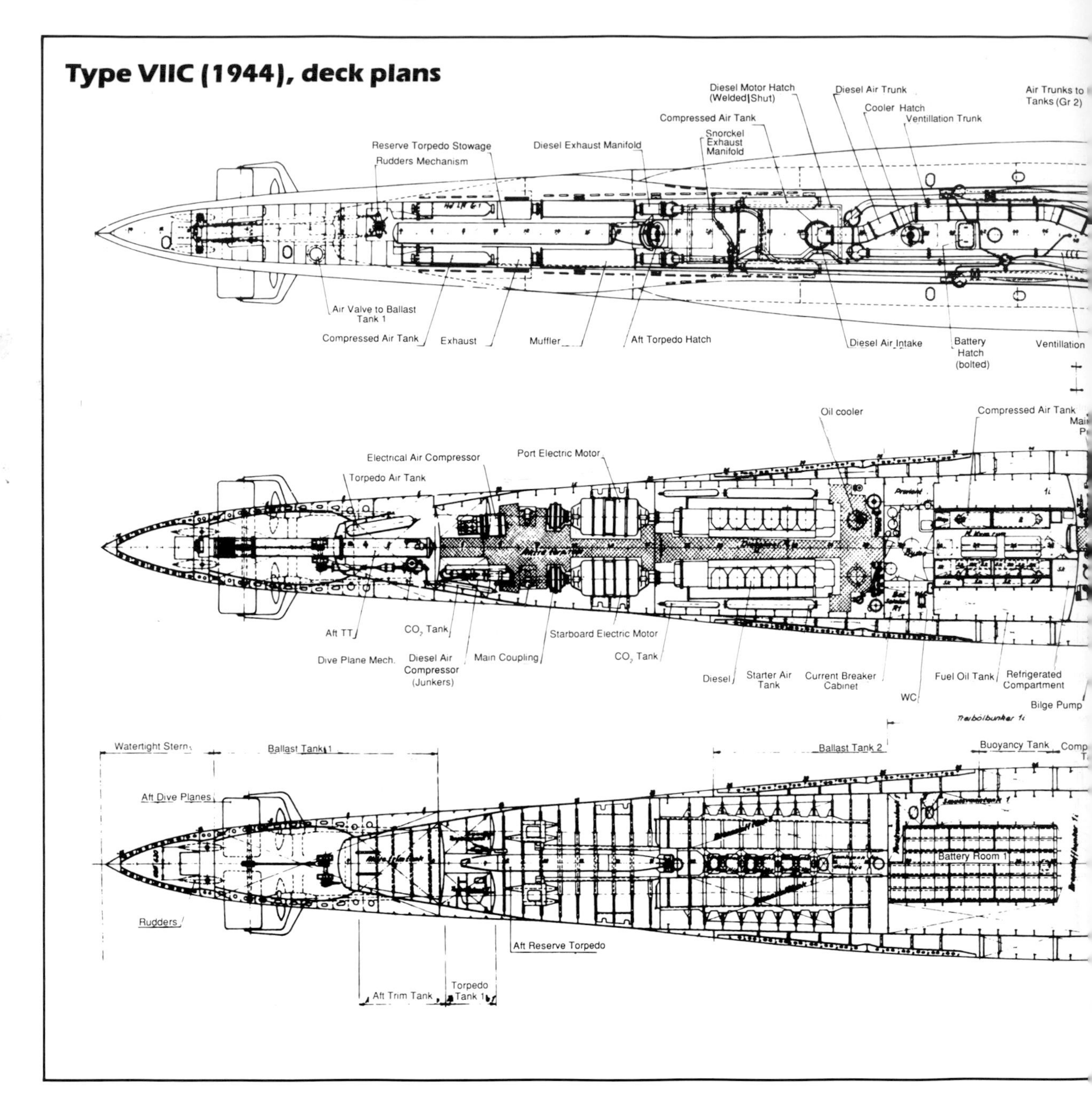

of the tower just below the edge of the bridge and just forward of the after edge of the bridge fairing. The main trunk providing air to the diesels was routed forward under the rear deckcasing and up inside the after end of the tower under the flak platform. Ventilation holes to let air into the trunk were located on the after sides of the tower wall, primarily on the starboard side. The magnetic compass was sited at the forward face of the tower, under a fairing that stretched about one metre forward. The earliest boats had antenna spreaders on both sides of the tower to help carry the antenna cables around the tower structure.

From this original form, the tower structure went through successive changes in response to a number of different stimuli. To remedy poor air supply to the diesels found in VIIAs and Bs, and to make that ventilation less susceptible to interruption in high seas, the air trunking on those boats was modified. Large external trunks were built up on both sides of the tower, starting under the Flak platform and extending up the after edge of the bridge. This effectively solved the ventilation problem and the air trunks on the C model and later marks were built in to the tower structure from the beginning of the series. Late in the war,

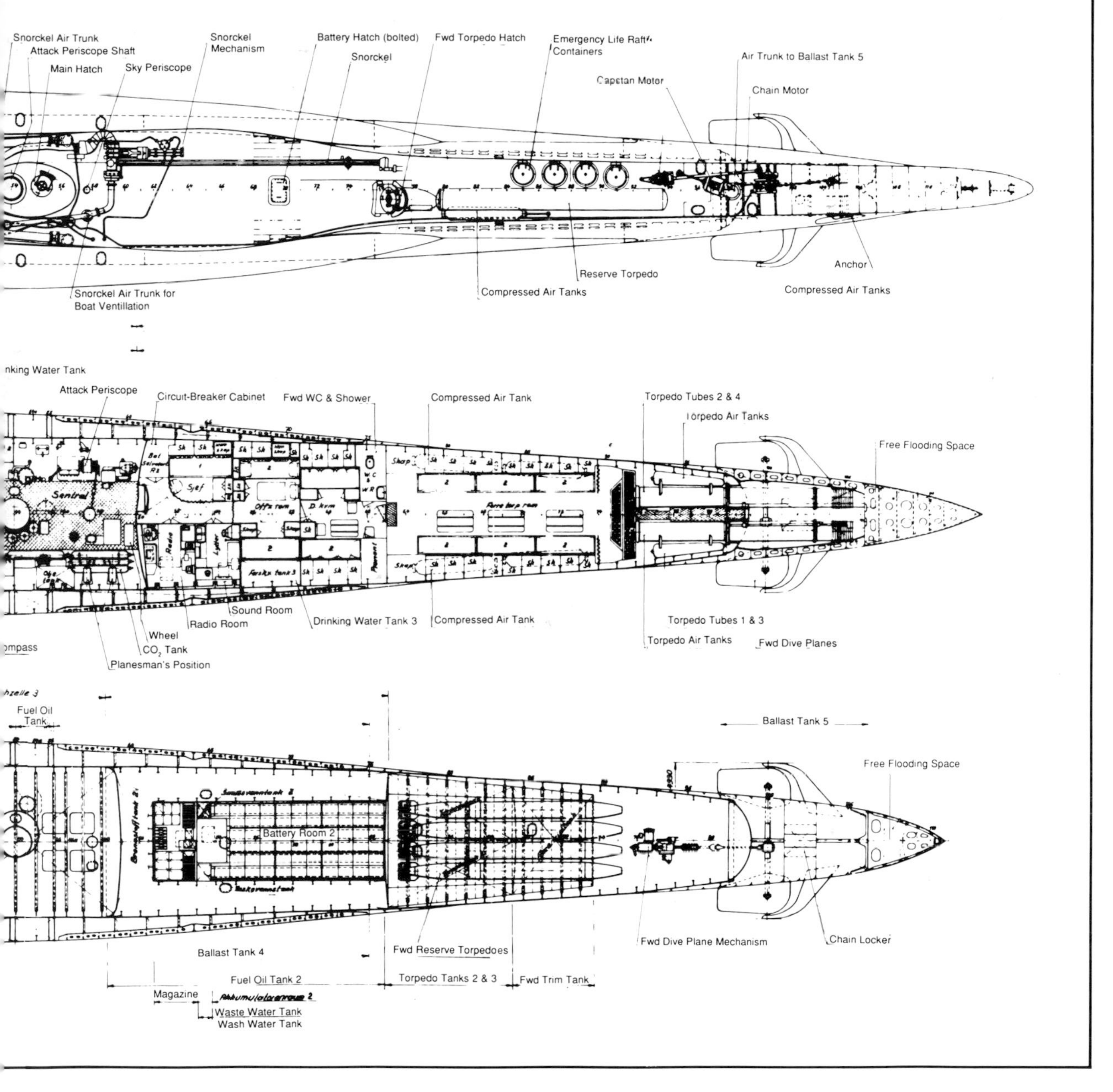

the adoption of the snorkel meant that fittings for the hinged air mast were added to the port side of the tower and additional air trunking was run along the tower side.

In an effort to provide the watch with better protection from the effects of rough weather, the forward edge of the bridge was modified in several distinct stages. The most common change was the addition of a spray deflector about halfway up the outside of the bridge. This was a flange, flat on top and concave on the bottom, about 15cm wide in front and tapering off on the sides. Later boats were completed with an additional deflector built into the top edge of the bridge. This was concave on its upper side and was separated from the edge of the bridge by a 1-cm gap. This deflector was retrofitted to some, but not all, early boats.

To improve the ability of the boat to communicate with and sense the outside world, the tower gradually became the site for an increasing number of electronic antennae. This started with the universal adoption of a telescopic rod antenna that was built into a housing which ran up the port side of the tower. Later on, as radars and radar detectors became common fittings in U-boats, their associated antennae were installed on top of, or on the front of, the tower. These installations are discussed later.

The increasing depredations of Allied aircraft led to the provision of armoured shelters on one or both sides of the bridge (*Kohlenkasten* – coal scuttles). These were small protected cubicles, open on the inside, large enough for men to crouch in. They were intended as protection if the boat had been surprised on the surface and was unable to dive before the aircraft attacked. There was a shelter large enough to accommodate five men on the starboard size of the tower and a much smaller one, intended for the watch officer, on the port side. Some boats went so far as to armour plate the entire tower, but this was not done extensively since the added weight high up on the boat had a seriously detrimental effect on stability. Even the armoured shelters were unpopular since they were thought to hinder the visibility of the tower watch in wet conditions. Also, they were considered to be superfluous because the crew couldn't both man the Flak guns and hide in the shelters.[5]

Yet it was in the Flak platform area aft of the bridge that the greatest changes took place. As the threat from the air increased, the number and size of Flak weapons was commensurately increased. More and bigger guns needed more space and the Flak platform was systematically extended, widened and sub-divided into multiple levels. These changes are described in detail later.

After Deckcasing. Like the forward deckcasing, the after deckcasing was a thin steel structure with hardwood decking. Once the Flak mounting on Type VIIAs was moved to the tower, the major feature of the after deckcasing was the external torpedo tube in the extreme stern of the boat. With the deletion of this feature in the B model and all subsequent variants, the after decking became relatively featureless. Despite the removal of the Flak mounting, all Type VIIs, at least until the middle of the war, retained the watertight container, right aft of the tower, that was used to store the barrel of that gun. Aft of this came the hinged deck plating giving access to the cook's hatch, the hinged hatchway over the after torpedo hatch and the removable deck plating over the after torpedo storage tube. The only remaining features were three pairs of retractable bollards, one on each side and one right aft.

The area between the upper decking and pressure hull aft of the tower was largely taken up by the ventilation trunking, which ran forward from the engine room to the tower, and the exhaust trunking and mufflers which ran aft to the exhaust ports on each side. The internal valves that sealed the exhaust trunks on each side where they passed through the pressure hull were the cause of some considerable anxiety at the beginning of the war. The seals on these valves proved inadequate in a number of boats and many commanders reported serious leakage if the boat were forced to dive deep.[6] The problem went undiscovered before the war because U-boats were prohibited from diving deeper than 50 metres on training dives. Once war patrols began, boats were routinely forced to dive to three or more times this depth. (*U49* dived to 170 metres during an attack in November 1939. Later in the war, dives of almost double that depth were commonly reported.) At those depths, many boats were forced to activate their pumps in order to maintain buoyancy. It is not known to what extent this problem contributed to the high rate of losses in the war's opening months, but it is noteworthy that loss rates dropped in 1940 after the exhaust valves were repaired.

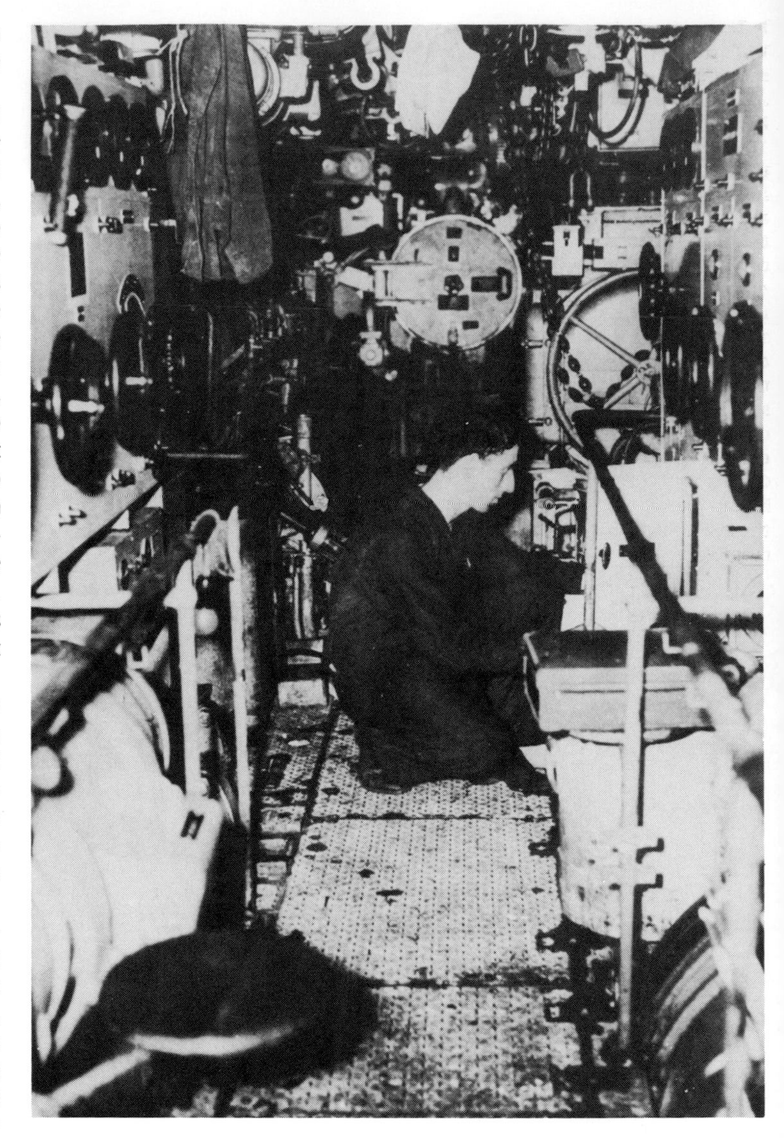

▲ Looking aft through the motor room into the after torpedo room in HMS *Graph* (ex-*U570*). The single after torpedo tube is located above the head of the RN sailor kneeling in the passageway. (via Albrecht)

▶ The bow of a Type VIIC, probably *U451*, is seen in final assembly at Deutsche Werke, Kiel, 14 December 1940. The external torpedo tube doors, here closed, can be made out below the two horizontal rows of flooding holes low on the bow. The two UT membranes can be seen, one above the other, directly above the foreplane. The second pair are directly aft. Two of the eleven holes for the GHG on this side can be discerned just aft of the lower UT membrane. (via Baker)

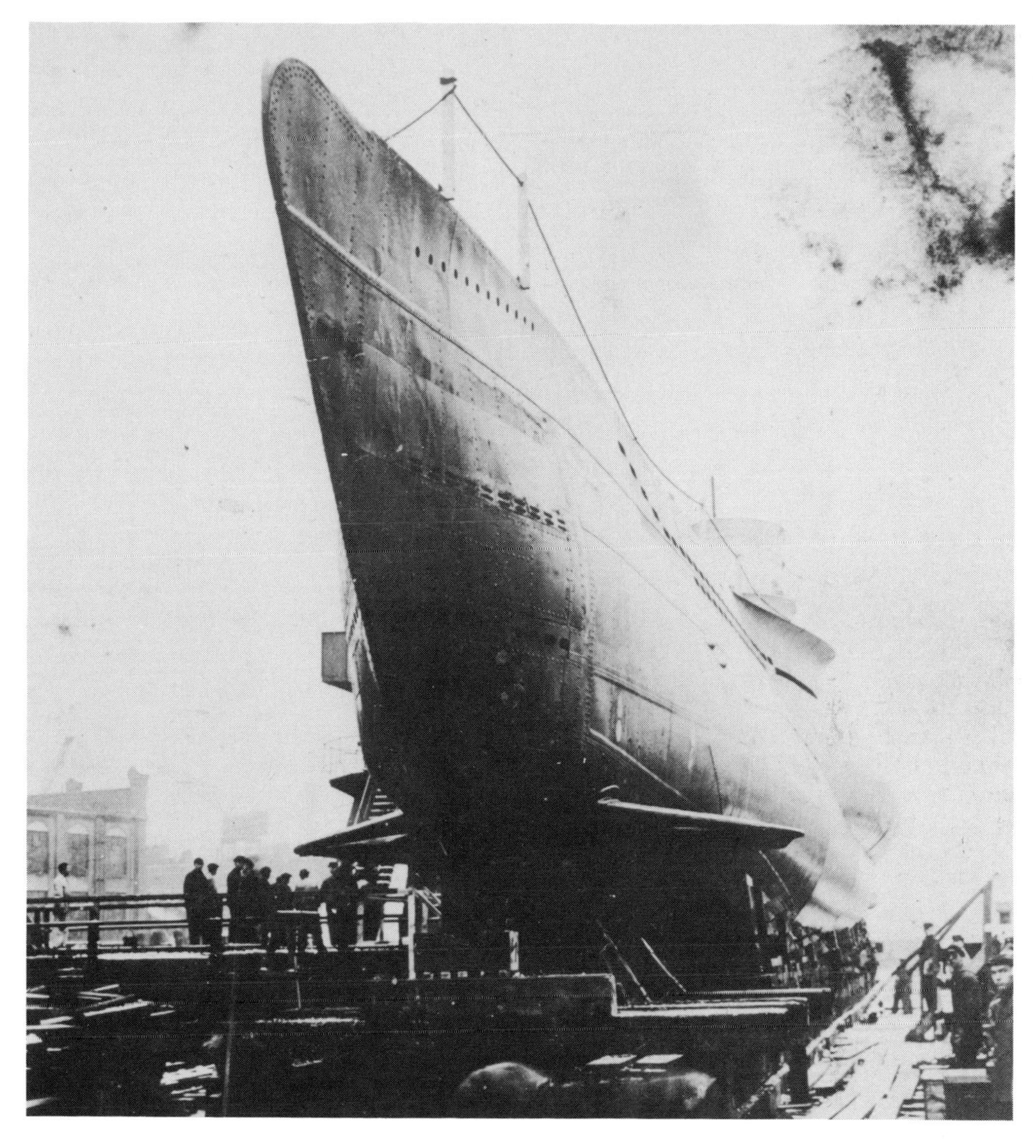

▶ A very late war boat, *U1305*, a C/41, is seen in captivity. The four watertight containers for life rafts are visible on the foredeck. Unlike most of the boats that surrendered to England, this boat wasn't scuttled. Instead, she ended up in Russian hands. (SFL)

Type VIIF

Glossary: Treibölhochbehalter, high fuel oil container; Mitte Torpedo Ausstossrohr, middle torpedo exit tube; Hecktorpedo und E.-Maschinenraum, stern torpedo and electric motor room; Dieselmotorenraum, diesel engine room; Unteroffizersraum hinten, NCOs' quarters after; Torpedolagerraum, torpedo store-room; Kombüse, galley; Zentrale, control room; Offiziers und Oberfeldwebelraum, ward room and warrant officers' quarters; Bugtorpedoraum, bow torpedo room; Rohr, tube; Frei durchflutet, free-flooding compartment; Wasserdichte Back, watertight forecastle; Treibölbunker, fuel-oil bunker; Tauchbunker, ballast tank (water or fuel); Untertriebzelle, negative buoyancy tank; Regelzelle, compensating tank (water); Regelbunker, compensating fuel tank (water or fuel); Tauchzelle, ballast tank (water); Kettenkasten, chain cover; Trimmzelle, trimming tank; Torpedozelle, torpedo tank; Trinkwasserzelle, drinking water tank; Torpedozelle, torpedo washing water; Dete-Anlagerraum, detection equipment room; Akkumulatorenraum, accumulator room; Schmutzwasserzelle, bilge water tank; Munitionskammer, ammunition compartment; Druckölbehalter, pressure-oil container; Kartoffellast, potato cargo; Gefechtspistolen, contact pistol; Motorenölvorratstank, engine oil storage tank; Gummboot, rubber dinghy; Sammeltank, collecting tank; Destillatbehälter, distilling chamber.

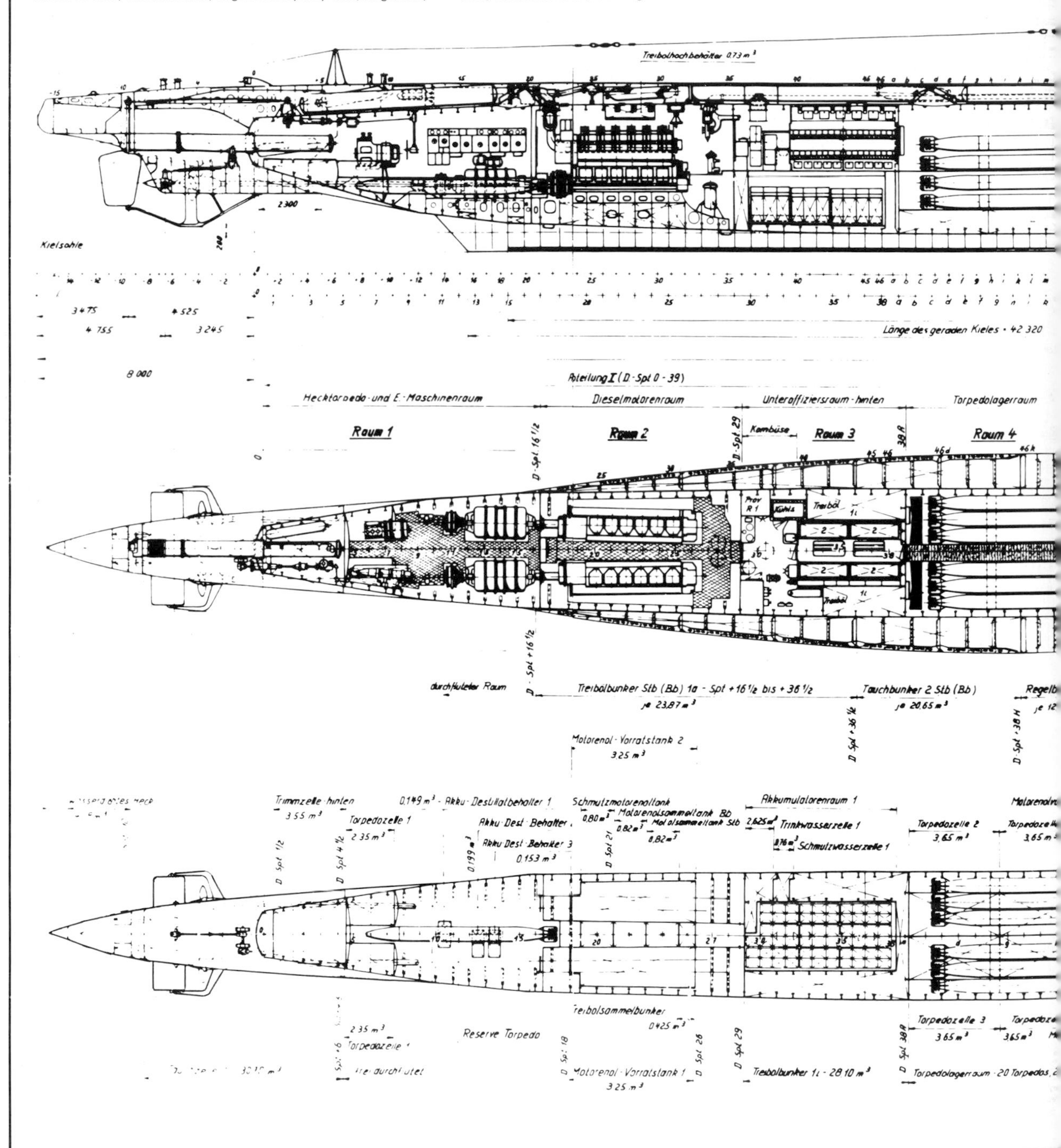

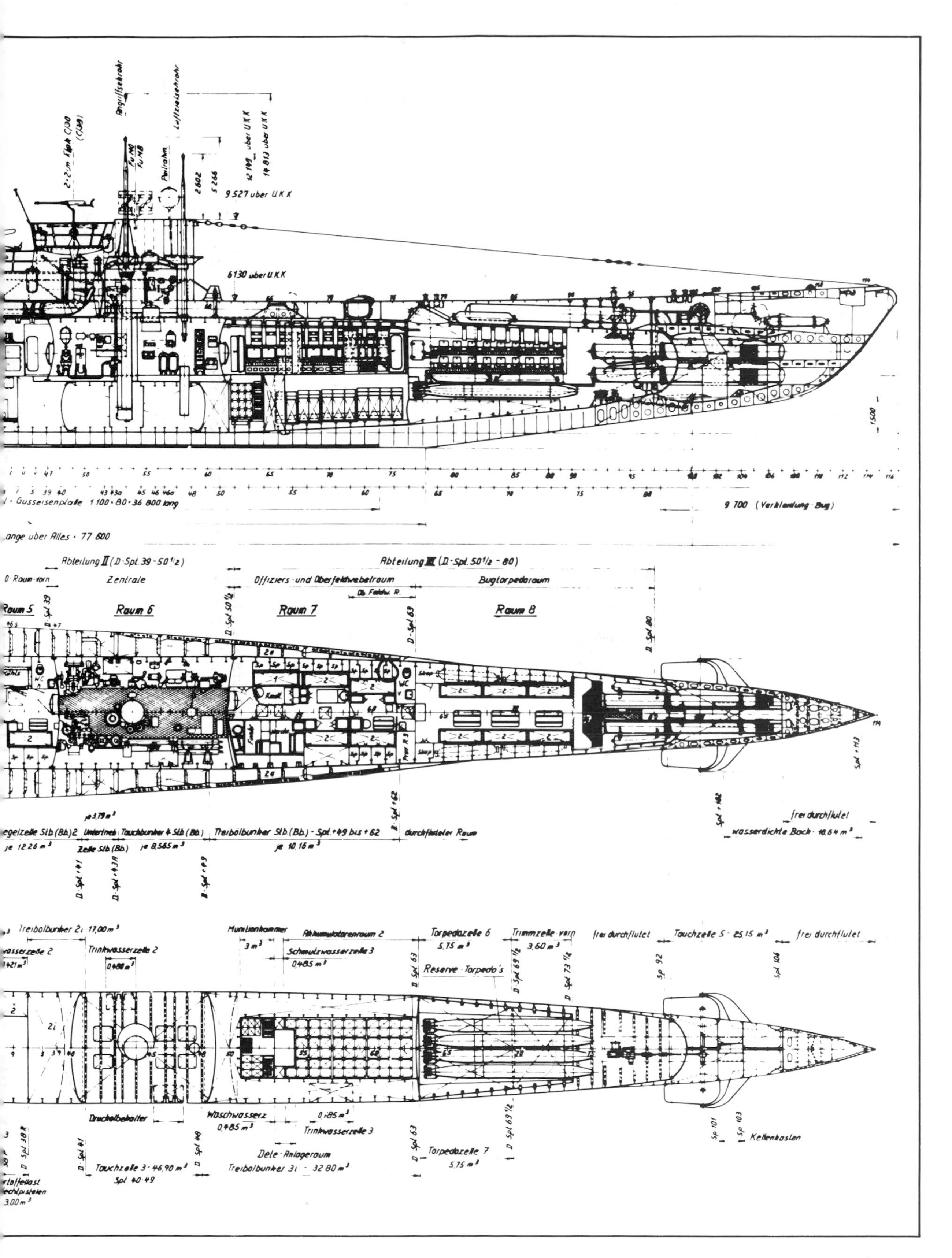
9 527 uber U.K.K
6130 uber U.K.K
Gusseisenplatte 1100 · 80 · 36 800 lang
9 700 (Verkleidung · Bug)
Lange uber Alles · 77 800
Abteilung II (D·Spt. 39 - 50 1/2)
Abteilung III (D·Spt. 50 1/2 - 80)
Zentrale
Offiziers · und Oberfeldwebelraum
Bugtorpedoraum
Raum 5
Raum 6
Raum 7
Raum 8
frei durchflutet
wasserdichte Bach · 18,64 m³
durchfluteter Raum
Treibolbunker Stb.(Bb.) · Spt. +49 bis +62
Torpedozelle 6
5,75 m³
Trimmzelle · vorn
3,60 m³
frei durchflutet
Tauchzelle 5 · 25,15 m³
frei durchflutet
Trinkwasserzelle 2
Reserve · Torpedo's
Schmutzwasserzelle 3
0,485 m³
Druckolbehalter
Waschwasserz.
0,485 m³
Trinkwasserzelle 3
Dele · Anlageraum
Treibolbunker 3 · 32 80 m³
Tauchzelle 3 · 46,90 m³
Spt. 40-49
Torpedozelle 7
5,75 m³
Kettenkasten

▲ *U373* comes into Brest, crew lined up for inspection. On the foredeck the bollards are in extended position and, immediately aft of the forward set of bollards, the KDB, seen almost end on.

◀ Crewmen relax on the after deck of a Type VIIA soon after its launch. The tower structure, seen from the rear, is in its original form. The mount for the 2cm Flak is still located on the after deck rather than on the smoking deck. The cook's hatch is open in the foreground, as is the hinged cover over it in the deckcasing.

▶ Another surrendered Type VII U-boat shows the foredeck configuration of many late war boats. Though it lacks the life raft containers, this boat does have the snorkel trough which characterized most later boats. (MacPherson)

▶ A Type VIIA with modified tower structure: the mid-tower spray deflector has been added forward, added air trunks run up the side of the bridge and the 2cm Flak mounting has been resited on the enlarged smoking deck. (via Baker)

◀ *U35*, a Type VIIA, comes into port. Crewmen take up docking positions at the bow and stern, hauling lines and fenders out of their storage spaces. The retractable capstan can be seen projecting above the deck casing between the two crewmen in the bows. (SFL)

▲ *U203*, an early Type VIIC pulls into St-Nazaire. This mark had the extended air trunking of the earlier marks built into the tower structure. It has had the prominent housing for the telescopic long-range radio antenna added to the port side of the tower. Otherwise, it looks the same as the tower on the Type VIIA in the preceding view.

Stern Section – The after end of the pressure hull is enclosed in the external stern section. This section provided streamlining for the blunt end of the pressure hull, housing for the after torpedo tube and mountings for the screws, aftplanes and rudders. The general shape of the external stern was a smoothly tapering form designed to ease the passage of water aft of the boat. The after torpedo tube emerged through the bottom of the stern section at the base of the housing that enclosed the control mechanisms of the aftplanes. These were rectangular structures, directly aft of the screw on each side, that were supported at their outer ends by a guard which extended from the drive shaft support just forward of the screw. Each rudder, directly aft of the aftplanes and in line with the screws, was hinged at the top and supported at the bottom by a guard which projected downward on each side from the aftplane housing. The large after dive tank was located inside the stern structure, surrounding the after torpedo tube.

Along the bottom of the boat, external to the pressure hull, ran the keel. Unlike the keel of a surface vessel, this really wasn't a structural member. It served no purpose in holding the boat together, this being done by the self-supporting circular pressure hull. Rather the keel was a convenient place to store the ballast weights used for crudely trimming the boat.[7] These ballast weights were cast iron ingots with a handle fashioned into one end to aid their lifting. They came in standard weights of 10, 25 and 50kg.[8]

◀ **KL Günther Prien, CO of *U47*, a Type VIIB, watches as his boat comes into port. He is standing on a step built into the inside of the bridge area as a footrest for the watch. To the right is the housing for the D/F loop and the binnacle. (ECPA)**

Dive

Diving or surfacing a Type VII U-boat was achieved by a precisely defined sequence of commands and actions that caused the boat's buoyancy to become greater than, less than or equal to that of the surrounding water as required. When the command to dive was given, the tower watch would head down the hatchway from the bridge, the last of the five pulling the hatch to behind him and spinning the wheel that seated the hatch. The process that drove air out of the boat's ballast tanks, allowing it to dive, didn't wait for the watch to come below. As soon as the dive order was given, the control room watch began to receive instructions from the LI. The flooding of ballast tanks was carried out in a precise sequence. Initially, the valves keeping the air in ballast tanks 5, 4, 3 and 2 were opened in that order.[9] The tanks were flooded from the bow aft in order to overcome the natural stern-heaviness of a U-boat. At the same time that the control handles for the head valves of these tanks were being swung to open position at the valve control board in the control room, the two planesmen seated on the other side of the compartment were turning their large wheels so that the foreplanes were canted downward and the aftplanes upward to lower the bow and raise the stern. Aft, in the mechanical spaces, the *Maschinisten* were switching off the diesels, shutting down the external valves on the ventilation and exhaust trunks and switching on the electric motors. Only after the desired angle of dive had been achieved would the aftermost ballast tank be flooded. At the same time, the angle on the planes was brought back to neutral. Once the tanks were sufficiently flooded to achieve the desired rate of dive, the top valves were again shut and, when the desired depth was reached, the forward dive planes were canted upward and the boat brought on to an even keel.

Movement to different depths underwater was achieved dynamically by use of the dive planes. Maintaining a depth was a matter of adjusting the amount of water in the ballast tanks. The density of water, and therefore the weight of the amount of water in the dive tanks, varies according to depth. To maintain any different depth, it was necessary either to add more water to the ballast tanks or partially vent the tanks by blowing air into them from the boat's compressed-air tanks.

Surfacing the boat was essentially a reversal of the diving process. Compressed air was blown into the ballast tanks, starting at the bow, while the dive planes were canted upward. It was not necessary to blow the tanks completely. In fact, great care was taken to keep from adding too much air both to conserve compressed air and to keep the boat under control as it surfaced. As the

▶ **A downward look into the bridge of *U373*, a Type VIIC, at Brest. This shows the standard mid-war configuration of the tower of a Type VII U-boat. The rod to the right is the top of the telescopic long-range antenna. That to the left is the CO's jackstaff, erected only in port to fly the long thin commissioning pennant. Aft of these are the gratings covering the diesel air intakes.**

▶ **Later in the war, a housing for the FuMO 61 (*Hohentweil-U*) radar antenna was added to the port side of the tower of most surviving Type VIIs, as seen in *U668*. This was a large mattress antenna, the top of which is seen end on projecting above its housing.**

Above: *U378* is seen under attack from the air. Its highly built-up bridge structure includes an enlarged set of Flak platforms, housing for *Hohentweil* on the port side and *Kohlenkasten* on the starboard. (USN)

Above right: An unidentified late-war boat, possibly *U475*, shows the armour plate added to some boats. The lower edge of the armour plate has been cut away to fit over the navigation light at the tower's side. (Rumpf)

▶ A crewman makes adjustments to the magnetic compass in this U-boat. The magnetic compass was housed in its own fairing at the forward edge of the tower.

▲ **Even though the mount for the after Flak gun was moved from the rear deck to the smoking deck very early in the Type VII's evolution, the watertight container for the 2cm gun's barrel was retained in production VIICs. This view of three Type VIICs in Norway after the battle for PQ17, shows a captured British Army major being taken ashore from the far boat. On each boat, note the convex hatch cover over the watertight container to the left and the hinged deck section to the right allowing access to the cook's hatch. (USN)**

boat broke the surface, the diesels were started up with a charge of compressed air from the engine room tanks and the electric motors were shut down. The complete blowing of the ballast tanks was accomplished by directing the exhaust gases from the diesels into the tanks.

A crash dive differed from the sequence just described only in that it involved a few more members of the crew. In order to dive faster, it was necessary to increase the downward angle of the bow more rapidly than simple flooding of ballast tanks and rotation of the dive planes could achieve. To increase the angle of the bow rapidly, it was necessary to make the bow heavier. The only movable ballast capable of rapidly adding weight to the bow was the off-duty crew. In a crash dive, all free crewmen were sent racing to the forward torpedo room, where they packed themselves in as best they could.

1. Single-hull boats had the ribs that braced the pressure hull on the inside of the pressure hull. Compare this to the design of double-hull boats, like the Type XXI, which had the ribs on the outside.
2. Atl, vol. 1, p. 15. Some early boats, particularly Type VIIAs, suffered from weak engine mounts which caused problems during the initial war patrols. The offending mounts were strengthened during refits in late 1939 and caused no further problems.
3. On 30 April 1943 the order was given that torpedo storage tubes should no longer be fitted in U-boats destined for operations in the North Atlantic, as reported in the KTB, 7 May 1943. 'This order was necessitated by the gradually increasing number of cases where, when the boats were depth-charged or bombed, especially at fairly great depths, the upper deck containers were cracked or started leaking ... and thus gravely endangered the boat ...' All other new boats were to receive stronger storage tubes.
4. U-boat veterans interviewed by the author universally agreed that the anchor was never used in any normal U-boat operations.
5. KTB, 1 December 1943.
6. Atl, vol. 1, pp. 15–16.
7. As opposed to the fine trim provided by the trim tanks.
8. WB. There were many rumours at the end of the war of boats that substituted gold bars for their iron ballast. One such was *U54*, which was sunk in the Kattegat in the last days of the war. All the survivors of that boat denied to other U-boatmen, as well as to the Allies, that they carried any gold.
9. All tanks and bunkers were numbered in ascending order, by type, from the stern. When identical tanks were found on both sides of the boat, they were given the same number and distinguished by port (*backbord*) and starboard (*steuerbord*) designations. Thus, the seven dive tanks in a Type VIIC were: 1 (in the external stern), 2 (port and starboard in the aft part of the saddle tanks), 3 (in the pressure hull under the control room), 4 (port and starboard in the fore part of the saddle tanks) and 5 (in the external bow).

Propulsion

A Type VII U-boat was driven through the water by its diesel and electric drive systems. These combined to give it the ability to be propelled either on or below the surface of the water. The transition from diesel drive on the surface to electric motors below the surface, or vice versa, was a complex operation involving the throwing of switches and the opening or closing of valves in precise sequence, closely aligned to the actions of diving or surfacing described earlier.

The diesels that drove a Type VII U-boat were a pair of 6-cylinder 4-cycle engines manufactured to nearly identical designs by MAN (Maschinenfabrik Augsburg–Nuremberg) or GW. They were extremely lightweight and powerful for their size. The basic power output for these units was 1,160bhp each. From the B model on, however, the diesels were fitted with compressors which increased the power output of each unit to 1,400bhp. MAN units were fitted with an exhaust-driven turbo-charging arrangement (*Büchigebläse*). GW diesels had a geared supercharger driven mechanically by the motor's drive shaft (*Kapselgebläse*). In general, the GW design was preferred as being more robust and reliable. There was even talk of replacing all MAN engines,[1] but in the event this never occurred. On the whole, both designs were highly successful, proving to be extraordinarily durable in operational use.

A second set of cams was provided with each engine to allow reversing the direction of rotation of the drive shaft, in order to slow the boat or move it backwards. Switching from normal cams to the reversing cams was a simple operation which required only stopping the engines and throwing a lever at each end of the cylinder bank.

The electric motors were standard naval units, built to identical design by Siemens, AEG or Brown-Boveri, designed to work on the direct current supplied by the boat's storage batteries. They were a double-commutator type motor rated at 500hp each. This gave 280rpm at 720 amps and 228 volts, resulting in a maximum speed of 7.4 knots. This level of energy output could be supported by the boat's batteries for only a half an hour. Creep speed (*Schleichfahrt*), the speed at which the motors made the least noise, was generally about 90rpm, though this differed slightly from boat to boat. This gave a speed of about 2.5 knots through the water. The electrical connection of each motor could be reversed. In drive mode, it would draw power from the batteries to drive the screws. With polarity reversed, it would generate electricity, charging the batteries as it was turned by its diesel. It could also be set to spin freely, neither driving the boat nor charging the batteries. This setting was controlled by the switchboards in the motor room.

Each motor was connected by a clutch to the drive shaft to the diesel engine immediately forward. Another clutch immediately aft of each motor controlled its connection to the propeller shaft. This allowed a large variety of possible configurations of diesel engines and/or electric motors depending on the needs of the moment.

◀ One of the *Maschinisten* leans over the top of one of the two diesels that powered a U-boat on the surface. Everything here, lifters, cams and couplings, was exposed so that it could be reached easily for adjustment or repair.

For instance, the normal configuration for high-speed surface travel (AK – *Außerste Kraft*) was to have both diesels operating and all clutches engaged, with both electric motors spinning freely. An 'unofficial' extra burst of power, giving about a half-knot of extra speed, could be achieved in emergencies by hooking up the motors in drive mode. This was called 'Zweimal AK' (twice AK), even though there was no such notation on the engine room telegraph. This speed was used only in emergencies because it rapidly drained the batteries, reducing the CO's tactical options. Economical surface drive generally involved shutting down one of the diesels and disengaging the clutch between it and the motor on that side, driving the boat with only the other diesel. The motor on the driven side was hooked up in generator mode and used to run the opposite motor, so both shafts were powered. Experimentation in extending the range of the Type VII so that it could operate off the coast of North America showed that shutting down one engine and running the other at most economical speed gave a speed of 6 knots. The working

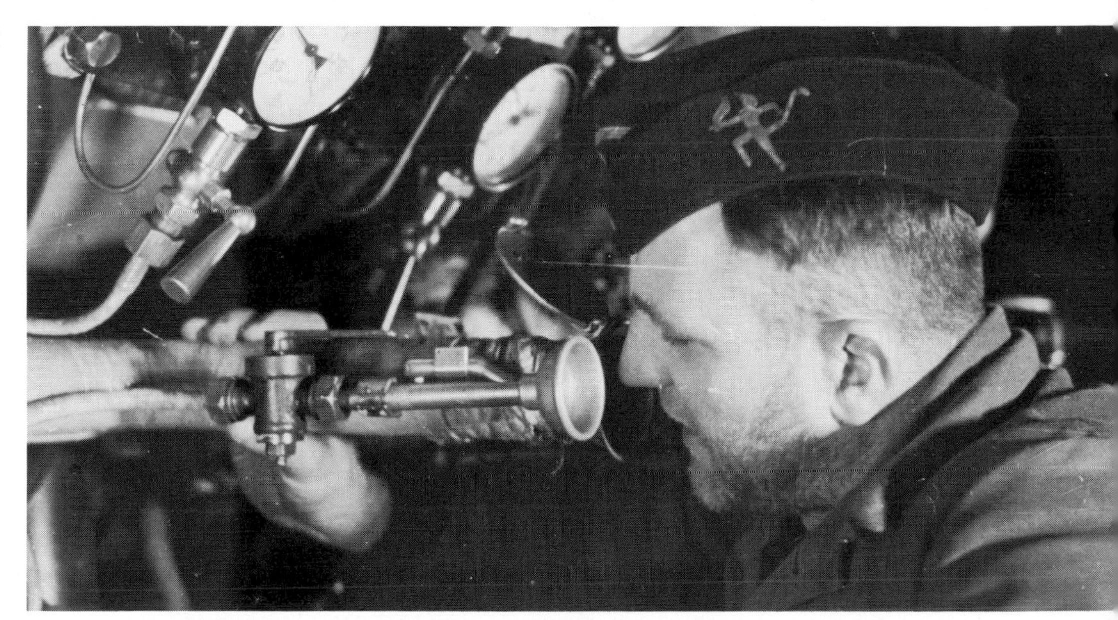

▶ A *Maschinist* in *U552* using the engine room voice tube.

▶ One of the *Elektromaschinisten* adjusts the levers that controlled the flow of electricity to the motors. The black gauges to the left are ammeters. The large dial just to the left of the crewman is an engine room telegraph repeater. Note the red emergency light just above the ammeters.

engine would be switched every four hours to equalize wear.

When a U-boat first surfaced, the highest priority was to recharge the batteries and fill the compressed air tanks. The batteries were charged by running the diesel and motor on one side in generator mode with the clutch between the motor and the screw disengaged. This allowed the engine to turn the motor on that side at high speed, giving maximum generating performance. Air was compressed either by the electric compressor or the diesel-driven Junkers compressor. The electrical apparatus was battery-driven and was intended primarily for use underwater. The Junkers compressor could only be run when the boat was surfaced.

The batteries which supplied the power to the electric motors were hardly distinguishable from those used in the First World War vintage submarines or, for that matter, from those used in today's diesel-electric boats. They were rubber-lined, lead-acid type batteries divided into cells and banks so that damage in one area would not mean the loss of all electrical power from a battery room. The forward battery room held 62 cells arranged in nine banks. The after battery room held one more cell in the same number of banks. Each battery room could supply approximately 11,000 amp/hrs of power. The boat carried spools of copper wire to be used for jumping disabled or contaminated cells.

Damage to the batteries' cells was a cause of considerable concern for U-boatmen. Not only could the loss of electrical storage capacity be limiting or disabling to a boat, but the danger always existed of spilled battery acid from broken cells mixing with sea water in the bilge. The combination of hydrochloric acid and salt water led to the release of poisonous and corrosive chlorine gas. The crew was issued crude re-breathers for exactly this eventuality. If the boat were damaged in a depth-charge attack, it was the unenviable job of the LI or the chief motorman to head down into the dark and reeking battery rooms armed only with wire, wire-cutters and litmus paper to test each cell for salt water contamination. Because the cells were arranged in series, to get the sum of all available power in the circuit, damaged cells had to be by-passed.

Snorkel

The number of possible combinations of diesel and electric motor was made significantly greater by the introduction of the snorkel in 1944. The concept wasn't new nor was it originally German. The idea of running a submarine powered by a fuel-burning engine using air supplied by tube from the surface had been around for as long as there had been submarines. The Germans captured a number of examples of a working snorkel when Holland was overrun in May 1940. In 1933, a Dutch lieutenant-commander, had convinced his navy to support a series of experimental installations of hinged air masts with a ball-float air cut-off which prevented the entry of sea water into the mast. His early installations used a separate, non-hinged tube for exhaust gases. This was altered in later examples to allow the exhaust mast to also be lowered. Altogether, nine Dutch submarines, *O19 – O27*, were fitted with various examples of his air mast design.

Dutch submarines from this series fell into both British and German hands as a result of the fall of the Netherlands to the Germans. Neither side saw much future in the idea and both navies removed the air masts from the Dutch submarines before putting the boats into service in their own navies. The Germans did test the air mast on *UD4* (ex-*O26*) in 1941 before removing it from the boat, but could see no practical application for it. It wasn't until early 1943 that the changing fortunes of the U-boat fleet brought the idea of the snorkel to mind again. A meeting in March 1943 between Dönitz and Hellmuth Walter, already well known for his decade of work on developing the Walter turbine drive for high submerged speed,[2] resulted in the resurrection of the idea of the snorkel. Walter's idea was for a float to which would be attached a pair of flexible hoses, one for intake and the other for exhaust.[3] A rigid snorkel design, resembling the Dutch model, with closely spaced, parallel intake and exhaust tubes was fitted to a pair of Type II boats and tested in the Baltic in August 1943. The air intake mast had a ball-valve similar to the Dutch design. The exhaust mast was curved over at the top to release the gases just under the surface of the water.

These tests were conducted to answer two specific questions. First, would the boat's diesels operate successfully under conditions of low intake air flow and high exhaust back pressure? The trials proved that this was a tractable problem. The high back pressure on the exhaust was handled by replacing the reversing cams of the diesels with a special set of snorkeling cams which significantly reduced the overlap of the inlet and exhaust ports in each cylinder (from 120° to 40°). Henceforth, reversing the screws could only be done with the electric motors. The back pressure problems also caused the abandonment of the use of the exhaust-driven Büchi turbocharger on those boats fitted with MAN diesels.

The second question relating to the use of the snorkel was whether the effects of the cutoff of outside air, and the resultant drawing of air from inside the boat, would be harmful to the engines or crew. In fact, this proved to be the case only when the pressure changes were repeated and

▶ **The crew of *U249* marches off their boat after surrendering at Weymouth at the end of the war. Note the clamp for the snorkel extending from the edge of the tower structure. (via MacPherson)**

rapid. In effect, the whole volume of the boat served as an air reserve which could keep the diesels running for several minutes with the head valve of the snorkel submerged.[4] Even the effects on the crew were far less than had been feared.

The trials showed that the snorkel was far more capable than originally envisaged. The device had originally been intended only to allow the re-charging of batteries while the boat remained submerged, and that most time would be spent running on electric power. In fact, it was discovered that boats could operate for prolonged periods snorkelling on diesel power at speeds of up to eight knots. In fact, higher speeds, up to 13 knots, could be achieved, but this resulted in the creation of disturbances in the water aft of the snorkel which set up dangerous sympathetic vibrations within the periscope and snorkel.[5]

Two different head valve types were tested in these initial trials. They shared the basic principle of having a buoyant float which dropped down when out of the water to open the air shaft and which, if the head of the snorkel dropped below the surface of the water, would float up to close the valve. The more common type was the ball-float type (*Kugelschwimmer*). In this design, a spherical float was housed behind the head of the air shaft. As it raised and lowered, it closed or opened the hinged clapper valve at the top of the snorkel. This type of valve proved to be responsive, especially after vanes were added to the ball-float to give some hydrodynamic boost to the closing action, though it was vulnerable to wave damage. The second type of head valve was the ring-float type (*Ringschwimmer*). This used a toroidal float enclosed within a cylindrical housing, open to the sea at the bottom and the air at the top, which surrounded the top of the air mast. This design was less vulnerable to wave damage, but was also less responsive. It had been adopted as the standard design by 1945, however, because its cylindrical shape proved much easier to cover with the better anti-radar coating (see page 131). Very late in the war, a simple electro-mechanical valve was proposed. This used water sensors on the mast, essentially open circuits that would be closed by being immersed in sea water, to signal the valve to close mechanically. This design was to be adopted for all subsequent snorkels, but the end of the war prevented its implementation.

The successful conclusion of the initial trials was followed within a month by the test of a snorkel with a hinged mast (*Klappmast*) in two new Type VIICs, *U235* and *U236*, then completing their working-up period. The mast was hinged at its base. In upright position, it ran up the forward port side of the tower, where it attached to inlet and exhaust trunks which ran back to the engine room. It folded forward into a trough in the deckcasing. The folding mast design was chosen because Type VIIs didn't have the necessary internal room at the after end of the tower, to install a telescopic snorkel such as was designed into the Type XXI.[6] The folding mast located forward of the tower was considered less desirable than the telescopic model because it partially restricted the forward view from the periscope.[7] Nevertheless, even before this second test was begun, the orders were placed for the

◀ *U953* alongside the pier at Bergen, Norway in February 1945. She is getting ready for a patrol, as indicated by the loading of a torpedo at the left. The fittings for the snorkel, the clamp at the top and the air trunking below, can be seen on the tower. (Werner via MacPherson)

◀ The snorkel is seen in raised position on *U235*. Note the extensive wooden scaffolding intended as camouflage.

general production and installation of snorkels for all front-line boats. The production mast differed from the test articles by replacing the curved tube at the top of the exhaust mast with a simpler arrangement whereby the exhaust mast terminated about 50cm below the inlet valve. Various methods were tried to spread the exhaust gases in the water so as to avoid tell-tale bubbles, but in the event, this proved to be no problem. The eventual solution was simply to drill a series of small holes near the top of the exhaust mast.

The first operational boat fitted with a snorkel was *U264* in February 1944, and additional boats were fitted with the device as the availability of parts and opportunity permitted. Those boats that received the snorkel early on, received it with enthusiasm.[8] At least now there was a chance of survival.

Early experience with the snorkel showed that a Type VII's batteries could be sufficiently recharged in three hours to power the boat for the rest of the day by running one diesel to charge the battery while driving the boat with the other at three to four knots. It was standard procedure to shut the diesels down every 20 minutes for a hydrophone check of the surrounding waters.[9]

By the time the Landwirt group of boats was sent against the Normandy Invasion in June 1944, still only nine of the 36 boats deployed were fitted with snorkels. A school was set up at Horten, near Oslo, in Norway in late 1943 to train U-boat crews in the operation of the device, but many crews made their first snorkel runs with little or no training. The following experience wasn't unusual:

> 'We got a snort in early August 1944.[10] It was fixed in raised position because the yard didn't have the parts to make it raise and lower. So, it extended permanently some four metres above the highest point of the conning tower. That was contrary to all basic rules. Normally, in a U-boat, the rule was your eyes should be the highest point.
>
> When we tried to use that snort for the first time, we'd had no experience or trials with it. Well, we had just dived after getting an aircraft warning and it was full of water.[11] We didn't know we were supposed to drain it and when we got to snorting depth and tried to start the diesels, that water just rushed down into the engines. It choked the diesels and forced all the exhaust gases into the boat. Guys were passing out. I still see the FT Mann (*Funker*) coming out of his shack and falling down. That could have cost us dear because of course we had to surface suddenly.
>
> When we had come up, there were two Lightnings and one had already made his attack along the track of the snort. Here we had a boat full of gas and we were panicky and there came the second one. Somehow we got the guns manned and gave him a good burst and he missed us by a bit.'[12]

Even experienced boats had trouble with snorkelling:

> 'The LI (Engineering Officer) had a tough job maintaining snort depth, especially if the seas came from the side. One wave pushed you up, so the LI would lower the boat and the next wave swept over the snort. Not that that was so bad. All this trouble with the eardrums, it was overblown! It never bothered me or my people. Maybe there were some who were very sensitive, but you read about bursting eardrums and bulging eyes . . . No, it never happened.
>
> A far more insidious thing was CO (carbon monoxide) which the diesels would put into the boat if the water pressure got too great for the exhaust to overcome. The snort was supposed to work with the exhaust only about half a metre underwater. When that increased to a metre or more, the counter-pressure on the exhaust forced the relief valves inside the boat to open and the CO got into the boat. You couldn't smell it or see it.
>
> We had some testing material onboard for the CO. Some phials which we opened to the air. Depending on the amount of CO, the contents of the phial changed colour, from white to light green to darker green and almost black. Well, we'd open these phials and watch them change colour but we didn't have a clue as to what it meant because they never let us have the scale we were supposed to compare the green to. That was ashore.
>
> If the snort slips below a metre deep only occasionally, then it's no problem. If you keep on dieselling, the air gets clean within seconds because the diesels are swallowing air from inside the boat at enormous volumes. One time we got a radar warning and had to go deep suddenly and shut the diesels down just after we'd taken some CO into the boat. Well after we'd been down for five hours, nobody

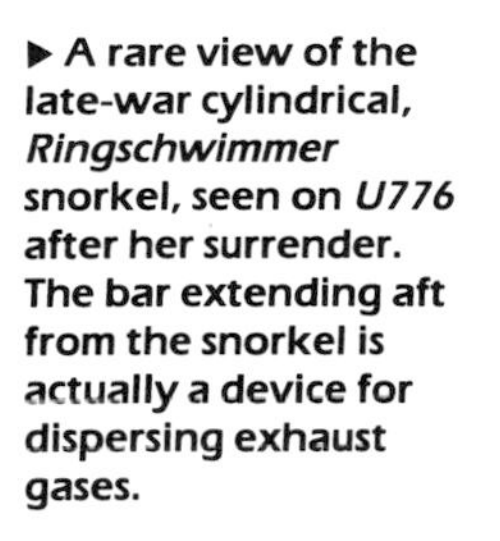

▶ A rare view of the late-war cylindrical, *Ringschwimmer* snorkel, seen on *U776* after her surrender. The bar extending aft from the snorkel is actually a device for dispersing exhaust gases.

on watch could stand up. Two or three people sort of stumbled into the Control Room half-conscious and brought the boat up in the middle of Biscay. That was fun!'[13]

A number of problems emerged as use of the snorkel became common. One had to do with the seemingly trivial problem of rubbish. A crew of 44 officers and men generated large quantities of rubbish whose build-up, if there were no means of easy disposal, could rapidly become a health problem as well as the source of a considerable stench. In the days before the snorkels allowed extended submerged patrols, rubbish disposal was easy; it was simply tossed overboard whenever the boat surfaced. When U-boats spent 24 hours a day underwater, there suddenly was no means of disposing of the accumulation. The options were few. The lavoratory was too complex and delicate to use for this purpose. That left a torpedo tube or the Bold ejector tube. Most boats used a torpedo tube to hold the accumulating rubbish, ejecting it periodically. This was known to U-boatmen as a *Müllschoss* (rubbish shot). The problem with this was that it reduced the available torpedo tubes by 20 per cent. Even if the tube being used for rubbish were empty, it still needed to be thoroughly cleaned before it could be used to launch torpedoes again. Using the Bold ejector preserved the original torpedo armament, but had its own problems. The rubbish had to be packed by hand into tin cans small enough to fit into the ejector tube. This was an unpleasant job at best, but many commanders preferred this option.

The problems of snorkelling weren't limited to the danger of asphyxiation or the difficulties of rubbish disposal. The ultimate problem with the snorkel was that it robbed a U-boat of its ability to act against the enemy. As long as a boat was forced to stay permanently submerged, its survival odds were certainly improved, but its chances of finding a target were reduced to almost nil.[14] That point couldn't be more simply shown than by the following report:

> '*U1199* has returned from its first operation out of Bergen. Her short report shows that the operation lasted 50 days, of which 31 were spent in the operational area off Peterhead and Aberdeen (AN 1895, 0131) close under the coast. Boat ran submerged the whole time, crew most enthusiastic about snorkel.'[15]

U1199 returned safely from this submerged patrol, but all it had to show for 31 days on station was a single sinking.

1. KTB, 20 October 1939. These were complaints primarily about the unsupercharged MAN version fitted to the A model.
2. The idea behind the Walter drive was to break down highly concentrated hydrogen peroxide (H_2O_2) into its constituent parts ($2 \times H_2O_2 = 2 \times H_2O + O_2$), water and molecular oxygen, in a catalytic chamber. The oxygen was used to burn fuel and the water sprayed on the resulting hot gases to produce steam which then drove a turbine. The problem wasn't the propulsion plant itself, which was small, light and relatively easy to design. The stumbling-block in the design was the concentrated H_2O_2, which was difficult to manufacture, more difficult to handle safely and needed to be carried in large quantities to give even the lowest acceptable range. The Walter-designed Type XVIII, intended to replace the Type VII, was double the size of the Type VII in part because it had to carry a complete standard diesel powerplant as well as the Walter turbine in order to achieve acceptable range and in part because of the amount of H_2O_2 it needed. It carried 124 tons of diesel fuel and 204 tons of H_2O_2, which gave it a range of 5,200nm on the surface and just 250nm submerged, but that submerged distance was covered at a speed of 24 kts! The Type XVIII design, with its H_2O_2 storage space given over to additional batteries, became the highly successful Type XXI.
3. Atl, vol. 3, p. 58. Hessler dates Walter's suggestion for the snorkel to November 1942. Most other sources give the later date.
4. TR-S. However, to avoid excessive pressure fluctuations within the engine room, it was necessary to keep all bulkhead hatches open.
5. TR-S & Rössler, p 204. A redesign of the snorkel, and indeed the whole external tower of the Type VII, was under way at the end of the war, which would have resulted in a more streamlined tower with the Flak platforms replaced by a housing for a snorkel which, when raised, provided protection for the periscope.
6. TR-S. In fact, the telescopic snorkel used in the Type XXI had a number of technical problems, particularly relating to the watertight seals between the telescopic sections. Also its round cross-section was more liable to self-induced vibrations than the tear-drop shape of the hinged snorkel. Planning was under way at the end of the war to fit all new construction, including Type XXIs, with a folding snorkel.
7. TR-S. Although the head valve of the snorkel was below the line of sight of the periscope, the wake caused by the snorkel head and the exhaust gases which rose to the surface both tended to obscure vision.
8. KTB, 24 February 1944. *U264* was lost on its first patrol with the snorkel before being able to report its experiences with the device. One of the next boats to receive a snorkel reported back favourably: '*U667* reported on putting in that it had a continuous submerged passage for nine days from 15 degrees West, using the snorkel apparatus. The commander was enthusiastic . . . ', KTB, 19 May 1944.
9. Atl, vol. 3, p. 58.
10. WB. Snort was common slang for snorkel.
11. TR-S. To prevent damage from water pressure at depth, a snorkel was designed to fill with water when it was in retracted position and the boat was submerged. When the boat resumed snorkelling, it was necessary to drain the water from the snorkel into the bilge.
12. WB.
13. WH.
14. KTB, 10 June 1944. The survival advantages of the snorkel were so obvious that 'on account of the great number of air attacks, above all on boats without snorkel, and the extensive damage caused thereby, for the present further sailing of those boats has been stopped'.
15. KTB, 5 Nov 44.

▶ A Type VII U-boat was led by its Commanding Officer. Most often he was a Kapitänleutnant, such as Kentrat, CO of *U74*, seen here at Lorient after returning from a patrol on 31 December 1941. The CO was the 'Old Man' in a crew of very young men. Most COs were themselves rarely older than 35 years, and they commanded a crew of younger men. KL Kentrat certainly looks the part of a U-Boat commander, with his clear eyes, hard stare and patrol's worth of beard. A U-boat's CO could almost always be distinguished by his white cap.

▶ Together with the four crewmen of the tower watch, the officers of *U575* assemble on the tower as the boat prepares to dock at St-Nazaire after a mission, 7 August 1942. From the left they are: three crewmen looking out forward, the IWO, who controlled the docking of the boat, with his megaphone for giving orders, the CO in his white cap and, on the gun platform, the IIWO and LI with the fourth watchman.

Crew

The primary component of a Type VII U-boat wasn't made of steel, but of flesh and blood. The crew of a Type VII was normally composed of 44 officers and men. This included four officers, four chief petty officers and the remainder petty officers and lower rates (known collectively as the *Pairs* (Lords) in U-boat slang). The boat was led by the Commanding Officer, who was normally a *Kapitänleutnant* (equivalent to Lieutenant in US Navy rank), though in some cases Type VII U-boats were commanded by an *Oberleutnant zur See* (equivalent to Lieutenant (jg)). In the informal atmosphere of an operational U-boat, the CO was generally addressed as '*Herr Kaleunt*'. The Executive Officer was known as the First Watch Officer (*Erste Wach Offizier* or IWO). He was called the '*Eins WO*' (pronounced 'Eyn-zwoe'). He was generally an *Oberleutnant zur See*. Besides being the second in command, he had specific responsibility for the torpedoes and the systems that aimed and fired them. The Second Officer was the IIWO (*Zweiter Wach Offizier*). He was generally a very junior *Leutnant z.S.* (equivalent to Ensign). His specific responsibility was for the deck and Flak guns. The last officer was the Engineer (*Leitender Ingenieur* – Lead Engineer). He was called 'LI' (pronounced 'Ell-ee') and generally held the rank of Leutnant (Ing). He was responsible for all the physical systems in the boat. Occasionally, a Type VII would carry one more officer, a Second Engineer. He would be an LI in training who had completed his required course work and was being sent on a mission to get a little 'seasoning' under an experienced LI prior to being assigned his own boat.[1]

The crew of a Type VII would assemble in stages as the construction of the boat neared completion. The first to arrive would be the CO and the LI, followed immediately by the engine room chiefs. This would generally occur about eight weeks before completion of the boat. These would go down into the hull each day, examining every weld and bolt as if their lives depended on them, because they did. This familiarization period was known as the *Baubelehrung*. Over the next few weeks the two watch officers, the rest of the petty officers and the bosun assembled at the building yard. Just prior to completion, the navigator and the Lords arrived, filling out the crew.

The entire crew, except for the officers, was divided into two divisions: the technical division and the seamen. The technical division was composed of the trained technicians who maintained and operated the complex systems that kept the boat operational. This included the diesel machinists, electricians, radio operators and torpedo mechanics of all rates. The rest of the

enlisted crew were considered part of the seamen's division. The distinction becomes important when attempting to understand the scheduling and assignment of duties among the crew.

The enlisted crewmen were led by the four CPOs (*Oberfeldwebel*). These included the navigator (*Obersteuermann*). He served as Quartermaster and was in charge of provisioning the boat as well as being responsible for the navigation. He also had responsibility for the conning of the boat and had direct authority over the boat's helmsmen. On many boats the *Obersteuermann* was also an essential member of the attack team, helping to determine how and when to take offensive action against convoys. The bosun (*Oberbootsmann*) acted as the senior NCO, being responsible for the conduct of the crew.[2] The *Obersteuermann* and *Oberbootsmann* also acted effectively as the third and fourth watch officers, taking their turns on the tower along with the IWO and IIWO. They were in charge of the seamen's division of the crew. The two other CPOs were the lead artificers for the diesels and the electric motors. Their ranks were *Diesel Obermaschinist* and *Elektro Obermaschinist*. They were responsible for the boat's propulsion systems, reporting directly to the LI. They had direct authority over the motormen and dieselmen who stood watch in the mechanical spaces and more generally had responsibility for the technical division of the crew.

Below these four served the 36 petty officers (*Unteroffiziere*) and men of the two divisions. While the proportions of ratings varied from boat to boat, generally there were two petty officers to every three seamen in a U-boat. The seamen did the work of the boat, standing watches, acting as stewards at mealtime and as labourers when torpedoes or supplies had to be moved. They included the bosun's mates (*Boots-mann* and *Bootsmannsmaat*), the helmsmen (*Steuermann*) and the remaining seamen (*Matrose*) including the indispensible cook (*Smut*). The technical division was filled out by the torpedomen (*Mechaniker* and *Mechanikersmaat*), the motormen and dieselmen (*Maschinisten* and *Maschinistensmaat*) and radiomen (*Oberfunkmaat* and *Funkmaat*).

The crew of a U-boat stood watches on a

Above left: The *Obersteuermann* in a U-boat was a jack-of-all-trades. Besides being in charge of provisioning the boat, he also was the navigator and he operated the attack computer during torpedo operations. In his role as navigator, he took any sun or star sightings required. The life jacket he is wearing was probably donned for the benefit of the photographer. The calm sea wouldn't necessitate this precaution.

Above: There was no typical U-boatman, but if such could exist, this crewman off *U201* seen at Lorient on 18 May 1941 might

qualify. Note the very unofficial plaid shirt seen under the collar of his overalls. Uniform restrictions were few in the U-boat service; men wore whatever was comfortable and kept them warm and dry.

▶ A watchkeeper from an unidentified boat. The scarf and gloves worn with standard U-boat overalls indicate that this photograph was taken in spring or autumn, but the weather was dry and calm. The Iron Cross Second Class on the pocket of his overalls indicates that he is a veteran. The lanyard hanging from his other pocket identifies him as a Bosun or a Bosun's Mate. Note also the lookout's large binoculars around his neck. (Via Schmidt)

Far right: Perhaps a more typical U-boatman than the last two smiling crewmen, this one appears to be concentrating intently on the horizon. He, too, wears a scarf and a knitted cap for his head against a cool wind. (via Schmidt)

number of different cycles depending on the assigned duty and the division. The seamen's division worked on a schedule based on eight-hour periods, dividing each day into three watches. This gave the seamen eight hours of duty, eight hours for sleep and another eight-hour period of which at least half was taken up with miscellaneous assigned duties. These included the periodic requirement to stand tower watch, if the boat were surfaced. The remaining four hours were for eating, hygiene, kit maintenance and such opportunities for relaxation as could be found in a U-boat. Only on rare occasions was tower duty required of the technical division, in part because they worked very different cycles. Tower watch was stood on four-hour cycles, timed to mesh with the seamen's normal eight-hour duty blocks. A watch would consist of four lookouts and the watch officer. The IWO and IIWO each stood two watches a day, two four-hour cycles separated by twelve hours. The *Obersteuermann* and *Oberbootsmann* generally stood one tower watch each per day, in addition to their regular eight-hour duty period.

The *Maschinisten* worked a completely different schedule, based on six-hour cycles. This meant they were generally exempted from standing tower watch, but put them on a gruelling six hours on, six hours off cycle which repeated every twelve hours. The four *Funkers* worked yet another schedule. The day between 0800 and 2000 was divided into three four-hour watches. The remaining twelve hours was split into two six-hour periods. Since two *Funkers* stood watch two at a time, they also averaged twelve hours of duty each day.

All these schedules and cycles held only during non-combat periods. When the enemy was in sight, all crewmen, even those 'officially' asleep, were awake and ready for instant response to the need to crash dive, to reload torpedo tubes or to repair damage to the boat.

Crew space in all Second World War submarines was cramped. Type VII U-boats were even more crowded than most because they were small boats compared to most other nations' ocean-going submarines. Ratings slept in the forward torpedo compartment. The twelve bunks

Above left: Four-fifths of a typical tower watch are seen on duty, each scanning his own quadrant of the horizon. Only the after lookout is missing from this view. Second from the left is the watch officer who had charge of the watch and kept an eye on the sky. The watch are wearing the thick leather coats issued to U-boat crews for cold weather. As long as the sea was calm, it was an effective garment.

◀ In rougher weather, the watch broke out their oilskins. These gave reasonable protection as long as the water wasn't breaking over the tower. In that case, nothing kept the water out. The elastic at the wrist and ankles of the wet weather suit then only served to hold in the water that came in at the neck and waist.

▲ With a boost from the sky periscope, a lookout on this 9. UFlot boat gets an extended view forward. U-boats were so low in the water that the normal radius of lookouts' vision was at the most 12 kilometres on a clear day. The added height might allow this lookout to see another kilometre or two.

◀ The return to base after a mission was the happiest part of a patrol, at least as long as the weather was nice and the RAF refrained from dropping a few bombs. *U437* is seen in the lock at St-Nazaire after a mission. The IWO guides the docking process while the other officers and the watch observe from the tower. Crewmen stand by on deck, ready to throw out the fenders which kept the boat from scraping the quay.

▶ The CPOs of *U48* relax while the boat is approaching the concrete U-boat pen faintly visible in the background. The variety of uniform worn by these CPOs was typical. Most wore the standard overalls like the *Oberfeldwebel* on the right. Some adopted the British Army officer's short field jacket which proved very popular among U-boatmen after large quantities of British battledress fell into German hands at Dunkirk.

there were sufficient for the approximately 22 seamen in a typical U-boat's crew. The *Maschinisten* were assigned two to a bunk because of their six-hour schedules. The remainder of the ratings were allocated two bunks for every three men. The system worked well except at the beginning of a patrol when the last two spare torpedoes forced one level of the bunks, three on each side, to be lashed up. Hammocks could be slung from the overhead to provide some accommodation, but generally that still meant that some of the Lords would sleep on torpedoes until the enemy had been found and two torpedoes fired off. The petty officers slept in their own *U-Raum* between the control room and the galley. Like the ratings they shared bunks, though theirs were available throughout the patrol. Their space did have one strong disadvantage, however. At every meal and every watch change, the narrow passageway down the middle of their space would be crowded with noisy stewards or *Maschinisten* squeezing their way past the folding mess tables on their way to or from the aft of the boat. One petty officer didn't sleep in the *U-Raum*. The leading *Mechaniker* slept in the forward torpedo room where he ruled the Lords and kept an eye on his precious 'Eels', as the torpedoes were affectionately known.

Only the CPOs and officers had their own bunks and only the Commanding Officer had a compartment to himself. The chiefs bunked in the small space just aft of the forward torpedo room and the head, just large enough for their four bunks. The officers' quarters were next aft, only marginally more spacious than the CPOs'. Only the Commanding Officer had a bunk without another bunk or the overhead just above and only he actually had a seat that wasn't someone's bunk and a worktable all his own that didn't double as a mess table.

1. WB. 'We had one engineer and that was it. Sometimes we had a second engineer, who was usually a very young *Leutnant*, for just one trip, just to get their feet wet. Then they usually commissioned a new boat.'
2. The CO, as commander, was ultimately responsible for crew discipline. However, the tradition in the German Navy was that the bosun attempted to resolve all disciplinary issues before they came to the attention of the CO. If the CO had actively to discipline a crewman, it meant that the bosun had failed in his duty.

▲ A pair of petty officers of *U236* are seen on deck as their boat approaches a U-boat pen. The single stripe on the collar of their overalls indicates that they hold the rate of Petty Officers, Third Class (*Maat*). The metal insignia on the cap was a common feature. Two such insignia weren't!

▶ When a U-boat, such as *U87* seen here at St-Nazaire on 8 July 1942, arrived home from a patrol, all crewmen who weren't on duty in the boat or on the tower, and didn't have docking duty manning the lines or bumpers, would assemble on the deckcasing aft of the tower for review by the flotilla staff and any other members of the official greeting party.

▶ The crew of *U712* drawn up for inspection, post-patrol. The Bosun leans on the railing to left, ready to call them to attention at the appropriate moment. (Von Ketelhodt)

▶ Sometimes, a special occasion called for special decoration. Such was the case when Kapitänleutnant Endrass of *U46* won the oakleaves to his *Ritterkreuz*, at that time the highest decoration given to U-boatmen. The cluster of oakleaves to the left was therefore quite appropriate. Note the canvas cover over the UZO on which Endrass is leaning.

◄ The flotilla staff tried to arrange a warm greeting for the crew once they got ashore. If there were some nurses in the area, they were often recruited to join the greeting party. A friendly, non-masculine face must have been a very refreshing sight after a long patrol.

◄ For some the most welcome of pleasures waiting back in port was a bottle of beer. The Kriegsmarine had similar policies to the RN regarding alcohol aboard ships. But even the limited official ration of alcohol was banned in U-boats where instant reaction was always a matter of life and death. So the bottle of Beck's had to wait for return to base. This crewman off *U588* is obviously enjoying his first beer in a month or so.

Right: The nurses would frequently greet the crewmen with small baskets of flowers or fruit. This crewman off *U753* looks more tired than elated by the greeting.

Far right: A cigarette on dry land was always welcome. So was a dish of ice cream, a delicacy that never found its way into a Type VII U-boat. Here Kapitänleutnant von Bülow, commander of *U404*, expresses his pleasure at St-Nazaire, 14 July 1942.

▶ Every bit as welcome as the friendly greeting was a chance to get the mail that had accumulated during the mission. Three crewmen in *U588* sit on the railing of the tower gun platform and begin catching up with news from home. This was early 1942 and the news had not yet turned bad.

Provisioning

The operation of a Type VII was limited by the expendable provisions carried by the boat. This included all materials that were used up during a patrol, including munitions (particularly torpedoes), fuel, food and water. Of these, the supply of torpedoes was the most limiting, at least at the beginning of the war. During this period, most patrols by Type VIIs were brought to an end by running out of torpedoes long before the remaining provisions were expended. By 1942, the range of the Battle of the Atlantic had been extended to the coast of North and South America and Africa. Before the war, it had been thought that only Type IXs would have to range over these distances, but the increase in defensive capabilities by the Allies in the Central Atlantic and the rich pickings to be had in the more remote theatres led the Germans to use their numerous Type VIIs over greater distances than they ever had been intended to cover.

Two factors allowed the use of Type VII U-boats in these more distant regions. One was the gradual discovery during the first two years of the war that Type VIIs were capable of considerably greater range than had been foreseen. By shutting down one of the diesels and running the other at most economical speed, Type VIIs could be operated off the coast of North America, at least as far South as New York City, without refuelling. Over these distances, it was generally shortage of fuel oil that limited a patrol's duration. It was rarely shortages of other provisions that caused Type VIIs to return to port. Type VIIs were now often returning from patrol with food in the larder and torpedoes in the tubes.

In order to exploit more fully the capabilities of Type VIIs over these long ranges, it was necessary to reprovision the boats at sea. There had been a system of supply ships specifically for the long-range Type IXs, but at almost the same time that the war was expanding to America, this surface supply network was being decimated by the Royal Navy.[1] This wasn't a wholly unforeseen circumstance and an initial group of six Type XIV supply U-boats had been under construction since early 1941. Therefore it was less than five months until the first of the Type XIV *Milchkühe* (milch cow) was ready for service. *U459* resupplied *U333*, a Type VIIC, off the US east coast on 19 April 1942, delivering a full load of oil as well as fresh food.[2] This system for resupply involved the two boats meeting in daylight, on the surface at a pre-designated location. A fuel delivery hose trailed by the Type XIV and kept afloat by inflatable rubber bladders, was hauled in aboard the Type VII, which would be sailing at low speed just aft and to the leeward side of the *Milchkuh*.

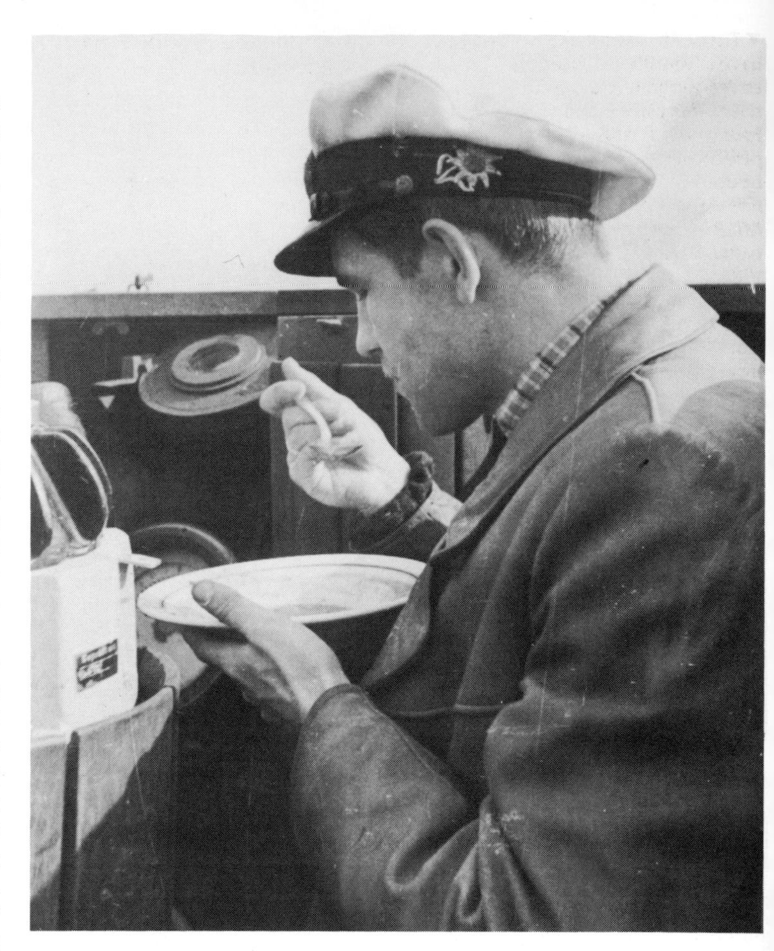

▲ In abstract terms, provisions defined the ability of a U-boat to fight the enemy. In more concrete terms, they meant a bowl of soup on the tower during a watch, as enjoyed by the Commanding Officer of *U706*.

Assuming all went well, fuel delivery would begin as soon as the hose was connected at the receiving end. The actual transfer of fuel took from an hour to five hours depending on how much fuel was being transferred, the weather and the competence of the crews. Other provisions, up to the occasional torpedo, were transferred by rubber dinghy or by line stretched between the boats. The transfer of torpedoes was a rare occurrence after 1942 because, even more than other forms of resupply, it required the opening of hatches to the extent that no reasonable chance of escape existed for either boat if an enemy appeared on the scene.

This scheme was used with great success until late July 1943, when a concerted effort on the part of Allied ASW forces sank nearly all the active *Milchkühe* and other resupply U-boats and brought the system to a halt. By then the Type VII had been effectively neutralized in the North

▶ The considerable size of a Type XIV becomes obvious in these views. The broad deckcasing allowed the free movement required by resupply activities, but it trapped a tremendous amount of air, making these boats very slow diving. The pair of 3.7cm deck guns were for decoration only. With no torpedo tubes and just those pop-guns, a *Milchkuh* had no chance of fighting its way past an enemy.

▼ Three U-boats meet in the Central Atlantic to resupply. (Actually there must have been four boats for this photograph to have been taken.) To the left is the Type XIV *Milchkuh*. The other two boats are Type VIICs. This many boats could only come together in 1942 far from either coast and from known convoy routes.

Atlantic. The loss of the resupply network only further confirmed that defeat. Resupply continued in the still quiet Central Atlantic west of the Azores for boats still operating in the tropics. This came to an end with the loss of *U488*.[3] The Germans experimented with underwater refuelling, but the numerous technical difficulties this involved, as well as the loss of the entire *Milchkühe* fleet, prevented this technique from being put into practise.

Food handling, storage and preparation on a typical Type VII U-boat was crude by almost any standards. There was only a tiny refrigerator and no freezing capability, so that any fresh food brought onboard at the beginning of a mission had to be consumed quickly before it became mouldy or rotted.[4] The storage of food was an art that was controlled by the *Obersteuermann*. Food was stored throughout the boat as evenly as possible, though most of the non-perishable food went into the larder that made up the port side of the small galley or into the after head on the starboard side of the same compartment. The rest of the food was distributed according to a set pattern. Hams, sausages and other preserved meats were stored between the forward torpedo tubes and from the overhead in the control room. These were out of the way locations that caused

◀ **The fuel hose was payed out over the stern of the Type XIV to be picked up by the Type VII which trailed astern and a lee of the *Milchkuh*. The inflated rubber bladders kept the hose afloat and made it easier to see and to retrieve. The crewmen here wear life vests, as the risk of being washed overboard by a wave or a twisting hose was very real. The valve in the foreground measured the fuel delivery so that the right amount could be passed and so the *Milchkuh* would know how much fuel it had left to deliver to other boats. (Albrecht)**

◀ **On the receiving end, hauling the hose aboard and controlling it in all but the calmest weather was difficult work. Here the hose has been looped over the pair of retractable bollards on the starboard side just forward of the deck gun and then run down the deckcasing to the fuel inlet valve aft of the tower. One of the watch officers observes while crewmen keep tension on the hose to prevent it slipping loose.**

the least inconvenience, since these items tended to last a long time and be consumed relatively slowly. Loaves of bread were stored in the forward torpedo room and the motor room, where they were very much in the way, but were consumed (or disposed of) quickly. Fresh meat and produce was stored in the refrigerator or pantry, the coolest places in the boat, but even there it lasted only days. Three rules governed the storage of food. It had to be securely stored so as to not come loose during enemy attack, evenly distributed so that its consumption disturbed the boat's trim as little as possible and it had to leave free access to all hatches and valves. As the food was consumed, its weight was recorded, along with any other consumables that had been expended, in the LI's daily weight report.

> 'Every morning I did a weight report. The cook reported what he had cooked and how many pounds he'd used and which of the various storage places it had come from. Every morning we went through the ritual of calculating how much weight had been taken from so far away from the centre of gravity of the boat, either plus or minus, and what effect did that have as far as the boat's balance was

▶ **The Navigator in *U571* takes a sun sighting while his boat manoeuvres close alongside the *Milchkuh* in order to transfer food and other provisions. Tinned goods were bundled together in net bags for the transfer. Bread and other materials that could be ruined by a dip in the sea were stored in sealed rubber bags.**

▼ **The transfer of torpedoes on the high seas was one of the least popular of activities. Not only did it mean leaving both boats open to attack, but these two crewmen got the unenviable task of shepherding the torpedo between boats in a rubber dinghy, while the torpedo floated alongside, marked by a pair of inflated rubber bladders.**

concerned. How much water did we have to move from one end to the other. Additionally, some water usually had to be pumped out of the trim tanks, because as we used up fuel it was replaced by water in the tanks making the boat heavier and heavier.'[5]

Once the fresh food was eaten or disposed of, the fare for the rest of the voyage was sausage and canned food, mainly *Kraut*. The cook was one of the most valued crew members, especially if he could make sausage and *Kraut* taste good. This was no easy trick in a U-boat where, very quickly, all food took on the taste of the boat, a not terribly pleasant combination of diesel oil, mould and bilge smells. The situation was made worse later in the war by the regular addition of a soya-based filler, called *Bratlingspulver*, which gave everything a bland flavour.

1. The sinking of the steamers *Atlantis* on 22 November 1941 and *Python* on 1 December 1941 effectively ended operations of the surface resupply network.
2. Type XIVs had an onboard bakery which could supply a Type VII with fresh bread, a great treat, enough to last several weeks.
3. KTB, 28 April 1944.
4. The obvious exception here were the Type VIIDs and Fs which had freezers as well as larger refrigerated compartments for the long-term storage of meat, eggs, etc.
5. WH.

Sanitation

A Type VII U-boat had two tiny heads (lavatories), one forward and the other aft, but for much of the voyage only the forward head was available as the after one was used for the storage of food and other goods. The head was a complex hand-pumped affair which became inoperable at depths much greater than periscope depth due to an inability to overcome outside water pressure. If a U-boat were held at depth greater than 25 metres for any length of time, buckets would have to be set out for the crew's relief. If an exploding depth-charge caused a bucket to spill into the bilge, a not uncommon experience, the smell became part of that boat's personality from then on.

All other aspects of sanitation were haphazard at best. The forward head was the larger of the two. It had a small antechamber ceremoniously called the wash room, but in fact the crew rarely had the opportunity to wash themselves. Fresh water on a Type VII U-boat was extremely limited, with barely enough for normal internal consumption, such as cooking, drinking and washing dishes. As a rule, none was left over for washing. The only exception was that water used for washing dishes was saved and occasionally recycled for use for crew bathing or shaving. Salt water soap was carried and could always be used, but was universally disliked by U-boatmen because it barely lathered and left a slimy film which was impossible to wash off. If a boat were

◀ **Long-ranged Type VIIDs were often sent to more distant tropical regions, allowing their crews the rare pleasure of a voluntary dip in the ocean. Here the crew of *U214* gets a chance to dive off the wide deckcasing and saddle tanks of this minelayer during one of its Caribbean or African patrols. (via MacPherson)**

◀ **Enjoying the U-boatman's equivalent of waterskiing, a crewman on an unknown Type VII hangs on to free-flooding holes for dear life while lying on the saddle tanks of his boat as it moves at high speed. The riskiness of this operation is attested to by the safety line tied around his waist.**

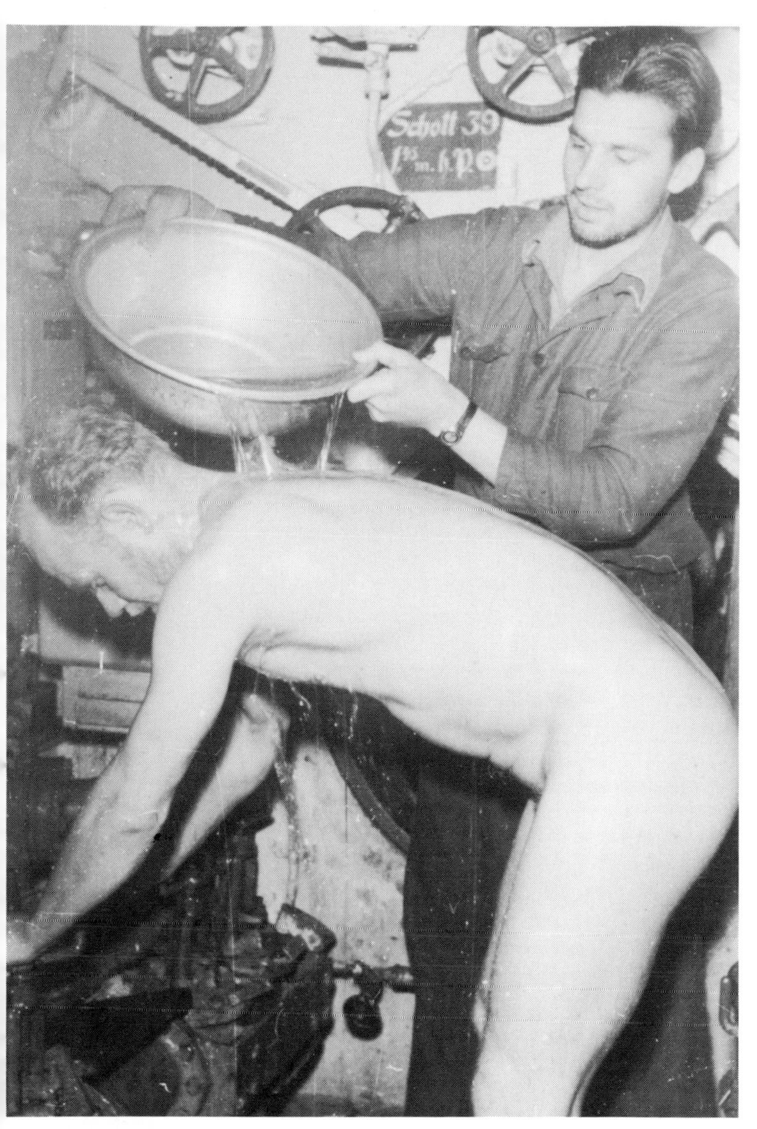

▲ A rare pleasure, a crewman gets a washdown at the after end of the control room of a Type VII U-boat with some of the precious washwater. After the cook had cleaned the dishes, the rinse water was saved for just this purpose. The lucky crewman is leaning against the main trim pump.

operating in tropical areas and was far enough away from an enemy airbase for safety, the crew would be allowed to swim by the boat. In general, shaving was neglected. Images of returning crews with a mission's worth of beard growth were common.

The health of the crew was generally in the hands of a *Funker* who had been through, at best, a few weeks training as a medical orderly. For the first four years of the war, Type VIIs almost never carried a doctor, though larger boats, particularly those used for resupply, such as the Type IXD or Type XIV, sometimes did so. In most cases, the lack of a real doctor was never noticed. The crew tended to be young and healthy and serious illness was rare. Even injury was unusual since U-boats tended to avoid firefights with the enemy. On those occasions when sickness or injury did occur, it was normal practise to attempt to set up a rendezvous between the Type VII and the nearest supply boat. More often, the treatment was just what could be delivered on the spot with the resources available. To supplement the barely trained *Funker*, there was a medical text on board each boat with information on the do-it-yourself diagnosis and treatment of most common injuries and ailments.

The most common complaints were skin and joint disorders related to the constant moisture aboard a Type VII. A U-boat was always wet and Type VIIs even more so because they lacked air conditioning or any other means to reduce the humidity in the boat. Once something got wet, it tended to stay wet. That included the crew. Those who had to stand watch, which meant most of the crew, went outside to get wet. The watch was supplied with oilskins to keep them dry on the bridge, but the effort was futile:

> 'When the breakers came over, everything got wet, particularly if you had your binoculars up. Well, of course, there were elastic bands at the wrists, but every so often you let down your arm and pour out the water.'[1]

But even if you didn't stand watch, you still had your chance to get soaked:

> 'If you didn't get wet on deck, you got wet down below when the boat surfaced. If you're underwater for a while, say 20 hours, all the pressure is released into the boat. You didn't dare release air out, so every little motor driven by compressed air, and there were quite a few, released their pressure into the boat. If you shot torpedoes, that's even worse. They were launched using 23 or 24 atms and this pressure, when the piston comes back, is released into the boat. The result is you have high pressure in the boat and moisture forms drops on all bulkheads. The moment you come up and the pressure is released, you get a brief shower. Everything gets wet.'[2]

The medical situation changed in mid-1943. The orders given by BdU for U-boats to engage attacking aircraft on the surface led to an inevitable sharp increase in serious combat injuries. BdU ordered that by July of that year, every second boat leaving port should have a qualified Medical Officer aboard. As of early June, sixteen MOs were at sea onboard supply boats, and a further thirteen were assigned to the remaining Type IXDs and XIVs. That left seventeen MOs for the almost 150 Type VIIs then operational.[3] The number of onboard MOs did increase slowly as the war progressed, but never approached the 50 per cent figure BdU desired.

1. EvK.
2. WB.
3. KTB, 6 June 1943.

Part Three: Weapons and Targeting Systems

The whole reason for the existence of a Type VII U-boat was the delivery of weapons against a chosen target. A U-boat had a variety of weapons to chose from in carrying out its mission of sinking enemy ships. The primary offensive weapon, of course, was the torpedo, but there were others available for use under the appropriate circumstances, and, increasingly, as the war progressed and life in a U-boat became more risky, defensive weapons proliferated as well.

The following sections describe the various weapons carried by a Type VII U-boat during the course of the war. They also describe the sighting and targeting systems available to aim those weapons at targets.

Torpedoes

Throughout the war years, Type VII U-boats carried a wide variety of torpedoes. These variants were developed in an attempt to give U-boats a tactical advantage in their attacks on increasingly well-defended targets. As the time available to the U-boat to aim torpedoes was reduced by aggressive defences, the ability to find the target was of necessity transferred to the torpedo itself. Advances in technology changed the role of the U-boat from one of active weapon delivery to a more passive one of simply carrying torpedoes within range. From that point on, the torpedo took over the job of finding the target.

Basic Torpedoes

A torpedo is itself a weapons system, reproducing in miniature some of the mechanisms used by a U-boat, including systems for propulsion, warhead detonation, depth keeping, course keeping and, in some cases, aiming. Each of these elements had been the subject of intense development during the inter-war years, but the upgrading of many of them was incomplete at the outbreak of war.

◀ A torpedo is lowered by crane into the loading trough on the foredeck of an unidentified Type VII U-boat. Given the shallow angle and position of the trough forward of the open torpedo hatch, this torpedo is probably a G7a destined for the forward external storage tube. The Type VII in the background has its tripod torpedo winch erected over its tower. (via MacPherson)

(Interestingly, the story of torpedo development in Germany and in America contains an uncanny number of parallels. Identical problems with detonators and depth keeping haunted the two navies and similarly circuitous roads were followed to correct the problems. The Japanese were unique in introducing new technology, oxygen propulsion, without particular difficulties in deployment.)

All the torpedoes developed for use by Type VII U-boats before and during the war were based on two propulsion designs. The older of these was a standard Whitehead-type steam propulsion torpedo known as the G7a (G model (ie., seventh model) – 7 metres in length – first subtype) and developed as the T1 series. These were powered by the burning of alcohol in air supplied from a compressed-air tank. This combustion gave off gases and steam sufficient to power a turbine which drove the single 6-bladed propeller. It had three speed settings depending on the desired range: 44 knots – 6 kilometres; 40 knots – 7.5 kilometres; 30 knots – 12 kilometres.

The other basic design was an electric drive torpedo known as the G7e and initially developed as the T2. The T2 was succeeded by the similar T3 and used as the basis for the T3a, T4, T5 and other later developments. This design was preferred by the Germans, despite the fact that it was slow and had a short range, because it left no wake of bubbles that could alert a defender to the location of the attacking U-boat. It had the additional advantage of being cheaper and faster to produce. Work had begun on this design in the early 1920s. Like German inter-war submarine research, development and testing of the design took place outside the country. With the help of German-owned engineering firms in Sweden, the initial trials were held in 1923 and final acceptance trials in 1929.

The G7e was powered by lead-acid wet cell batteries driving an electric motor of approximately 100hp, in turn driving a pair of 2-bladed counter-rotating propellers. Course-and depth-keeping gyroscopes were powered by compressed air. When the batteries were properly charged and pre-heated electrically to 30°C before firing, a G7e could reach five kilometres at 30 knots. Without pre-heating, the range and speed both dropped, to three kilometres at 28 knots. Midwar, an improved G7e (T3a) was introduced with increased battery capacity which incremented range by 50 per cent (to 7.5 kilometres).

Both basic designs were housed in almost identical packages, which is not surprising since they were intended to be fired from the same torpedo tubes, stored in the same spaces and handled by the same gear. They were 54cm (21in) in diameter and 7.16m (7.8yds) in length. The G7e was slightly heavier at 1,608 kilograms. Both carried warheads of 280kg of explosives (or were supplied in training versions with dummy warheads of similar weight). At the beginning of the war both designs were supplied in a basic configuration (T1 and T2) fitted with standard guidance and the Pi 1 detonator pistol.

Standard guidance for a German torpedo meant depth and course control by gyroscopic stabilization. Torpedoes could be directed to turn from the course on which they were fired to any other up to 90° off that base course in 1° increments. (Later in the war this course change ability was increased to 135°.) Actually, the very first patrols of the Second World War were conducted with torpedoes whose course couldn't be altered. They had the correct course change mechanisms, but by mistake were not fitted with steerable fins. BdU was not informed of this fact until the evening of 13 September 1939.[1] When told, he was infuriated at the apparent lack of concern and commensurate care on the part of the Navy's Torpedo Directorate, the organization responsible for the production and testing of torpedoes. It would not be the last time he would make that complaint.

The new course taken by the torpedo would be maintained until it found a target or sank at the end of its run. Upon reaching the target detonation was the responsibility of the Pi 1 pistol. This was developed just prior to the beginning of the war, but was insufficiently tested before its adoption as the standard detonator. It added a new magnetic influence detonation feature to a standard electrical contact pistol. The contact pistol was set off by a central firing pin closing the firing circuit, caused by physical contact with a target, activating an electrical detonator. Four angled 'whiskers' were supplied to handle glancing blows. The magnetic exploder was a dip needle type based on the design of the British Sinker Mk 1(M) mine developed late in the First World War and deployed without much success during the last days of that war. The firing circuit was complete except for a gap which could be closed by a pivoting magnetic needle. Under the influence of an external magnetic field, the needle dipped, closing the circuit. The minimal electrical current needed to detonate the warhead was supplied by a small spinning-armature generator driven by a 5-bladed propeller at the nose of the pistol. This self-contained power supply to the pistol allowed the Pi 1 to be fitted to both G7a and G7e models without modification.

The magnetic influence detonator set off the warhead when it registered a magnetic field of sufficient strength, such as that generated by the steel hull of a ship. This allowed the torpedo to be set to run up to three metres below the keel of the target. If the magnetic pistol were properly calibrated, it would detonate the warhead directly below the target. This was far more effective in destroying a ship than an explosion along the side of the hull. While an explosion alongside a ship will generally open a hole in its side and possibly lead to fatal flooding, most of the energy of the blast is expended in creating a glorious plume of water and explosive gases. An explosion under the hull of a ship directs almost all of this energy upward toward the keel. The effect with most merchant ships would be to break the keel of the ship, an almost certainly mortal blow. That is, if the magnetic pistol had worked.

The effect of the Pi 1's inadequate testing was that almost as soon as the first patrols set out against the British, reports came back of inexplicable torpedo failures. A sampling of these reports includes:

> '4 Oct 39: *U35* reported two spontaneous explosions of G7as.[2]
> 13 Oct 39: *U47* reported that its first spread of three torpedoes fired at HMS *Royal Oak* in Scapa Flow resulted in only one detonation and that one of such low order that it wasn't noticed by the British.
> 18 Oct 39: Various boats reported an attack on a convoy. Four or five ships were sunk, but two torpedoes exploded at the end of their run, another two were surface runners and two more exploded spontaneously upon arming [all torpedoes had a propeller device as part of the detonator that only armed the warhead at a safe distance from the U-boat, generally 500–700 metres].[3]
> 25 Oct 39: *U48* entered port. It reported five torpedo failures which cost it several possible sinkings.'[4]

By now, BdU's complaints were getting tiresome to his superiors and on the same day that *U48* entered Kiel, a Torpedo Inspectorate was established to study the spate of seemingly unrelated failures. At that time, BdU stated flatly that 'at least 30 per cent of torpedoes are duds' and that 'The torpedo problem is . . . the most urgent of all problems of U-boat warfare'.[5]

From the beginning, BdU suspected that the fault lay at least in part in the Pi 1 pistol. The magnetic influence detonator was a sensitive device which had to be set up correctly in order to operate. The strength of a ship's magnetic field is determined in part by the size of the ship. The pistol set up was therefore based in part on the estimated size of the target. However, a ship's magnetic field will also vary directly in proportion to the strength and direction of the earth's magnetic field and these in turn are influenced by the target's position on the face of the earth. The Pi 1 had a field strength setting that had to be set according to a geographic zone chart issued to all boats. (The strength of the magnetic field required to pivot the detonator's dip needle was controlled by this field strength setting.) In general, the setting changed the farther north the boat went, although, since the earth's magnetic pole is offset from the axis of rotation, the relationship between position and magnetic zone was complex, influenced by longitude as well as latitude. An error of as little as 30 nautical miles could mean a difference of one zone and the difference, according to the Torpedo Directorate, between successful detonation and a failure. Consistently, throughout that winter and early spring, the Directorate would claim that faulty estimation of target size or poor navigation or both was the real problem, not the Pi 1.

As early as 2 October, a cutout switch was added to the Pi 1 which allowed it to be set for contact detonation only (AZ setting – AZ being short for *Abstandzündung*, literally contact detonation) as opposed to the normal dual setting (MZ – *Magnetischerzündung* – magnetic detonation). At this time, BdU ordered that the AZ setting, together with the shallower depth setting required for contact detonation, was to be used exclusively.[6] The new Torpedo Inspectorate reported that its initial studies had traced the problem in the G7e to a faulty cable layout. The problems in the G7a remained unexplained. They claimed that the cable layout problem had been resolved in new production G7es and that boats should be able to fire torpedoes safely at either setting.[7] It was not to be that simple.

Besides the correct zone setting, the Pi 1 also had to run at the correct depth in order to function properly. The magnetic field of a metal object such as a ship falls off rapidly (based on the inverse square of distance). If a torpedo armed with a magnetic detonator passes too far under the target, it will fail to explode, even if set correctly. The Pi 1 was designed to detonate two metres below the keel of its target. Thus, the torpedo failures could also be explained by faulty depth keeping and the spate of surface runners tended to indicate that this might be a problem too.

Nevertheless, the Torpedo Inspectorate's most recent claim that the problems with the torpedoes were resolved led BdU again to authorize the use of the MZ setting.[8] Immediate reports of continued failures[9] caused the immediate reimposition of the ban on magnetic firings.[10]

> 'We were thus back where we were in 1914–18. But I had to make this difficult decision to abandon the much-vaunted, much-discussed magnetic firing in order to avoid losing boats, directly or indirectly, through our own weapons . . .'[11]

Switching permanently to the AZ setting equally failed to resolve the problem. Many

▲ A torpedo is winched down through the forward torpedo hatch into the forward torpedo room. This scene is taking place in the Mediterranean, still early enough in the war that the U-boat still mounts its 8.8cm deck gun, which has had to be swung athwartships to keep it out of the way. The boat is probably *U458*, seen sometime in 1942. (USN)

torpedoes still failed to detonate despite obviously correct firing solutions. In a typical case, *U25* reported four torpedo failures when firing at a stopped target at short range.[12] Frustration began to creep into the official reporting of day-to-day activities. The KTB entry for 7 November 1939 read:

> '*U46* entered Kiel. It sank one tanker of about 5,000 tons. The result is rather meagre, but the CO's verbal report tells quite another story of the patrol. The boat was in convoys three times. On one occasion the CO fired at a wall of several overlapping ships – failures. It had a stationary cruiser at inclination 90 off its bows. Again several failures, which finally warned the cruiser and it made off. Seven shots were quite definitely failures and not attributable to errors in drill. In spite of this, due to the CO's determination, the boat still went on searching for the enemy and attacking. The boat could have sunk 30,000 or 40,000 tons; it actually sank 5,000. The crew are naturally somewhat depressed. Several patrols like this will turn keenness into indifference, if all efforts are to no purpose.'[13]

The only possible conclusion was that the depth-keeping ability of at least the G7e was indeed faulty and that torpedoes were consistently running deep.

To counter this problem, BdU ordered that depth settings on all torpedoes be set at two metres less than the presumed draught of the target. But, in order to avoid the risk of a surface runner, this setting couldn't be less than three metres in calm weather and four metres in a swell. Thus, targets of less than five to six metres couldn't be attacked. This meant that U-boats had no weapon effective against destroyers and other escorts.[14]

On 5 November, a new version of the Pi 1, the Pi A-B, with a stabilized magnetic needle, was introduced. Depth was to be set at draft of the target plus one metre. BdU again authorized firings using the MZ setting. The first boats out with the new pistol (*U28* and *U49*) both reported continued failures. BdU again ordered his boats to revert to AZ firings only.[15]

This cycle continued several more times through the autumn and winter of 1939/40. The pistol was 'improved' by insulation of the copper cap and smoothing of the thrust collar. Neither change helped.[16] They tried lowering the zone setting by two notches. This made the pistol less sensitive, a move which decreased the number of premature explosions and increased the number of failures. There was no overall improvement. In late January 1940, the Torpedo Inspectorate went so far as to claim that it was improper storage of G7es that was the cause of all the problems. They reasoned that storage of the electric torpedoes with batteries charged had caused the steel casings to become magnetized and that degaussing the stock of torpedoes would solve all the problems.[17] It didn't. In fact, the frequency of premature detonations increased markedly after the degaussing, some boats experiencing up to 50 per cent failures.

Operation 'Weserübung', the German invasion of Norway in April 1940, was the last straw. Again and again torpedo failures caused simple shots, often at prized targets, to fail. The Germans time and again had major Royal Navy units in their sights and, in frustration, watched them sail away undamaged. On just one day, torpedo failures off the coast of Norway allowed the heavy cruiser *Cumberland* and two destroyers to escape from certain destruction.[18] The problem proved even worse in the narrow waters of Norway's fiords, where premature detonations often left the attackers dangerously exposed to counter-attack. On 16 April, BdU ordered all boats out of the fiords, even though this significantly increased the difficulty of finding targets.[19] 'It becomes increasingly obvious that the failure of the torpedoes is the cause of our lack of success . . .'[20]

This may have been obvious to BdU, but the admission by the Torpedo Directorate that this was indeed the case came slowly and grudgingly. After months of trying simple solutions that had no beneficial effect, only gradually did it become clear that the torpedoes suffered simultaneously from a number of problems, each of which contributed to the overall problem. The fact that the problems were the result of multiple, independent causes explained why no single remedy, such as switching from MZ to AZ settings or changing the depth setting, had resolved the problem. And because no one solution would resolve the overall problem, when solutions to the contributing problems were finally discovered and implemented during the spring of 1940, the improvement wasn't sudden and dramatic but rather was characterized by a gradual reduction in complaints.

> '17 Apr 40: The Torpedo Directorate admitted that an undisclosed percentage of G7es issued to the fleet had been fitted with a new, untested 4-bladed arming propeller in place of the normal 5-bladed model. It apparently failed to supply enough power in some cases. Approximately 10 per cent of these failed to arm properly.[21]
> 17 Apr 40: At the same time, the Torpedo Directorate admitted that the effect of unplotted ore deposits and other factors made magnetic firing in fiords, close in to shore or in Zone 0 (north of 62'5°N) totally unpredictable.[22]
> 19 Apr 40: The G7e was tested again for depth keeping. It was discovered that when set to run at two metres, it actually ran at between 3.5 metres and 4.7 metres.[23] It was not until later that the true cause was found, that the high air pressure frequently found in submerged U-boats was causing the air chambers in G7es [that were used to control the torpedoes' depth] to overfill. [High-pressure air was released into the boat as a side-effect of the firing of torpedoes and by the use of power-assisted controls. It was also done deliberately to add oxygen to the boat's air when long submergence raised CO and CO_2 levels dangerously high.] This had the result of disturbing the setting of the gyroscope that controlled depth keeping.[24]
> 15 May 40: The Pi 1's firing pin was found to be liable to premature release, leading to early detonation, even in the AZ setting. The Pi 1's contact pistol was a needlessly complex affair, directing the normal backwards thrust of the firing pin through 180° by a series of levers before it would make contact with the firing circuit.[25] BdU demanded that the simple contact detonation pistol used by the British [examples of which were obtained when HMS *Seal* was captured] be copied.'[26]

◀ A Lord takes a cigarette break during the loading of torpedoes. The crewman wears the leather jacket that was standard issue for heavy work aboard a U-boat. The torpedo is in its trough in the background, suspended from the tripod winch by a harness which was attached to each side of the torpedo's afterbody. (ECPA)

▶ Seen from the tower, the job of loading a torpedo still looks dirty and difficult. The open hatches, the amount of miscellaneous equipment required and the number of crewmen on deck explains why this job was rarely carried out at sea, even early in the war when Allied air power had not yet begun to dominate the scene. (USN)

Far right: Only the fins and propellers of this G7e protrude from the torpedo hatch after lowering into the boat. The end of the loading trough is at the bottom. Once inside the boat, the movement of torpedoes became even more difficult because the space was cramped and gravity became an enemy rather than a friend. (SFL)

This, in fact, wasn't done. The Pi 1 was retained. Indeed, as the problems that plagued the tor-

pedoes were, one-by-one, resolved, confidence in the weapon proportionately increased. On 23 May 1940, BdU concluded that the AZ setting had become reliable enough that MZ could be permanently abandoned.[27]

The U-boats now had a generally reliable torpedo, but it was one that was much less effective than BdU desired. The whole idea behind the magnetic influence exploder had been to provide U-boats with a torpedo powerful enough to sink the largest targets with a single shot. This was particularly critical for Type VIIs with their limited torpedo capacity. Being forced to use only contact detonation meant accepting a considerably less effective weapon. BdU ordered a study to determine the exact effect of switching over to contact detonation. The results of studying 816 reported hits during the period January to June 1942 showed that 40 per cent of victims went down after one hit, 38 per cent required one or more additional torpedoes before sinking and the remaining 22 per cent got away after one or more hits.[28] BdU was hardly pleased with the results.

Another spate of torpedo failures occurred in February 1941, when attacks on two convoys, OB 288 and OB 289, were far less successful than they should have been. In the second of these attacks, *U552* reported on 23 February 1941 that she fired seven torpedoes in three salvoes, all of which failed to detonate. BdU reached the conclusion that these were torpedoes that had been stored over a very cold winter in North Germany and that this exposure must have led to the failures. All the boats that experienced the failures, with only one exception, had come directly from German bases rather than from France. The problem disappeared as suddenly as it arose with the arrival of March and warmer weather.[29] Finally, in late 1942, the Pi 2 (also known as Pi G7h or Pi 39h) was introduced for G7es. Pi 2 was an improved Pi 1 that drew its electric power from the G7e's batteries rather than making its own. BdU decided to try out the new pistol in the Mediterranean since there seemed to be a preponderance of large targets there that would provide a proper test for an operating magnetic detonator. On 4 November 1942, BdU ordered that the first fifty Pi 2s be sent to the Mediterranean with all possible speed.[30] This was done despite some known limitations of the pistol. It had been shown in tests to be ineffective at high angles of incidence, less than 20° or greater than 150°, and was overly sensitive to longitudinal disturbances, therefore being liable to premature detonation in seas greater than four or five or in the vicinity of exploding bombs or depth-charges.[31] The actual introduction of the Pi 2 took place almost simultaneously from western France and La Spezia in December. By February 1943, all boats leaving Germany and Norway also carried torpedoes equipped with the new pistol. Each boat was to be equipped with six G7es armed with Pi 2s as soon as production of the new pistol reached projected levels.[32] The original set of instructions on the use of G7e fitted with Pi 2, known as the T3, deliberately set the running depth of the torpedoes too shallow, in an attempt to limit the impact of possible MZ failures. As a result, however, by 20 March 1943, BdU was able to identify only four sinkings that could be positively attributed to the MZ feature of the pistol. Therefore a new set of orders was struck that increased the depth settings to be used. The results were completely satisfactory and the T3 with MZ detonation became briefly the standard torpedo for Type VII U-boats.[33]

G7as were given a different magnetic pistol, the Pi 3, which needed no external power source, being based on the Italian SIC design. Development of this pistol began in January 1943 in Italy, with the first operational example being ready in August of that year. Unlike the Pi 2, the Pi 3 used completely separate MZ and AZ units, the former being embedded in the torpedo and not therefore serviceable at sea. Deployment of Pi 3-equipped G7as was slow due to the collapse of Italy and the need to transfer production to Germany. In general, the Pi 3 was less successful than the Pi 2. One nagging problem was the tendency to explode at the end of the run.[34] On 2 August 1944, the problems had reached the point that the use of the Pi 3's MZ feature was discontinued.

Advanced Torpedoes

As the war progressed, the stiffening Allied defences made the close approach to a convoy increasingly dangerous. The longer it took to line up a target, the greater the risk to the U-boat. What was needed were torpedoes that took less time to aim, and did more of the job of finding targets. (It is interesting, and not at all surprising, that weapons designers in the 1980s have reacted in exactly the same fashion to improving air defences. In order to aid in the survival of attack aircraft and their pilots in the dense, multi-layer modern air defence environment, increasing responsibility for identifying and destroying targets is being placed in 'smart' munitions.)

Germany responded to this need with the development of new torpedoes that fall into two separate lines of evolution. These were:

Anti-Convoy Torpedoes

In September 1942, the leaders of the U-boat Arm watched from a tender as the first test runs of a new type of torpedo were tried out against a convoy of German merchant ships in the Baltic. The ships were aligned in the same way that the Allies organized their convoys, a short, broad pattern of ships arrayed in parallel columns with escorts circling around them. The new torpedoes were fired from a U-boat in normal attack position off to the side of the convoy. In the place of a warhead was a bright light which allowed the course of the torpedoes to be tracked from the ships in the convoy. By pre-arrangement, the merchant ships fired off coloured flares when a torpedo passed beneath them. The course indicated by these flares was a very unusual one. Each torpedo started out normally, on a course set to intercept the convoy. Once it had passed through the convoy, however, it made a 180° turn and ran under the convoy's rows from the other side. Each torpedo repeated this manoeuvre several times before its fuel gave out. Flares filled the sky as the spread of torpedoes passed under ship after ship.

The revolutionary torpedo tested that day was called the *Flächenabsuchender Torpedo* (shallow searching torpedo), most often contracted to FaT.[35] It replaced the standard guidance unit of a G7a with a special unit which, in addition to the standard course setting up to 135° from the original course at the beginning of the run, guided the torpedo into its characteristic back-and-forth course (see Figure 1). The length of the initial straight leg could be set to any multiple of 100 metres, from a minimum of 500 metres up to the full 12.5km range of the torpedo. The direction of the turn could also be set, the diameter of the turn being fixed at 300 metres. Turns were set to be made in alternate directions, giving a 'ladder' course. The length of the back-and-forth legs could be set to either long (1,600 metres) or short (800 metres). The mean speed of advance in the back-and-forth phase was approximately seven knots for short legs and five knots for long legs.

The length of the legs established for FaT were not intended to cover the full width of an average convoy. At the time that FaT was introduced, an average convoy would number between 40 and 60 merchant ships, arrayed in parallel columns of four or five ships. Thus, given average spacing between ships and columns, a convoy could easily cover an area of two nautical miles in depth and six nautical miles in breadth. The escorts covered a pair of concentric circles around the convoy. The inner defence stayed in position within a mile or two of the outer edges of the convoy. The outer escort had freer reign, generally staying about 10 miles from the centre of the convoy, but able to range 30 miles out or more as circumstances required.

It was immediately obvious to the admirals who watched the test that this was a major new weapon in the war against merchant shipping in convoys. FaTs were ordered into production with the greatest possible speed and the first operational models were delivered to the U-boat fleet in November 1942. As with the new Pi 2, BdU decided that the need was greater in the Mediterranean and that the FaT should be introduced there first.[36] However, the introduction of the FaT involved more than just the delivery of the new torpedoes. Crews had to trained in the use of a radically new weapon and boats had to be physically modified to fire it. Changes had to made to the attack computer and to the torpedo tubes to allow the setting of the various parameters of a FaT's course.[37] In the event, the first U-boat to leave port with FaTs was *U553*, which left St-Nazaire on a North Atlantic patrol on 23 November 1942.[38] Its sailing meant that new instructions had to issued to all boats as there was considerable fear that firing FaTs presented a danger to other U-boats nearby. A U-boat intending to fire a FaT was ordered to issue a 'FaT Warning' message on the medium-wave band that was to warn off all other boats for a period of half an hour. If a U-boat were within a convoy when it heard a FaT Warning message it was to leave the area at high speed or dive to at least 50 metres.[39]

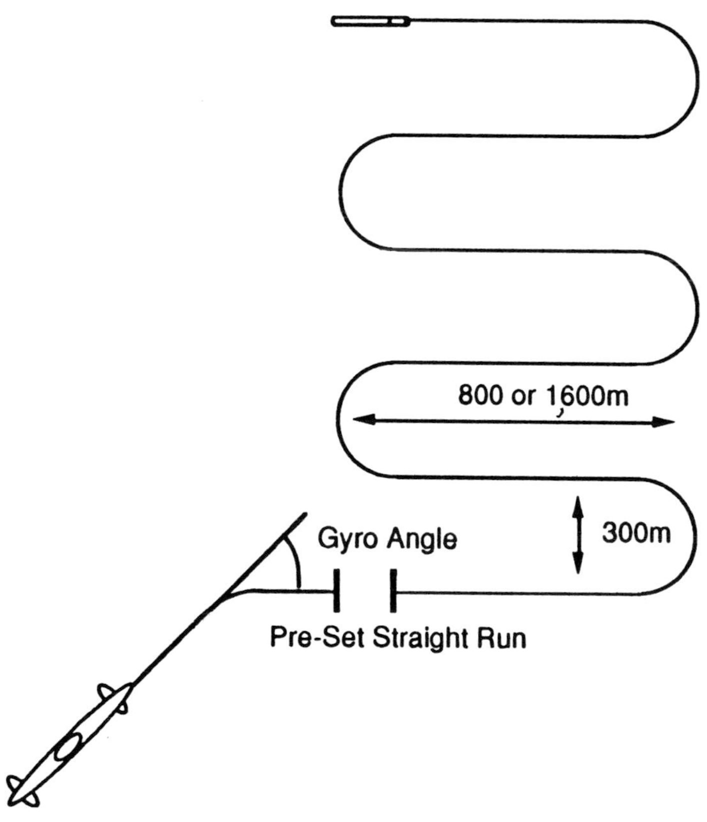

The introduction of FaT was good news for the U-boat fleet at a time when good news was needed. BdU, in August 1942, had redirected the bulk of U-boats from the American coast back into the main battleground of the North Atlantic. Against the increasingly effective defences protecting convoys, these boats found it harder and harder to manoeuvre into effective attack position and escape in safety. Now, it was no longer necessary to work out as exact a firing solution as had previously been required. If the torpedo missed on its first pass through the convoy, there were always more chances. The only effective defence against the FaT was to force U-boats completely out of firing range of the convoy. Generally FaTs were intended to be fired within a distance to the convoy equivalent to half or less of the full range of the torpedo.

The results obtained with the first deployed FaTs were very favourable. A report of a convoy attack dated 16 March 1943 showed that four FaT hits were obtained by *U435*, two of them after runs of more than eight minutes. No record of sinkings was associated with the hits.[40] Nevertheless, there were severe restrictions on the use of the FaT. Since it was an air-driven torpedo, its use was restricted to night attacks. More importantly, the number of G7as produced each month was only 350, and after the demands of other uses were taken into account, only 100 FaTs could be made each month. BdU therefore decided early in 1943 to develop the FaT II based on the G7e, despite the much shorter range of the electric torpedo. The FaT II was designed to operate similarly to FaT I except that it was restricted to long leg or circle run settings. This latter setting was intended to allow the FaT to be used as a stop-gap anti-escort weapon, until the first acoustic torpedoes became available. The idea was that a FaT II would be fired from the stern tube in the path of a pursuing escort, where it

Figure 1: FaT – 'Ladder' Course

▲ **An unidentified Type VII U-boat pulls into a bunker at a French Atlantic port. This must have been still relatively early in the war, soon after the first of these U-boat pens was completed, as shown by the presence of a deck gun and the fact that a torpedo is being lowered into the forward external storage tube, which is angled upward to receive its load. By the end of 1942, deck guns had disappeared and use of external torpedo storage had been discontinued. (NARA)**

would loiter running a small loop until the escort ran into it.[41] The first FaT IIs were introduced to the Mediterranean and Norway in May 1943 and to the Atlantic in June.

As a result of these changes, Standing Order No. 40, which directed what types of torpedoes were to be carried, was changed on 10 May 1943. From then on, all Type VIIs were to carry four FaT Is and six T3s forward and two FaT IIs aft.[42]

The range of the G7e was so short as to restrict severely the usefulness of the FaT II. The obvious solution was to extend the range of the base torpedo. This was done in February 1944 with the operational introduction of the T3a. This new version had its range lengthened by 50 per cent, to 7.5 kilometres. This went a long way towards addressing the weaknesses of the FaT II.[43]

If there were a weakness in the FaT, it was the fact that it still required the attacking U-boat to attain a position roughly alongside the convoy. Only from such a position could the ideal intercept angle of 90° to the line of advance of the convoy be achieved. The farther off from that angle, the lower the chance of a FaT's success. Given the increasing presence of air cover over convoys, the ability of U-boats to manoeuvre on the surface in the vicinity of convoys was decreasing. But it was only on the surface that a U-boat could overtake a convoy and gain a broadside position. It would have been much safer for the U-boat if it could launch its torpedo from whatever position it encountered a convoy. Ideally, it could then submerge before the convoy's escorts could react. What was needed was a FaT that was as effective from any bearing on a convoy.

That improved FaT appeared in the spring of 1944. It was called the *Lagenunabhängiger Torpedo* (bearing independent torpedo), commonly referred to as the LuT. The LuT added two features to the FaT. First, the capability to perform a second course change at the end of the initial straight leg was added. Thus a LuT could be fired from any position around a convoy and have its course adjusted to perpendicular to the target's line of advance at the end of its run-in. Hence the name LuT; It could be fired with equal effectiveness from any bearing on a convoy. (It must be noted that in practise, shots from either quarter or directly aft of a convoy were much less likely to succeed because the torpedo had to overcome the convoy's speed of recession. The ideal attack position with a LuT was ahead of the convoy to either side.) Also, the length of the back-and-forth legs of a LuT's course could be set to any length from 1,600 metres down to zero. This had the effect of allowing variance of torpedo speed of advance from five knots to 21 knots.[44]

By the end of May 1944, 35 U-boats had been modified to fire the LuT. Like the FaT, it required the modification of the attack computer and torpedo tubes. By the beginning of July 1944, the number of LuT-modified boats had only increased to fifty.[45] At first, only a T3a version was produced, though a G7a model came later. The first operational reports indicated that the LuT was an effective substitute for the FaT. On 29 June 1944,

U984 reported a LuT attack on a two-column convoy west of the Bay of Biscay. A double shot of LuTs resulted in a hit on an 8,000 BRT freighter in the near column and another hit on a 7,000 BRT steamer in the far column. Both sank, the former after being finished off by another torpedo.[46]

Despite this success, the introduction of the LuT did not have the same dramatic effect as the introduction of the FaT. This was because its introduction coincided with the overall defeat of the U-boats in the North Atlantic. Even a weapon as effective as the LuT was insufficient to counter the fact that any approach to a convoy by a Type VII U-boat had become terribly dangerous.

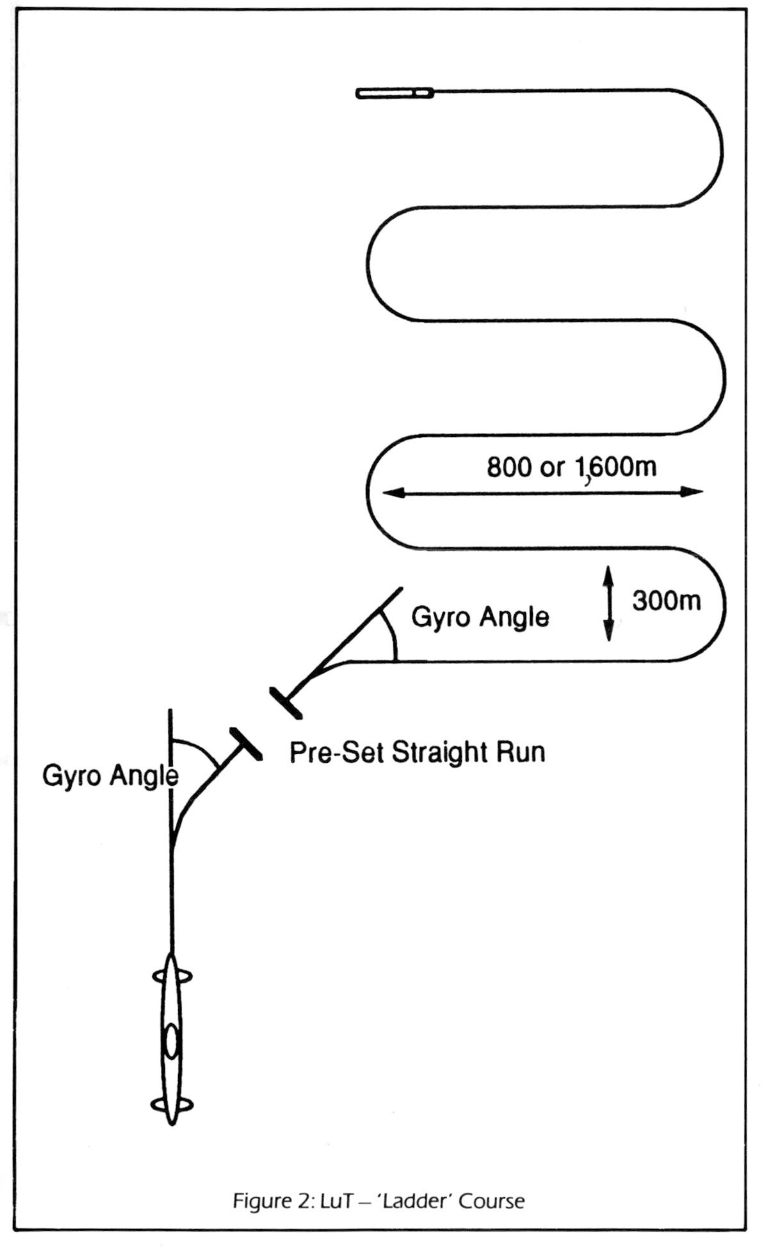

Figure 2: LuT – 'Ladder' Course

Acoustic (Anti-Escort) Torpedoes

The same desire to provide a weapon for use against convoys that led to development of the FaT and LuT led also to the development of a series of acoustic torpedoes which became the major anti-escort weapon of the later stages of the war.

For a long time it had been realized by U-boatmen, in their sound-rich underwater environment, that targets were heard long before they could be seen. Some commanders claimed that a good hydrophone operator could aim torpedoes as accurately by that means as he could with his eyes. Starting with this idea, it was relatively simple to design an apparatus that combined a pair of acoustic sensors in a side-by-side arrangement and connected this seeker to a torpedo's steering mechanism. The torpedo would be steered toward whichever side registered the stronger signal. Thus, if fired from somewhere on the quarter of a target, it would tend to steer a snaking course toward the target, its guidance system oversteering and then correcting in successively finer adjustments until finally striking the target in the vicinity of the noise source.

Work on the concept of an acoustic homing torpedo began as early as 1934, but progressed only slowly. Initial testing of a prototype began at TVA – Eckernförde in 1940. The first production test models weren't available until February 1942. The torpedo that was being run through these final acceptance tests at Gotenhafen was called the T4 Falke (Falcon). The intended target of this torpedo had been escorts, but it was realized that, because of the torpedo's slow net forward speed and its lack of MZ pistol, it could really only be used against slow, deep-draught targets, such as merchantmen moving at between seven and thirteen knots.[47]

Acoustic homing as implemented in the T4 was a guidance technique of elegant simplicity, yet it was such a novel technology that many teething problems had to be resolved before it could become effective. At this early stage of the technology's evolution, the T4 was far from being a reliable weapon. It's greatest weakness was tactical rather than technical. Because of the nature of sound propagation underwater from the propellers of a moving ship, the sounds of these propellers are strongest aft of the source and far weaker forward of it. Thus the T4 was an effective weapon only when fired from the target's quarter. Yet, this wasn't a position in which U-boats often found themselves when encountering a merchant ship in a convoy.

Two T4s were issued to each of six U-boats in February and March 1943. Firing was restricted to the after torpedo tube of these boats because of a perceived danger of the torpedo arming in the tube. (Because the nose of the T4 was taken up with the acoustic seeker, it couldn't use the standard propeller arming system of conventional torpedoes.) This, combined with the requirement to be aft of the target in order to attack with a T4, severely restricted its use. Of this first batch, a number of successes were nevertheless obtained. On 16 March 1943, *U603* and *U758* both used the T4 with success while attacking the convoy HX 229. The T4 was released for operational use as of 1 July 1943, but only five boats actually left port with T4s before it was succeeded by the T5 *Zaunkönig* (Wren).

The T5 differed from the T4 in having a faster net forward speed (24.5 knots v. 20 knots) and in using the Pi 4 pistol which combined MZ with AZ detonation. The seeker was more sensitive, being capable of picking up the propeller noises of a typical escort ship running at a speed of 15 knots at a range of 300 metres. All T4s and T5s were built on T3a chassis, giving them an overall range of 7.5 kilometres. The room taken up by the seeker head somewhat restricted the space available for the explosive warhead. This was reduced to 274kg from the normal weight of 280kg for a T3a. Due to a short arming range of only 400 metres, needed to make the torpedo effective against an approaching escort, the firing U-boat had to crash dive as soon as a T5 was fired.[48]

The T5 was extensively tested before and after being released to combat boats. A veteran involved in that testing for more than seven months recalls:

> 'In the spring of 1943, the big disaster happened in the Atlantic. So the U-boat command decided to hold the boats back for a while. We were detached to the trials of the T5 at Gotenhafen. Our boat was lying there during the day in the harbour at a special pier where the TVA was located. This was a special section that did torpedo research work. Top Secret. Surrounded by barbed wire. Guarded by a boat day and night.
>
> A big crane loaded us up every day with torpedoes. We put them right in the tubes. We carried no reloads. This was only done when it was dark. Then we went out. We weren't told much at first. Just how to shoot these torpedoes. There was a target ship, about 2,500 or 3,000 tons, not very big. It was a recovery ship for seaplanes. It had a big crane running on two tracks. They had divers on board to help recover the torpedoes. It was a fast ship. It could run at 22 knots on two diesels. This was the ship we shot at.
>
> We were shooting in all kinds of weather and at all kinds of angles. Now, we shot mostly from the stern so it would pick up the noises better. Shooting distance was from 2,000 metres all the way down to 600 or 800 metres. We were told never to aim at the ship, always behind it. We were shooting at angles that would have been impossible with a conventional torpedo. We were shooting at angles only 5° or 10° off the base course of the target. We always sighted the ship with our UZO, which was connected to a new version of the attack computer. Later we increased the distance, but never more than 2,500 or 3,000 metres and always 50 or 100 metres behind the ship; 10° or 15° behind.
>
> Before we fired each shot we were told exactly what they wanted. We had a special crew aboard with ultra-shortwave radios. They always told us, "Now, Number 2, please 100 metres behind."
>
> We were doing that for more than seven months and we shot more than 500 torpedoes in that time, starting in April 1943. After we knew enough about it, we were finally formally introduced to the T5. We were taken into the hall there and they showed us the torpedo. There was a T5 on a stand with a pivot and some small motors. We were told to make a noise with our keys about a metre away from the nose of it. When you made the noise, it started to turn towards you. It was the damndest thing.
>
> Finally the crews came from the front boats, just the IWO usually, and we introduced them to that torpedo. They came aboard and we would take them out at night. The practise torpedoes had lights instead of the warheads and we would get reports from the target ship that they saw it coming about 10 or 20 metres from the propellers or engine room. They learned the little tricks, the mechanics of it and how to use the new computer.'[49]

The T5 proved to be an effective anti-escort weapon, though never as effective as the Germans believed. The first boats sailed with T5s in August 1943. Albert Speer had managed to get the initial production batch of 80 torpedoes to the fleet months ahead of schedule. The first use of T5s in combat occurred on the night of 19 September 1943. *U305* claimed a Royal Navy destroyer that night during an attack on a convoy in square AK (just south of Greenland, midway between there and Iceland). This was followed by a spate of similar reports as Gruppe Leuthen converged on the convoy. By 20 September, the reports had been compiled by BdU. The Germans recorded seven destroyers sunk and three more probably sunk from the convoy's escort.[50] The actual results were much more modest. The British only admitted the loss of three destroyers and the damaging of another.[51] Either way, it gave the U-boats a valuable new weapon against a convoy's surface escorts. While the battle now became more dangerous for the escorts, it still didn't improve the meagre successes enjoyed against the real target, the convoy's merchant ships.

The T5 could be, and often was, fired from

▲ *U73*, **a Type VIIB, is being towed to the torpedo dock at a French port. The torpedo loading trough has been erected aft and the after torpedo storage tube has been opened prior to loading a spare torpedo.**

considerable depth based only on hydrophone readings.

> 'The great number of recent unsuccessful submerged attacks also shows that boats were not able to break through the screen without being located or picked up on the hydrophones. For this reason, in future attacking at periscope depth will have to be given up and attempts made to fire blind from a great depth with the new specially designed torpedoes. Even if the available hydrophone and location apparatus do not at present give a definite estimate of enemy course, speed and formation, nevertheless in the event of approaching or being passed over by the enemy, the best possible use must be made of even defective data . . .
>
> The following procedure is to be used in the future:
>
> (a) As up till now it has only been possible to fire torpedoes at depths up to 22 metres, remain as far as possible at a depth of 20 metres in case torpedo attack is possible.
>
> (b) Under normal circumstances tubes are only to be loaded with FaT and T5s. These have the advantage in that when fired according to uncertain firing data, they usually hit something when there are a number of ships together.'[52]

The limiting factor on the depth at which torpedoes could be fired was the amount of air pressure capable of being supplied by the boat's compressed air tanks.

After firing a T5, almost any explosion heard was assumed to be a hit on the targeted escort. (The Germans officially recorded a hit rate of more than 50 per cent for the T5.) Such was most often not the case. While the T5 was indeed a marvellous machine which gave the U-boat a valuable weapon against escorts, and despite the rigours of the testing described above, it was far from infallible. The sensitive Pi 4 pistol fitted to T5s was known to be liable to premature detonation in turbulent water. Because its snaking course often caused it to cross the wake of the target, T5s were constantly subject to premature detonation due to the turbulence.

An additional problem was related to the T5's short arming range. On the theory that T5s would be used primarily as a last-ditch defence against a rapidly closing escort, its arming range was set at 400 metres. In practice this meant that there was a real danger that the loudest screws in the vicinity would be the U-boat's own and that the T5 would home in on the firing boat. BdU therefore issued orders that U-boats firing T5s were to crash dive immediately to at least 60 metres' depth. If the T5 were fired from the stern tube, the only option to diving immediately was to reduce speed to the silent range. In practice, these precautions proved to be a major nuisance. Some T5s were indeed fired at short range from the stern tube at a pursuing escort. U-boat COs didn't need orders to tell them that the only safe tactic in this case was to dive immediately and to well below 60 metres, because, if the torpedo missed, a depth-charging was almost certain to follow. However, an analysis of T5 firings showed that most were fired at ranges of about 3,000 metres, obviating the need for the short arming range and the crash dive.[53]

Even with these known weaknesses, the T5 put a real scare into the Allies. It led inevitably to tactical and technical countermeasures. The Allies learned early on that T5s could be detonated prematurely by a depth-charge dropped nearby and this tactic was initially employed as a defence. Through interrogation of survivors it was learned that the T5's acoustic sensor operated at 24.5kHz. This was the primary sound frequency generated by the propellers of a ship moving at 15 knots, the normal 'working' speed of convoy escorts. Therefore, the tactic was introduced of dramatically increasing or decreasing an escort's speed when it was known to be in the vicinity of a U-boat. These were known as 'High Safe Speed' or 'Low Safe Speed'. These were effective tactics, but worked only when a U-boat was known to be near. Maintaining a much higher or much lower speed than 15 knots wasn't practical in normal operations. On the technical side, this led to the development of foxers, acoustic decoys meant to be towed behind escorts that made more noise than the ship's propellers and therefore lured the T5 away from its real target. The first foxers were introduced at the end of 1943. Designed to be towed in pairs, one on each quarter of the escort, they made a noise that was easy to identify. U-boats that heard towed foxers reported that they sounded like 'a continuous heavy rattle, singing note, heavy humming with cracks like an overloaded spring'.[54] The foxer was a simple device composed of a pair of closely-spaced steel tubes which, when towed, set up sympathetic vibrations, generating the varied noises heard by U-boats and T5s. While foxers proved extremely effective in luring T5s, they weren't very popular with escort commanders for three reasons. First, the very noise they made attracted U-boats. Foxers could be heard at greater range than normal screw sounds. Secondly, the noise made by the foxers rendered ASDIC/sonar useless. Thirdly, because they had to be towed at some distance behind the ship, and because the noise making was automatic, the only way to silence a foxer was to haul it in, a slow and laborious process, or stop the ship. Nevertheless, the countermeasures to the T5 applied by the Allies worked to a great extent. According to Allied accounting, of the approximately 640 T5s actually fired in combat, just over 6 per cent actually found their target.[55]

The success of the T5 led to another revision of Standing Order No. 40 in April 1944. From then on, Type VIICs operating in the Atlantic were to load three T5s forward along with five LuTs (or two FaT Is and three FaT IIs, if the boat were not LuT-capable) and two T5s aft.[56]

An upgraded version of the T5, known as the T11 *Zaunkönig II*, was introduced in April 1944. It was tuned more specifically to the frequency of ships' propellers, making it effectively more immune to foxers than the T5. The Allies responded in kind late in the war with an improved foxer, which had the advantage of being towed singly, rather than in pairs.

Loading and Storage

The handling of torpedoes was easily one of the dirtiest jobs on a Type VII U-boat. Torpedoes are large, heavy and awkward and covered with thick grease to ease their sliding in and out of the torpedo tube, yet they are delicate devices that need to be handled with utmost care. If any damage were done to the Eels during any of the handling, the entire reason for the existence of the U-boat would be nullified.

▼A 7th Flotilla boat pulls into St-Nazaire in 1940. The crew is lined up on the foredeck. The captain, resplendent in his white cap and gloves, holds the voice tube to the control room. At his elbow is the UZO with the large waterproof sighting binoculars clamped in position. In front of that is the head of the sky periscope. (NARA)

Just prior to leaving on a patrol, torpedoes were loaded from the torpedo dock (or occasionally from specially equipped barges) using the dock's heavy winch. A dismountable trough for sliding the torpedoes into the forward and after torpedo hatches was erected by the crew and the torpedoes lowered into place one at a time from dockside. Each torpedo was inspected by the ranking *Mechaniker* and then covered with a coating of grease to ease its passage through the torpedo hatch. As the new torpedo was slid inside the boat it was caught by the chains of one of the torpedo hoists so that, once clear of the hatch, it could be lowered into the proper storage position. This hoist was an ingenious apparatus which allowed the transfer of torpedoes within the torpedo room. It had two chain winches that lifted the torpedo fore and aft. The winches could be slid fore and aft in tandem allowing torpedoes to be hauled in and out of the tubes. The after torpedo hoist was fixed on the centreline of the boat, but the two forward hoists could also be moved from side to side to allow them to service all four torpedo tubes and reach any of the stowed torpedoes.

All Type VII U-boats had five torpedo tubes and left port carrying one torpedo in each tube. Additional torpedoes were carried internally and externally as reloads after any of the originally loaded torpedoes had been fired. The Type VIIA carried up to six reloads, all internally and all in the forward torpedo room. Four of these were stored under the floorboards of the compartment. The other two were suspended by chains or stored on cradles at the sides of the compartment. These last two reloads were very unpopular with the Pairs because they were always in the way, requiring that a full row of bunks be lashed up and preventing the crew's mess tables from being erected. Needless to say, life was very uncomfortable for the Lords until the first two torpedoes were fired off. No reloads were carried for the after torpedo tube and no after torpedo hoist was shipped since the after torpedo tube on Type VIIAs was external to the pressure hull and could only be loaded from the outside.

Type VIIBs and subsequent marks carried three additional reloads. One of these was under the floor of the after torpedo room and allowed reloading of the now internal after torpedo tube. The other two were stored externally in storage tubes sited between the pressure hull and the deck casing. One was right aft on the centreline. The other was forward and towards the starboard. These two torpedoes could be brought inside the boat during a patrol after at least two of the internal load had been expended. Besides the collapsible loading trough, all boats now carried a dismountable tripod winch which was erected over the tower, facing forward or aft as appropriate. The storage tubes were angled with the tower end raised, so that a torpedo could be winched out of the tube, manhandled into the trough and then loaded just as at dockside. Needless to say, this could only be done during daylight, in the calmest of weather and in an area where the risk of enemy interference was considered negligible, since a submarine loading torpedoes had multiple hatches open and large numbers of crewmen on deck. These requirements restricted the use of these external storage tubes to a great extent, especially as the war progressed. Additionally, there were restrictions on the type of torpedo that could be stored in the external tubes. Only G7as could be stored externally because they didn't require the same regular maintenance as G7es.

Once safely stowed in cradle or torpedo tube, the work of handling torpedoes was far from over; quite the opposite, moving torpedoes was a daily operation. Not only did the torpedo tubes have to be reloaded after firing, but every four to five days each electric torpedo, which made up the bulk of a U-boat's load, had to be serviced to assure that it would be ready to fire when needed. Servicing included checking the batteries for fluid level and recharging them as required. General practice was to service one torpedo a day on a rotating basis. The boat would generally be submerged to keep it as steady as possible and the trim adjusted forward or aft to let gravity assist the Lords' muscles in moving the torpedo in or out of the tube.

Not only did the torpedo itself have to be moved, but the German torpedo tube employed a free-floating piston which provided the actual push to propel the torpedo out of the tube. This was a heavy (approximately 75lb), greasy steel spindle positioned between the torpedo and the inner torpedo tube door. This had to be hoisted in and out of position each time a torpedo was moved. The piston had a pair of crossbars welded to the back as hand holds. Torpedoes were launched with compressed air at approximately 24 atmospheres of pressure. This was sufficient to propel the torpedo well free of the boat before its own motor took over. The piston was retained in the tube by an ingenious arrangement. The torpedo tube had a pair of grooves on opposite sides and the piston a pair of corresponding flanges which slid down the grooves. Water filled the grooves when the forward torpedo tube doors were opened. As the piston was propelled forward by the charge of compressed air behind it, the water pressure that built up in the grooves acted against the rapidly dissipating force of the expanding air behind the piston, bringing it to a halt just before the end of the tube. A relief valve would then automatically open at the back of the tube and water pressure would force the piston back. It would land against the rear hatch with a series of bumps that told the Lords that the torpedo had launched successfully. This process would force the air behind the piston into the boat, increasing the air pressure within the hull if the boat were submerged. (Later types, such as the Type XXI, bled the air into a reserve tank rather than letting air pressure build within the boat.) After that, the forward inner tube door was closed, the water from the front of the tube bled into the bilge and the tube was ready to be reloaded.[57]

Compressed air at the pressures used in Type VII U-boats was sufficient to launch torpedoes at depths of 22 metres, and later in the war it was not uncommon for T5s to be launched from those depths. The later Type XXI used higher air pressures that permitted torpedoes to be launched from 100 metres or below.

Fire Control

Once a target had been sighted (by lookouts or by some sensor), the torpedo fire control systems of a Type VII U-boat came into play. While late in the war it was possible for Type VIIs, particularly, those few equipped with *Balkon Gerät*, to attack a target without ever gaining visual contact, it was generally considered prudent that a target should be seen in order to be attacked. Range to target is an essential ingredient in any firing solutions and range could only be obtained by using one of the two available sighting devices. This sighting was done by attack periscope if submerged or by *Uberwasserzieloptik* (UZO) if on the surface.

The attack periscope was the larger and the aftermost of the two periscopes that protruded from the control room of a Type VII U-boat. Unlike the smaller sky periscope (and the attack periscope on US submarines of this period), the eyepiece of the attack periscope did not rise and fall as the height of the periscope was adjusted. Rather, the eyepiece was sited at a fixed height in the small conning tower located directly above the control room. Conventional periscopes, such as those used by the US Navy and by the Germans for the sky periscope, used a simple prism arrangement. One prism in the periscope's head bent incoming light 90° downward and a second at height of the eyepiece bent the light another 90° back to the original direction. The distance between the two prisms was fixed, making range calculations simple, based on image focus. The Type VII's attack periscope used the two prisms of a conventional periscope and added another adjustable double prism. Light that entered the head was directed down to the bottom of the periscope and reversed 180° in direction back up to the eyepiece by the double prism. The configuration of the double prism was controlled by mechanical linkage to the height adjustment mechanism of the periscope, compensating variances in periscope height.

Watertight hatches above and below were located in the forward part of the conning tower, allowing passage between the control room and the tower. The after section of the conning tower was given over to the attack periscope and the torpedo attack computer. The commander's position at the attack periscope was actually quite efficiently laid out despite the limited space. The CO was provided with a simple metal bicycle-type seat facing the periscope and the eyepiece. Seated, straddling the periscope, the Commander controlled the rotation of the periscope with foot pedals on each side. His right hand rested on a knob which controlled the angle of the upper prism. This could direct the centre of his field of view vertically from 15° below horizontal to 70° above. On the left side was a lever which controlled the height of the periscope. Other levers controlled the magnification, either 1.5 or .6, and the sun filtering. The eyepiece was threaded to allow the connection of a still or motion picture camera. The view through the eyepiece gave the standard crosshair reticle, marked off in degrees of elevation and deflection. It also showed the range scale and the bearing from the current course. The commander's seat folded up when not in use. When extended, the internal mechanisms of the periscope controls were exposed. To protect this delicate apparatus the seat was always kept stowed when not in use.

The UZO was located toward the front of the external tower, between the hatch and the sky periscope. It was actually composed of two parts, a pair of large rangefinder binoculars and a permanently mounted rotating bracket set in a ring marked off in degrees. The binoculars were generally in the possession of the watch officer and were mounted on the rotating bracket only when actually needed for surface attack computation. They had to be taken inside the boat before diving because they weren't waterproof at depth.

Both the attack periscope and the UZO were linked to a mechanical analog attack computer (essentially a glorified adding machine) located at the after end in the conning tower. It was manned by the *Obersteuermann*. When the target was properly lined up, the necessary mechanical connections were made to the gyro compass and the UZO or attack periscope. This connection provided the attack computer with data about the current position and speed of the boat and the bearing of the target. Target range, speed and heading and the rate of turn of the U-boat, if any, had to be entered using dials located on the front of the attack computer. Once the required data was entered and the computation process initiated, a firing solution was achieved within seconds. From this point on, any change in the speed or course of the boat or the bearing of the target were received by the attack computer and the firing solution automatically recalculated. The required settings were passed automatically to the torpedoes in their tubes, with courses adjusted to allow for approximately a ship length spread in a salvo of four torpedoes at the set range.

The actual firing of torpedoes was done from a control panel in the control room, sometimes personally by the torpedo officer (generally the IWO). More often he would be in the conning tower, with the CO, *Obersteuermann* and helmsman, and would yell his firing instructions to a rating at the control panel. This panel had switches that designated the tubes to be fired, status lights reporting the readiness of those torpedoes and a firing button. The firing was initiated by a single button, but to prevent mutual interference the torpedoes were not fired simultaneously. The firing circuits enforced an automatic 1.2-second delay between multiple firings. A second identical control panel was located in the forward torpedo room as backup in case the primary panel failed to fire the torpedoes.

Upon the launch of torpedoes, the appropriate torpedo trim tank in the bow or stern was flooded with the appropriate amount of water to compensate the weight of the now absent torpedoes. (A single G7e weighed 1,600kg.) This was done even as the torpedoes were being fired to prevent the boat from broaching the surface, to prevent the following torpedoes from broaching and to keep trim in case a crash dive was required.

1. KTB, 14 September 1939. Actually, the authorization to make angled shots was only given to boats on 7 September.
2. KTB, 4 October 1939. The reference makes it clear that this wasn't the first such complaint.
3. KTB, 18 October 1939.
4. KTB, 25 October 1939.
5. KTB, 31 October 1939.
6. KTB, 21 January 1940. This is a long exposition on the torpedo problems, at that time far from resolved. This was point 4 of 16 separate points raised by BdU in this entry.
7. Ibid., Point 5.
8. Ibid., Point 5.
9. Ibid., Point 6. *U46* was the first to report continued failures on 18 October 1939.
10. Ibid., Point 6.
11. Ibid., Point 6.
12. KTB, 31 October 1939.
13. KTB, 7 November 1939.
14. Op.cit., Point 7. This order was given on 20 October 1939. On that day, the Torpedo Inspectorate first admitted the likelihood that torpedoes were running two metres deep.
15. Ibid., Point 9.
16. KTB, 19 November 1939 and 21 January 1940. Point 12.
17. KTB, 21 January 1940. Point 15.
18. KTB, 11 April 1940. This is part of an inquiry into the repeated torpedo failures.
19. KTB, 16 April 1940.
20. KTB, 17 April 1940.
21. Ibid.
22. Ibid.
23. KTB, 19 April 1940.
24. 10 years, pp. 92-93. *U94* reported on 30 January 1942 that during a routine inspection of torpedoes, the balance chamber was found to contain high-pressure air when it was supposed to contain air at normal sea level pressure. The fault was found to lie with an inadequate seal around the torpedoe's rudder shaft which ran through the chamber. The increased air pressure could only be balanced by water pressure at deeper than normal depths.
25. 10 Years, p. 97.
26. KTB, 15 May 1940.
27. KTB, 23 May 1940.
28. 10 Years, p. 94.
29. Atl, vol. 1 p. 69.
30. KTB, 4 November 1942.
31. Atl, vol. 2, p. 84.
32. KTB, 10 May 1943. Assembly rate was to be 300/mo by April.
33. Ibid.
34. KTB, 15 July 1944.
35. Rössler, on p. 217, states that FaT was an abbreviation of *Federapparat Torpedo*, which might be translated as spring-operated torpedo.
36. KTB, 8 November 1942.
37. Ibid. At first, only two tubes on each boat were to be modified to fire FaTs.
38. KTB, 29 November 1942.
39. KTB, 10 May 1943, Standing Order No. 306.
40. KTB, 16 March 1943.
41. KTB, 10 May 1943. This is from Appendix 4 dated 28 March 1943. The circle setting of the FaT II was actually just the short leg setting set to loop, that is to turn always in the same direction, always to the left.
42. Ibid.
43. KTB, 1 July 1944. Appendix entitled 'Summary of the development of the torpedo arm in operational U-boats'.
44. KTB, 15 June 1944.
45. KTB, 15 July 1944.
46. KTB, 5 July 1944.
47. KTB, 24 September 1943.
48. Ibid.
49. WB.
50. KTB, 20 September 1943.
51. SW, p. 176, Note 4. This information is supplied by the translator, Lieutenant-Commander R.O.B. Long, RNVR. See also, 10th, p. 229. The actual escorts sunk were the destroyer HMCS *St. Croix*, sunk by *U641* on the afternoon of 20 September 1943, the corvette HMS *Polyanthus* sunk that night and another corvette, HMS *Itchen*, sunk by *U666* on the evening of the 22nd.
52. KTB, 28 December 1943, Standing Order No. 34.
53. Atl, vol. 3, pp. 26–27.
54. KTB, 1 December 1943.
55. Preston, p. 135. This data varies by source. Jürgen Rohwer gives the figures as 610 T5s fired at targets and a maximum of 1/3 hits for damage. (The figures from Rohwer are cited in CO, p. 162. Cremer refers to an unspecified post-war study by the well-known naval historian.)
56. KTB, 15 July 1944.
57. WB and WH.

Mines

During the First World War, the Germans had successfully deployed anti-ship mines from submarines, the entire UC series of boats being designed specifically for the laying of such mines in British coastal waters. They anticipated that such weapons could again perform well in any repeat engagement. Faced with a severe shortage of U-boats and the undesirability of committing scarce hulls solely to the minelaying task, however, the Germans developed, between the wars, a series of mines that could be launched from standard 54cm torpedo tubes.

The TM (Torpedomine) series of mines were handled and stored identically with torpedoes, but, being shorter than the torpedoes they replaced, more TM mines could be carried than the number of displaced torpedoes. The initial model, the TMA, was 3.64 metres long, so two TMAs substituted for one torpedo in a U-boat's torpedo tubes. The TMA was a standard buoyant moored mine with magnetic influence detonation. It was designed to be laid in waters of up to 270 metres depth. The detonator was an exploder very similar in design to the dip needle Pi series torpedo pistols. Power was supplied by a storage battery. Like the torpedo pistols, mine detonators had zone settings keyed to geographic location which had to be set immediately prior to laying. Being a moored mine, much of the volume of the mine apparatus of the TMA was taken up with the buoyancy chamber, mooring cable and the mechanisms designed to float the mine at the correct depth beneath the surface. It had room only for a relatively small 215kg explosive charge.

This version was soon replaced by the smaller and simpler TMB. The TMB was a new design, based on a totally different operating concept; a heavier-than-water ground mine, intended for much shallower waters than the TMA. The TMB had a length of 2.31 metres. The total weight was 740kg, of which 580kg was the explosive charge. The whole of the larger charge allowed by the ground mine design was needed to give the mine a chance of sinking its target, even at the much shallower depths at which it was intended to be laid. The smaller size allowed three to be fired from a torpedo tube at one time, effectively increasing mine stowage by 50 per cent. By the start of the war, the TMB had become the standard U-boat mine. (Size of the mine, dictating the number that could be placed in a torpedo tube at the same time, was critical, because it determined the number of mines that could be laid. Typically, Type VII U-boats carried only one tube-load of mines, sacrificing four torpedoes to carry eight TMAs or twelve TMBs.

At the beginning of the war, when the rules of engagement placed on U-boats by Hitler made the carrying out of standard attack missions problematical, BdU on a number of occasions opted to use his U-boats to plant TMBs off English ports. The first such operation was by *U26*, a Type IA, a boat slightly larger than a Type VII. The next was by *U32*, a Type VIIA, assigned the task of laying mines off Portsmouth on 10 September 1939. Immediately, as *U32* was *en route* to her assigned target, fears arose for the fate of *U26*. The British claimed to have sunk a minelaying U-boat on the same day that *U32* left port.[1] In the event, this turned out not to be true, but the fear it raised was genuine. The danger to such relatively large boats operating in the shallow waters required by the TMB couldn't be ignored. Foremost on the minds of BdU and of KM staff was the risk of capture of cipher materials, meaning the Enigma machine. *U32* was immediately ordered to lay her mines in the deeper and less heavily defended Bristol Channel. For all future minelaying operations, U-boats would land their most sensitive materials, encoding their communi-

▲ U-boat life in winter was far from glamorous. KL Bielfeld, CO of *U703*, is dusted with snow, as are the large surface sighting binoculars mounted on the UZO to the left. (USN)

cations with the old-fashioned AFB hand cipher system.[2]

The next round of such operations, leaving port in mid-October, involved *U26* and *U31*, another Type VIIA, setting the pattern for these missions. BdU always saw minelaying as a useful, but necessarily secondary, form of U-boat warfare. For this reason, his older, less capable boats were assigned to the task. He would have liked to have employed the smaller and generally less useful Type IIs exclusively, but they had two fewer torpedo tubes, making them of significantly less value as minelayers. *U31*'s mission was to lay a mine barrage at Loch Ewe. There she encountered no patrol but ran into a net system, possibly one of the most dreaded forms of anti-submarine defence. The boat was temporarily entangled in the nets, but pulled herself free and laid her mines outside the defences.[3]

As the results of these initial minefields began to filter back to Germany, through the efforts of B-Dienst which monitored British radio traffic, it became increasingly obvious that the TMB wasn't as effective as had been hoped.

> 'Information received so far on the effects of the minefields laid by U-boats shows that not all ships which run into the fields were sunk. We must therefore try to lay the mines in shallower water and reduce their sensitivity so that they are only exploded by largish ships.'[4]

Dönitz called in a mining expert, who suggested that TMBs be laid no deeper than 25 metres and that new zone charts be produced that would reflect a coarser setting of the exploder. His main point, however, was that these would not really resolve the problem. Only increasing the size of the TMB's explosive charge would result in an effective mine. Dönitz took this advice, ordering investigation of the possibility of a more powerful mine, even if that meant reducing the per tube load to two or even one.[5]

The first of the new mines, named TMC, was ready for testing on 29 November 1939. It was similar in design and operation to the TMB, differing only in size of warhead and, consequently, length and weight. The TMC was 3.39 metres long and weighed 1,115kg, of which 1,000kg was warhead. The only negative feature was the length, which reduced the per torpedo tube load to two. So simple was the conversion from manufacturing TMBs to TMCs, that the Mining and Barrage Directorate promised Dönitz a full load of eight TMCs for *U32* to lay off the Clyde by 10 December. In fact, *U32* didn't sortie until 28 December, but this was due to mechanical difficulties with the boat rather than delays in delivering the mines.

Mining operations continued at the same pace, approximately four or five missions per month, throughout the winter and spring of 1940. Bad weather and severe icing served to limit normal U-boat operations. During 'Weserubung', minefields were laid in Norwegian waters as well as British. The ending of this initial mining offensive came gradually during the spring. The causes were a combination of factors. The conquest of France and the opening of the French Atlantic ports to U-boats put increased emphasis on more normal operations. Perhaps more importantly, the prospect of an increased number of new U-boats forced BdU to commit an increasing number of older boats to his training flotillas. The first to go were the nearly useless Type IIs, but the remaining Type VIIAs followed during the summer and autumn of 1940. (Only four Type VIIAs were sent to the Baltic, the other six, and both Type IAs, were lost in action during the first year of the war.) With no more old boats to commit to mining operations, there followed an almost total hiatus in mining missions until the emergence of the dedicated minelayers in 1942.[6]

This early mine offensive had involved a total of 34 mining missions and the mines laid accounted for 115 ships totalling 395,000 tons. The best known victims were the battleship HMS *Nelson* and cruiser HMS *Belfast* which were damaged on 4 December 1939 by mines laid by *U21* in the Firth of Forth.

After the beginning of the war, when the severe limitation on resources committed to U-boat construction had eased slightly, BdU turned his thoughts to dedicated minelayers, like the UC boats of the First World War. One entire class, the Type Xs, were intended from the beginning as long-range, ocean-going minelayers. BdU, however, was never in favour of such large, and therefore, he believed, vulnerable U-boats. Why put all your eggs in a few large baskets? Better, many smaller ones. With this in mind, he ordered the development of a minelaying variant of his favourite class of boats. The result was the Type VIID.

The Type VIID differed from the standard C variant in having five vertical mine tubes in an additional hull section added aft of the conning tower. Each tube was capable of holding three moored magnetic mines which were intended to be placed by being dropped out of the bottom of the tube while the submarine was submerged over the intended emplacement site. Otherwise, they were functionally identical with the standard Type VIIs, except for somewhat extended range and reduced speed. The mines sowed by the Type VIIDs, like those carried by the Type XBs, were different from the tube-launched series. Designated Type SMA (SM = *Schachtmine* – shaft mine), they were larger in all dimensions compared to the tube-launched series. Like the TMA, the SMA was an anchored mine, so that of the total weight of 1,600kg, only 350kg was explosive. Each mine was 2.15 metres long and had a diameter of 1.33 metres.

When the Type VIIDs were ready for operations in 1942, the SMA wasn't. Problems with the mine resulting in premature detonation, prevented its release for operational use and not until March 1943 were SMAs actually deployed.[7] It was to be April before they were laid by Type VIIDs.[8] Mining operations continued throughout 1943 and well into 1944. The Type VIIDs, and a few Type VIICs, were sent out at regular intervals to lay mine barrages of TMBs, TMCs and, in the case of the VIIDs, SMAs off the British Isles, America, Africa and in the Caribbean. Typical of the laying instructions for these boats were the following for *U373*, a Type VIIC, for a mission off Port Lyautey (now Kenitra), Morocco, dated 28 June 1943:

> '12 TMB, time setting 80 days, delay clockwork one day for two mines, three days for two mines, five days for four mines and six days for four mines, response value 10 millioersteds, two mines to fire at first activation, two at second activation, three at fourth activation and five at sixth activation (five blue, four red and three green). Maximum depth of water at which mines can be laid is 20 metres, minimum is 12 metres. Distance apart of mines should be 400 metres.
>
> Torpedoes are to be carried in the tubes on the way to the operations area. Tubes are to be reloaded one day off the laying area. One bow tube is to remain loaded with a torpedo. Enemy traffic is to be observed before laying the mines. The Commanding Officer is to make every effort to lay the mines as close as possible to the entrance.'[9]

Type VIIDs generally carried a full load of torpedoes and fifteen SMAs on their first few missions. However, two new torpedo mine types were carried by Type VIIDs on some later missions.[10] When *U214* was sent with a load of fifteen SMAs to mine the Caribbean entrance to the Panama Canal, it also carried six EMS periscope mines. These were examples of a new floating mine designed to sink after 72 hours. The EMSs were to be laid outside the area mined by SMAs, so as to drift with the current. They became active only ten minutes after launch. The crew was urged to use extreme caution, since the mines' rubber horns were extremely sensitive.[11]

On a mission against Trinidad in January 1944, *U218* was fitted with fifteen SMAs, five EMSs and four of yet another type, the MTA. This was a combination of mine and torpedo meant to be fired like a conventional torpedo. It was powered by a conventional torpedo motor and could be set to run any distance up to seven kilometres in 200 metre increments. At the end of its run, it would sink to the bottom and act as a small bottom mine such as the TMB or TMC. The running speed was 18 knots. The accuracy of firing was +400 metres in distance and 1.5° in bearing. The intended running depth was six metres, though the water depth had to be at least eight metres throughout its intended course. The water depth at the end of its propelled run couldn't be deeper than 20 metres for the mine to be effective. The warhead armed after a run of 115 metres.[12] This mine was intended as a replacement for the TM series mines. The laying of those mines had always exposed U-boats to extreme danger since they could only be laid to good effect in the shallow water near a harbour entrance. The MTA was devised in an attempt to make the laying of these shallow water ground mines safer since now the laying U-boat could place the mines in shallow water while remaining safely in deeper water miles off the coast. The obvious disadvantage of the MTA was the loss of accuracy in laying position. BdU's KTB contains no record of the operational effectiveness of the MTA.

1. KTB, 10 August 1939.
2. Ibid.
3. KTB, 31 October 1939.
4. KTB, 11 November 1939.
5. KTB, 14 November 1939.
6. Mining operations did continue but at a very low level. For instance, the KTB on 13 July 1941 records: 'The CO of *U69*, KL Metzler, carried out an operation in the south with a Type VII. He carried out with caution and great skill the very difficult task of laying mines in Takoradi and Lagos, so that the British Admiralty was forced to close both harbours.'
7. KTB, 8 March 1943. This mission was by *U117*, a Type XB.
8. KTB, 19 April 1943. This mission was by *U217* to Land's End.
9. KTB, 15 July 1943. This order was dated 28 June 1944 and signed by Hessler.
10. These mine types are mentioned in only one source, the KTB. The description is necessarily sketchy, since the KTB contained only operational orders, not technical details.
11. KTB, 31 August 1943.
12. KTB, 31 March 1944. The operational order was dated 12 January 1944.

Deck Gun

The standard deck gun of the Type VII U-boat was an 8.8cm naval gun. The official name for the weapon was the 8.8cm *Schiffskanone* C/35 in *Unterseebootslafette* C/35. Despite having the same calibre, it was a completely different weapon from the famous 8.8cm Flak gun of the German Army which was later used widely as an anti-tank gun and as the main armament of Tiger tanks. The shells of the two weapons were not inter-

▶ **The crew of *U571*, a Type VIIC, lounges on deck, while a fair assortment of Army and Navy brass looks down from dockside at La Rochelle. The pristine state of the paint and boat indicate that this is probably just before or after its first patrol. Also, both gunsights are in place on the 8.8cm mount, something rarely seen in more experienced boats. Note the tompion in the gun's muzzle and the lanyard wound loosely around the barrel. (NARA)**

changeable. Rather, this gun was a development of the 8.8cm weapons used extensively in the German Navy before and during the First World War as a quick-firing medium calibre gun. During the course of that war, it was given a modified mount which allowed higher elevation and was used as an anti-aircraft weapon.

The mount for the 8.8cm was located on the foredeck, on the centreline, just forward of the conning tower. The deck plates surrounding the mount had a pattern of narrow friction strips (approximately 2cm wide) of textured material to provide surer footing for the gun crew in rough weather. The strips were laid in a radial pattern of 16 spokes, each approximately one metre long. Between each of the spokes was a pair of short strips of the same material making up two concentric rings. On most boats, the outer ring of strips were eliminated forward of the mount and the spokes there were shorter.

The gun crew consisted of three men: aimer, layer and loader. The aimer and layer took up standing positions next to each other at the gun sight. Each had a padded open harness at waist height that he could lean into. Control wheels just beyond the harnesses caused the gun to traverse or elevate. The aimer's position was behind the sight, directly in line with the gun. He was responsible for the horizontal deflection of the gun. The layer's position faced the gun, at right angles to and on the outer shoulder of the aimer. He looked down at an angle into the sight. His responsibility was for the correct elevation of the gun, controlling the range of the shot. There were identical positions for aimer and layer on each side of the gun, so that they could take a position on the lee side of the mount in rough weather. The layer's harness, which projected outward from the gun toward the side, could be folded inward when not in use. A gun sight was provided for both sides of the mount. The sights were considered waterproof, but they were generally stowed inside the boat for safekeeping (so they wouldn't be knocked loose during depth-charging) and were brought up on deck only when the gun was to be manned. The sights were fastened in place by a large set screw in the appropriate mounting on the side of the gun. The third crew member was the loader, whose position was behind the gun barrel. He operated the breech, loading shells and ejecting spent casings. All three members of the gun crew could strap themselves to the gun mount with leather straps in rough weather. The gun commander, generally the IIWO, would be stationed in the tower. He selected targets and determined when and how many rounds to fire.

Three additional crewmen made up the full on-deck gun crew. These were Lords whose job was to pass shells to the loader from the tower. Other crewmen inside the boat passed up the shells through the main tower hatch from the shell locker which was located below the deck plating by the forward circuit-breaker cabinet, just forward of the control room watertight door. (A few ready use rounds were stored in a watertight container just forward and to the port of the gun mount.) The shells themselves were single-piece rounds combining projectile and a brass cartridge case filled with propellant charge. Each all-up round weighed 20lb. The effective rate of fire was between 15 and 18 rounds per minute. The

▲ **The gun on *U552* has obviously seen some use, as can be attested by the five silhouettes of sinking ships stencilled in white on the barrel. Such victory marks were rare on U-boats, more from the lack of opportunity than lack of exuberance. (ECPA)**

◀ **A closeup of the 8.8cm mount on *U84*, a Type VIIB, seen at St-Nazaire on 8 July 1942. This gun has been given a name, a practice that was rare but not unheard of. Note the padded braces for the aimer and layer. The layer's braces are turned inward, as was common practice when the gun was not in use. (NARA)**

mount allowed fire at up to 85° elevation, but there are few recorded instances of the 8.8cm being used as an anti-aircraft weapon. The maximum range of the gun was 11 kilometres, but this range was never fully utilized since the maximum distance that a boat's lookouts could spot a target's mastheads was just 12 kilometres.

Bringing the gun into action was an intricately choreographed activity. The three main members of the gun crew would be called on deck by the CO. (In action, or at any other time at sea, no-one came on deck without the CO's authorization. The more people up top, particularly if they were some distance from the hatch, the longer it took to crash dive.) They would bring the gun sight up from below, if it wasn't already in place. While the aimer and layer attached and cleaned off the sight, the loader would unseat the waterproof tompion which sealed the gun's muzzle. This unscrewed with a large wingnut. There was a receptacle at the base of the mount of the same diameter as the muzzle where the tompion could be secured when the gun was in use. Additionally, the tompion was attached to the mount by a lanyard which prevented its loss if the gun crew were in a hurry. The loader would, if necessary, open the ready use container and chamber the first round. Otherwise, he would wait for rounds to be passed up from below. To prepare the gun for diving the procedure was put into reverse. The tompion would be re-attached. It was usual practise to wind the lanyard around the gun barrel. The mount would be locked in fore and aft position and the sight taken below.

The 8.8cm gun was obviously a weapon that was useful under very restricted conditions. It could only be used in situations when there was no threat of attack from the air and when the target was believed with a high degree of certainty to be unable to return fire. (U-boats were notoriously vulnerable to shell fire of any kind. One hole in the pressure hull, which was made of high-tensile steel, not armour plate, left a U-boat unable to dive and virtually defenceless.)

To Dönitz the gun always was a secondary weapon but one that had a definite role to play, at least early in the war. Two months after the war began, he stated:

> 'Of its nature, the U-boat is intended to fight with torpedoes and not with guns. Her strength is in being able to make a surprise attack and her protection is in deep diving. A full-scale torpedo attack always promises success; a gun action, which is always full-scale as soon as the boat is within range of the enemy guns, does not by any means promise the same results. Nevertheless it must not be forgotten that she needs her guns to stop the ship and break resistance when she is not from the first in a position to fire a torpedo at the enemy. It takes a long time to haul ahead and it is not always possible. To renounce the use of guns altogether would therefore lower the chances of success considerably.'[1]

At the beginning of the war the deck gun was a real option as a weapon against merchant targets for many commanders. Certainly, the ability to use the gun could extend a patrol, since the number of torpedoes carried was one of the principal restrictions on the duration of a patrol. Further, the rules of engagement imposed on U-boats at the very beginning of the war made normal torpedo attacks problematical.

While British propaganda during the war made it seem that the Germans started the war with the same policy of unrestricted commerce warfare as had ended the previous war, such was not the case. The orders given to U-boat commanders at the outbreak of war required strict adherence to prize law in the case of merchant shipping.[2] All merchant ships were to be stopped and searched. Only ships of hostile nationality and neutrals carrying war materials to hostile ports could be sunk, and then only after the crew was safely free of the vessel. Once that had been accomplished, it was often as easy for a U-boat to use its deck gun as a torpedo to finish off the target. Passenger ships were never to be sunk. The only exceptions were ships of known hostile nationality, armed merchant ships (which effectively made them auxiliary warships) and ships of any kind or nationality in a convoy guarded by hostile war ships. These could be sunk without warning. Thus it was as much an acute embarrassment to BdU as it was a propaganda coup for the British when Lemp in *U30* sank the liner *Athenia* without warning on the first day of the war.

The first result of the sinking of the *Athenia* on the German side was an even tighter interpretation of the prize rules.[3] Yet, such tight restrictions on the action of U-boats couldn't last. The U-boat arm had been strangled by political restrictions in the last war. BdU was determined that his wolves be given free rein. The loosening of restrictions was gradual over the first months of the war, but the trend was always in the direction of greater freedom of action:

> '18 Sept 39: Raeder proposes the announcement of a danger zone around England where British ships only may be sunk without warning. BdU objects on the grounds that this was no improvement over normal prize law.[4]
>
> 23 Sept 39: Returning U-boats reported that merchant shipping was using radio when stopped and that, in some cases, aircraft had arrived overhead soon thereafter. This was a wrinkle never envisioned in the prize rules.[5]
>
> 24 Sept 39: Merchant shipping using radio when stopped may be sunk without further warning.[6]
>
> 26 Sept 39: The Royal Navy co-operated by announcing that all merchant shipping would soon be armed.
>
> 28 Sept 39: All neutrals are warned not to act suspiciously. They shouldn't follow a zig-zag course, use their radio or fail to stop when requested to, travel darkened at night or travel in convoys.
>
> 1 Oct 39: The Royal Navy orders all merchant ships to attempt to ram a U-boat on sight.
>
> 2 Oct 39: Danger area announced around England where darkened ships may be attacked without warning.[7]
>
> 4 Oct 39: Danger zone extended to 15°W. Ships known to be armed may be attacked without warning.[8]
>
> 19 Oct 39: Danger zone extended to 20°W.[9]
>
> 27 Oct 39: U-boat crewmen are ordered never to board a merchant ship being stopped. The target's crew are to bring the ship's papers to the U-boat. Ships are to be sunk by torpedo only.'[10]

This last order, while far from clear, effectively brought an end to the widespread use of the deck gun to stop merchant vessels. The steady imposition of a convoy system on British shipping was an equal factor. For a while yet, commanders would opt to use their gun to finish off ships that had been torpedoed but which were taking their time about sinking. A few shells to the waterline was often enough to hasten the process. The gradual loosening of restrictions on the rules of engagement[11] meant that most U-boatmen never saw the deck gun in action, though they all seemed to hear of others who used it:

> 'Our Type VIIs had the eighty-eight mm, we called it 'acht-acht', but it was not used later on in the war. Only in the Mediterranean was it still used and by boats on the Murmansk run and the ones that were stationed up on Novaya Zemlya.'[12]

A number of factors, besides this easing of the rules of engagement, led to the gradual abandonment of the deck gun as an attack weapon. In the North Atlantic Allied airpower soon made any surface attacks too dangerous and use of the deck gun as an offensive weapon effectively ceased. The last recorded gun attacks took place in the spring of 1942.[13] On 14 November 1942, BdU ordered the removal of deck guns from Type VII U-boats to compensate the weight of the increased Flak armament.[14]

1. KTB, 23 October 1939.
2. KTB, 3 September 1939. 'In radio message T.O.O. 1400 Naval War Staff ordered: "U-boats to make war on merchant shipping in accordance with operations order." This should exclude any misunderstanding, as the operations order expressly orders war against merchant shipping in accordance with prize law.'
3. KTB, 4 September 1939. 'Radio message from Naval War Staff to all U-boats: "By the Führer's orders no hostile action is to be taken for the present against passenger ships, even if in convoy." There is no definition of the term passenger ship. Nor do I think that it could be defined in any way which would be of practical assistance to COs.'
4. KTB, 18 September 1939. BdU's point was that the enemy wouldn't co-operate. They'd just flag their ships as neutrals and sail them with impunity through the danger zone. There was no law against lying about your nationality.
5. KTB, 23 September 1939.
6. KTB, 24 September 1939.
7. KTB, 2 October 1939. 'This will be a great relief to U-boats.'
8. KTB, 4 October 1939. SKL reserves sole judgement of which ships are armed or not. Passenger ships not to be attacked, even if armed, unless they are known troop-ships.
9. KTB, 19 October 1939.
10. KTB, 27 October 1939. This is a contradictory order, since torpedoes only are to be used to sink ships, even 'after resistance has been quelled with gunfire'.
11. For the record, it should be noted that all restrictions on sinking merchant shipping in the danger zone around England were not lifted until 17 August 1940.
12. EvK.
13. KTB, 3 April 1942. *U552* off Cape Cod: '3 April sank 'Atwater' (2438 BRT) in CA 5714 by gunfire'.
    KTB, 19 June 1942. *U701* off Hatteras: 'Surprised by patrol boat in the mist. Sank her after a gun action lasting 1.5 hours.'
14. KTB, 16 June 1943.

Flak Guns

The offensive weapons carried by U-boats gradually diminished in importance as increasing Allied airpower forced U-boats on the defensive. From the beginning, Type VII U-boats, had carried a 2cm gun intended at least in part for anti-aircraft defence. (Anti-aircraft guns in German usage were called Flak, a contraction of Flugzeugabwehrkanone.) As the war progressed, these weapons were resited, increased in number and calibre in a continual attempt to provide U-boats with adequate defence against attack from the air.

The original arrangement of Flak guns on Type VIIAs and early Type VIIBs was a single 2cm mounting located on the after deckcasing just aft of the tower. The official nomenclature for the gun and mount was '2cm Flak C/30 in LC 30/37'. The location of the gun in this position, where its crew would be unable to get below rapidly in any emergency, indicated that it was primarily thought of as an anti-ship weapon and only secondarily as a Flak gun. Further, due to a belief that the gun wasn't adequately waterproof, the entire breech and barrel assembly had to be dismounted and stored in a watertight container in the deckcasing before the boat dived, and then re-mounted when needed after the boat resurfaced.

This siting for the 2cm gun didn't last long. Its disadvantages, whether the gun was to be used against aircraft or ships, were so obvious that remedy was demanded by BdU. By the beginning of the war, all Type VIIs already launched had the 2cm resited to the after end of the tower and all subsequent boats were built to this configuration. The tiny open smoking deck found at the after end of the tower of these early boats was enlarged into a circular platform approximately two metres in diameter. At the same time, the decision was made to leave the gun permanently mounted rather than stowing before each dive.

The Flak armament of all Type VII U-boats remained at this state until mid-1942 when a gradually increasing number of attacks from the air, particularly during passage of the Bay of Biscay, brought the problem of Flak defence to BdU's attention.

> 'Increased danger from the air in the Bay of Biscay makes an alteration of orders for procedures on approach routes necessary . . . But as the danger of unexpected attack by radar-equipped aircraft is greater by night than by day, in future boats shall proceed by day, and submerged only in the extreme sections when daylight is not sufficient for the whole journey.'[1]

Once the increased danger of air attack was recognized, the search for remedies came rapidly.

▲ *U36*, a Type VIIA, soon after its launch in 1936. Like the remaining early Type VIIs, this boat carried a single dismountable 2cm Flak gun on its after deckcasing. That mount, minus the gun, can be seen in this view just aft of the tower. (via MacPherson)

► A Type VIIC is commissioned, 11 May 1941. The circular Flak platform known as *Turm 0*, was now standard for all Type VIIs. The weapon is the 2cm C/30.

On 16 June 1942, BdU held a conference in Paris among representatives of all concerned OKM departments.[2] One result of that conference, the development and deployment of radar detectors, is treated in detail on pp. 122–7. The other major outcome was the decision to upgrade the Flak armament of U-boats. In the short-term, the existing Flak platform (*Turm 0*) on U-boats was to be widened and the single 2cm gun replaced by a pair of twin 2cm MG151 mountings. The MG151 was a small, low muzzle-velocity cannon developed for the Luftwaffe. As soon as the materials were available, all boats were to receive a second Flak platform (known as the *Wintergarten*) with a twin 2cm C/30 mounting, below and aft of the existing one. Until this twin mount was available, boats were to keep their single 2cm C/30. This arrangement was to be the basic Flak defence suite, known as *Turm 1*. For the longer-term, BdU ordered the development of a naval

Above left: The size needed for the Flak platform of *Turm 0* was irrespective of the size of the boat. The two near boats in this view are Type IXs while the rear boat is a Type VII. Despite the significantly larger tower structure of the Type IXs, the Flak platform on both boat types was the same size. (via Albrecht)

◀ The 2cm Flak gunner stood, or rather squatted, in the shoulder harnesses at the rear of the mount, which were offset to the left of the gun barrel. His left hand is on the trigger lever. His right hand would operate the cocking/clearing handle. The loader shoves a magazine into place from the left.

▲ The C/30 version of the 2cm Flak gun was fitted on an LC 30/37 gun mount, seen on *U85*, a Type VIIB, at St-Nazaire. This was a short mount really better suited to surface than anti-aircraft usage. To shoot at any significant elevation, the gunner had to squat. However, the gun was balanced for Flak use, with most of the weight to the rear of the pivot. Note the 7.92mm (30cal) MG34 mounted on the

bridge structure, just this side of the CO.

Above right: The CO of *U566*, Kapitänleutnant Borchardt, watches the docking of his boat by the IWO, Brest, 30 June 1942. A 7.92 mm MG34 is mounted just forward of the IWO on the tower structure. This small calibre machine-gun didn't have much use on U-boats, particularly this late in the war. Earlier, it had been occasionally useful for close-range counter-battery fire against armed merchantmen. It certainly was too small to be useful as a Flak weapon.

▶ The introduction of *Turm 1* with its second level of Flak platform, preceded by quite a bit the availability of the MG151s that were supposed to be fitted to the upper platform. As an interim measure, U-boats, such as *U632* seen here, were fitted with *Turm 2*, which mounted single 2cm C/38s on both platforms.

◀ *U604*, a Type VIIC, was attacked by the aircraft of VB129 off Bahia, Brazil, on 3 August 1943. Its strengthened Flak armament failed to ward off the attackers. The two circular platforms of *Turm 2* can be plainly seen in this view from one of the attackers. This attack failed to sink *U604*, but the damage was such that she was scuttled eight days later. (USN)

▶ *U338* was experimentally fitted with a very unusual suite of Flak weapons before she went on operations. Together with whatever weapons were mounted aft of the bridge, she had a small bandstand added to the front of the tower for a twin 2cm MG151. This gun had the advantage of being very small and thus easy to fit into odd locations such as this, but it was also ineffective and was thus never widely adopted. (SFL)

◀ Some of the crew of *U712*, a Type VIIC, gathers for this portrait on or aft of the two platforms of *Turm 2*. Note the ever-present lookouts on the bridge. Even at this moment of apparent relaxation, the threat from the air had to be always kept in mind. (Von Ketelhodt)

version of the Army's 3.7cm Flak gun, as well as ordering completion of testing of the experimental 3cm gun.

These plans were modified a number of times during the following months in the light of experience. On 28 September 1942, BdU reported to Hitler that the MG151 was inadequate due to poor range and penetrating power. The one boat that had been fitted with the *Turm 1* Flak suite, *U553*, had failed all tests. Further, even the 2cm C/30 was barely adequate due to insufficient stopping power and a poor reliability record.[3] Not only was the weapon unsatisfactory, but the very shape and size of the added Flak platform caused problems. The CO of *U553* complained that the *Wintergarten* caused added spray to be generated in a crossing sea which increased the boat's visibility and that when submerged, its hydrodynamic effects made depth maintenance more difficult. Until the 3.7cm gun was ready, BdU recommended the adoption of the more reliable 2cm C/38. He had no remedy to the problems with the platform itself, which he felt was a necessary evil.

Since development of the 3.7cm gun was likely to be slow, BdU continued looking for alternative weapons. A pair of 2cm quadruple mounts (*Flakvierlinge*) were procured from the Army and mounted experimentally in U-boats. As a result of these tests, a new official Flak suite was planned, to be composed of a pair of twin 2cm C/38 mounts on the upper Flak platform and a 2cm Flakvierling (to be replaced by a 3.7cm mount when it became available) in the *Wintergarten*. Since neither the twin nor quadruple mounts for the C/38 were immediately available, an interim standard, known as *Turm 2*, was adopted. This had a single 2cm C/38 on the Flak platform and another in the *Wintergarten*. The fitting of *Turm 2* to Type VII U-boats began in December 1942, but was slowed by some minor bugs in the C/38, which took until mid-January 1943 to iron out.

Deliveries of *Flakvierlinge* had progressed to the point that a pair of Type VIICs were fitted with the gun in March and April 1943. Pending successful completion of tests with the weapons, BdU developed a plan for the delivery of 24 of the new guns to the fleet by mid-July and another 24 by mid-September. *U758*, the first of the test boats, reported complete success with the mount on 4 June 1943. BdU hadn't waited for this word. In mid-May, he ordered a speeded-up delivery schedule that would have 150 of the new guns to the fleet by August. With the availability of twin[4] and quadruple C/38s, the new standard suite was adopted as *Turm 4*.[5]

Even as these developments were taking place, the situation in the Bay of Biscay continued to deteriorate to the point that, in early 1943, BdU decided on a series of stopgap measures to protect U-boats until the extended bridge and increased Flak armament could be applied to all boats. The third and fourth *Flakvierling* mounts available were installed, together with the first experimental 3.7cm gun, on a specially designed air defence U-boat, *U441*, also known as *Flak-U1*. Actually *U441* was not the first boat intended as a Flak U-boat. The idea had originally come to BdU while deciding the fate of *U256*. That boat had returned to port in September 1942 in badly damaged condition and there was some question as to the economics of trying to rebuild it. BdU decided to take it in hand and reconstruct it as a Flak U-boat with the two Flak platforms of *Turm 4* and another Flak platform with another *Flakvierling* forward of the bridge. It was also to carry a battery of 8.6cm line-carrying rockets described in the next section. Only five torpedoes, intended mainly for self-defence, and only enough fuel for operations in the Bay of Biscay were to be carried. When the reconstruction of *U256* was delayed, it was decided on 16 April 1943 to take *U441* in hand for the same conversion. This was completed rapidly, and on 22 May 1943, *U441* sailed with orders to attack enemy aircraft in the Bay and to provide escort for less well armed U-boats.[6] Two days after she sailed, *U441* encountered an RAF

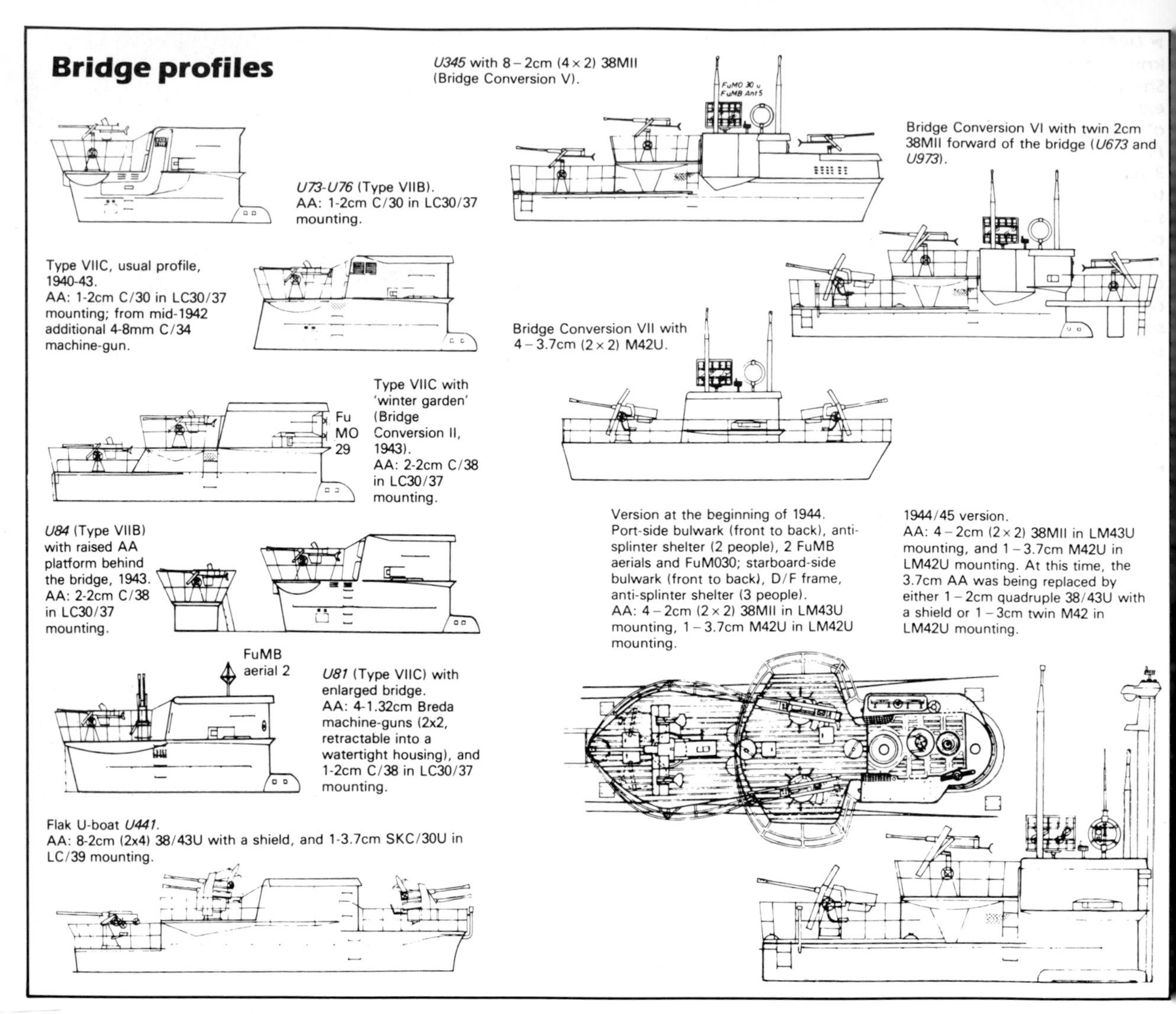

Bridge profiles

U73-U76 (Type VIIB).
AA: 1-2cm C/30 in LC30/37 mounting.

Type VIIC, usual profile, 1940-43.
AA: 1-2cm C/30 in LC30/37 mounting; from mid-1942 additional 4-8mm C/34 machine-gun.

Type VIIC with 'winter garden' (Bridge Conversion II, 1943).
AA: 2-2cm C/38 in LC30/37 mounting.

U84 (Type VIIB) with raised AA platform behind the bridge, 1943.
AA: 2-2cm C/38 in LC30/37 mounting.

U81 (Type VIIC) with enlarged bridge.
AA: 4-1.32cm Breda machine-guns (2x2, retractable into a watertight housing), and 1-2cm C/38 in LC30/37 mounting.

Flak U-boat *U441*.
AA: 8-2cm (2x4) 38/43U with a shield, and 1-3.7cm SKC/30U in LC/39 mounting.

U345 with 8 – 2cm (4 × 2) 38MII (Bridge Conversion V).

Bridge Conversion VI with twin 2cm 38MII forward of the bridge (*U673* and *U973*).

Bridge Conversion VII with 4 – 3.7cm (2 × 2) M42U.

Version at the beginning of 1944. Port-side bulwark (front to back), anti-splinter shelter (2 people), 2 FuMB aerials and FuM030; starboard-side bulwark (front to back), D/F frame, anti-splinter shelter (3 people).
AA: 4 – 2cm (2 × 2) 38MII in LM43U mounting, 1 – 3.7cm M42U in LM42U mounting.

1944/45 version.
AA: 4 – 2cm (2 × 2) 38MII in LM43U mounting, and 1 – 3.7cm M42U in LM42U mounting. At this time, the 3.7cm AA was being replaced by either 1 – 2cm quadruple 38/43U with a shield or 1 – 3cm twin M42 in LM42U mounting.

Sunderland. *U441* shot down the attacker, but not before the Sunderland had damaged the U-boat sufficiently to require two months of repairs.

BdU noted with satisfaction the shooting down of the Sunderland and seemed to ignore the implications of *U441*'s serious damage. On 29 May, he ordered that the next few returning boats should form themselves into groups:

> '... in order, in case of enemy air attacks, to be able to counter the enemy when surfaced, *which has proved to be most practical*, with heavy and successful gunfire, all boats returning in a position West of 16° should continue the return passage together, through the Biscay area in groups up to four boats.
>
> The measure taken ... today for boats on return passage will be introduced by way of experiment for outgoing boats, this being passage together through the Biscay area in groups of between three and six boats. FdU West will see that these measures are carried out and has received the following instructions in this connection:
>
> (1) Naval CinC has ordered the experimental introduction for outgoing boats, at the earliest possible moment, of the method of proceeding *together* in daylight and on the surface in order to ward off enemy aircraft attacks.
>
> (2) *Points to be remembered*:
>
> (a) Minimum number of boats three, maximum number six ...
>
> (c) Proceed together, surfaced, by day under the orders of the most senior Commanding Officer. Strict orders not to submerge in case of aircraft attack but to ward off attack with all guns.
>
> (d) Proceed submerged at night with prescribed speeds and rendezvous for next morning.
>
> (e) If it is not possible to use guns, disperse or proceed submerged according to the orders of the most senior Commanding Officer ...'[7]

▶ *U441* was also known as U-Flak-1. She was given the first experimental models of both the 2cm *Flakvierling* and the 3.7cm M42, fitted on to a unique tower structure which placed one of the *Flakvierlinge* forward of the bridge. *U441*'s career as U-Flak-1 was short. Two days after sailing on 22 May 1942, she shot down an RAF Sunderland, but was seriously damaged in the process. (USN)

This move proved to be ill-conceived. The evidence provided by a few successful defensive actions by U-boats against aircraft was given far too much weight.[8] The first few groups of outbound boats crossed the Bay of Biscay without incident, but this situation changed on 13 June 1943.

> '*U564*, in an outward bound group of five boats was attacked by a Sunderland in BE 9453 (WNW of Cape Finisterre) and subsequently unable to dive. The aircraft was shot down. *U185* remained with the damaged boat to give assistance and the other three continued on their outward passage. When *U564* was fit to proceed at 12 knots, it started for home with *U185*. It was still unable to dive. It was intended that both these boats would be met by the destroyers *Z 24* and *Z 32*, which were to leave Verden at 0800, 14 June.'[9]

The story continued the next day:

> 'One of the two destroyers which put out to give assistance returned because of engine trouble. The rendezvous was ordered for 2100 in BF 7566 (close into the Spanish coast Northwest of Cape Ortegal). During the afternoon, *U185* and *U564* were several times attacked by aircraft. One aircraft shadowed constantly. After a further bombing attack in BF 7549, *U564* sank. *U185* took the Commanding Officer and 18 other survivors on board. It met the destroyer as planned and continued on its outward passage after it handed over the men.'[10]

BdU realized his mistake:

> 'On the basis of of recent experience in Biscay, the following order has been given to the boats. With immediate effect groups of U-boats will proceed through Biscay mainly submerged and will surface only to charge batteries.'[11]

BdU's attention turned back once again to improving the Flak defence capability of individual boats. On 30 June 1943, he ordered that no boat was to leave on patrol that hadn't been fitted with *Turm 4* including the *Flakvierling*. He accepted that this would mean a delay of up to four weeks in the sailing of some boats.[12] Additional Flak U-boats came into service and were deployed. *U621* sailed on 29 August and *U953* and the long-delayed *U256* sailed on 8 October. Three more boats, *U211*, *U271* and *U263*, were also in the process of conversion, but the number of Allied aircraft continued to increase over the Bay of Biscay, overwhelming the defensive capabilities of even the Flak U-boats. The RAF adopted the same tactic against them as it had against the U-boat groups. The first aircraft to find a Flak U-boat, or a group of surfaced U-boats, simply shadowed the target, rather than trying to attack immediately and drawing the full weight of defensive fire. Only after additional aircraft showed up was the attack made, from multiple directions simultaneously. The irony in this, of course, is that this was Dönitz's own *Rüdeltaktik* used against himself. On 11 November 1943, BdU finally admitted defeat. The Flak U-boats were no longer able to fulfill their assigned mission in the Bay of Biscay, and they lacked the fuel capacity to operate farther afield. Also, the standard Flak armament for Type VIIs had increased to the point where they were not much inferior to the Flak U-boats' in defensive firepower. The seven Flak U-boats were ordered to be converted back to normal attack boats, fitted with *Turm 4*.

The 2cm *Flakvierling*, which now was standard equipment, never really fulfilled its promise as a defensive weapon. The Army mount proved to be insufficiently robust for U-boat requirements and was replaced by a specially designed naval mount (M 43), developed by Hanomag, in all fittings. This new mount resolved some of the reliability issues but didn't make the gun more effective. The twin 2cm C/38 mount became standard in all boats as of October 1943. It was a reliable and handy weapon but suffered from the same lack of stopping power. In its original mount, it was fitted without an armoured shield. This left the gun crew without any protection from the gunfire of aircraft. BdU ordered the fitting of an armoured shield in October 1943. This involved an extensive revision of the mount.

The last major development in Flak armament was the introduction of the production version (M 42) of the 3.7cm gun, which finally began in November 1943. By 1 December, eighteen boats had been able to exchange their 2cm *Flakvierlinge* for single 3.7cm mounts. The 3.7cm was enthusiastically received by U-boat crews, because for the first time, it gave them the ability to stop an attacker before it could deliver its weapons. This was because the 3.7cm's shells were more than twice as large as the 2cm's (0.73kg v. 0.32kg) and had more than twice the effective range (2.5km v 1km). The major disadvantage of the bigger gun was that it fired much more slowly (50rpm v. 240rpm). Another problem that emerged with the fitting of the 3.7cm together with the twin C/38s in armoured mounts was that of ammunition supply. It was difficult to bring ammunition to the 3.7cm past the twin 2cm mounts on the upper platform. The only solution BdU had to offer was to build ready storage containers into the *Wintergarten*, which was all very well until the limited storage in these containers was used up.[13] Some very late VIICs were fitted with a twin 3.7cm mount.

▶ A February 1945 view of *U953*, a Type VIIC, shows the widened upper Flak platform with its two twin 2cm mounts to advantage.

◀ *U338* reverted to early standard *Turm 4* armament of one Flakvierling on the lower platform and a pair of twin 2cm C/38s on the upper. The eight 2cm barrels looked impressive and put up a heavy volume of fire, but the light 2cm shell was insufficient to stop an oncoming attacker before it could deliver its bombs. (USN)

◀ The later *Turm 4* standard used a 3.7cm gun in the place of the *Flakvierling* on the *Wintergarten*. This recent view of *U995*, the only surviving Type VII, shows the widened upper Flak platform allowing the siting of two twin C/38 mounts at that level. (Albrecht)

By this time, the number of patrolling aircraft had increased to the point where every surviving boat had a tale to tell:

> 'We had the two Flak platforms, one right behind the bridge and one lower and behind. On the upper we had on either side a double 2cm, *Doppellafette* we called it, and the other had a double 3.7cm manned by two men, one on either side. They would rush to their positions at the guns as soon as we came up, the gunners of the 2cm at their shoulder harnesses and the 3.7cm in their seats. They just had to hear the order to fire and they started shooting.
>
> Well, that one that almost got us in the Bay, we had no signal on him on our Naxos. We thought he was gone and suddenly he's 200 metres away with his spotlight[14] about 10 or 15 metres off the water, this spotlight he had right between his wheels. That's when he started shooting, but we got him. He came down flaming. Just about took my head off. His bombs were a little bit too far. He came about 20° off the port quarter. He tried to put his row of bombs a little bit across our path, so he'd have a good chance with two. The best angle was 5° or 10° off. Then he has a good chance to put one right beside us. His last bomb was 10 or 15 metres off our stern. Then he came over us and down about 100 or 200 metres on the other side. He came flaming down into the sea. We had already started our dive and so we tried to snort again. We came up again right away and the next guy came. We didn't get him but gave him such a good shot with our 3.7cm that he turned away. He dropped his bombs, but not close enough.'[15]

At least one other gun type was fitted to some Type VII U-boats operating in the Mediterranean; single or twin 1.27cm (.50cal) Breda machine-gun mounts. This gun was popular, but was too lightweight to be an effective Flak weapon.

At least three more standard Flak suites were experimented with before the introduction of the snorkel allowed U-boats to remain submerged more or less permanently. *Turm 5* added a Flak platform forward of the tower structure, that faired into the tower. *U362* was experimentally fitted with this tower design. *Turm 6* was similar except that the forward Flak platform was on a separate pedestal, in order to reduce the spray generated by the forward gun mount. *U673* and *U973* were fitted with this design. *U973* reported that diving time and depth keeping were both adversely affected by the added Flak platform. All boats reported reduced surfaced stability. *Turm 7* went farthest in strengthening Flak armament, adding a Flak platform which completely encircled the tower. This provided room for four single 3.7cm mounts, two forward and two aft. There is no record of which boats, if any, were fitted with this design. The first two of these designs used the standard *Turm 4* configuration aft of the tower. Few boats, if any, besides those already noted, were fitted with these tower designs.[16]

1. KTB, 16 July 1942.
2. KTB, 16 June 1943. Much of the following details come from this entry entitled: 'Survey of Measures to be Adopted for the Improvement of U-boat Anti-Aircraft Armament'.
3. The US Navy reached the same conclusion about the 20mm Oerlikon gun which was its standard light AA weapon. These guns were known as 'doorknockers' to US sailors due to their inability to stop an oncoming kamikaze. By war's end, the number of 20mm guns on US ships was rapidly declining.
4. KTB, 1 December 1943. The first 40 twin C/38 mounts were delivered to the fleet on 15 July 1943.
5. *Turm 3* was a modification just for Type VIIDs. It was composed of two single 2cm C/38s side by side.
6. KTB, 22 May 1943, Operational Order Atlantic No. 55.
7. KTB, 29 May 1943. Italics added by author.
8. KTB, 7 April 1943 and 13 April 1943.
9. KTB, 13 June 1943.
10. KTB, 14 June 1943.
11. Ibid. Despite this evidence of the danger of group passage, the idea was tried several more times with returning boats before it was finally totally abandoned on 2 August 1943.
12. KTB, 30 June 1943.
13. KTB, 1 December 1943.
14. This was the Leigh Light airborne searchlight mounting, first used in 1942.
15. WB.
16. KTB, 29 February 1944.

Experimental Weapons

The Kriegsmarine experimented with a number of novel weapons as the war began to turn against the Axis. These were primarily defensive weapons intended to enhance a U-boat's ability to survive in an increasingly hostile environment.

The continuing German experimentation with rockets and missiles, dating back to the 1930s, was the primary source of these novel weapons. The first attempts at using rockets as weapons from a U-boat came about by pure coincidence. The Commanding Officer of *U551*, KK Fritz Steinhoff, just happened to be the brother of Dr Ernst Steinhoff, a researcher working on problems of small rocket guidance at the *Heeresversuchsanstalt* (Army Experimental Establishment) at Peenemünde which was developing artillery rockets for the German Army. As a result of conversations between the brothers, the idea arose of trying out an installation of artillery rockets in *U551*. During its working-up period, *U551* was detached briefly to Peenemünde where, from 31 May to 5 June 1942, she went through a series of experimental launches of 30cm *Wurfkörper Sprengraketen* from a rack for six rockets installed on the after deckcasing. The last of the experimental launches took place while the U-boat was submerged at periscope depth. The experiments proved that rockets could be launched from U-boats, even when submerged, but showed little promise of producing a useful weapon. No further similar experimentation followed these initial trials.

As the presence of Allied aircraft came increasingly to dominate the operational lives of U-boats, the interest of BdU turned to means of using this fledgling rocket technology to defend his boats. Before the first of the Flak U-boats, *U441*, deployed to the front, it was equipped with a battery of 8.6cm line-carrying rockets. The idea was that the rockets would be fired in the path of

◀ **All that added firepower didn't help against surface escorts. *U744*, a Type VIIC fitted with *Turm 4*, came up against a Canadian escort group on 6 March 1944 and, not too surprisingly, lost the engagement. A crew from HMCS *Chilliwack* tried to board the U-boat, but it was sinking too fast. (MacPherson)**

an attacking aircraft, each rocket trailing a length of wire intended to ensnare the aircraft. In theory, a barrage of rockets would either entangle the attacker in the wires causing it to crash or, failing that, at least cause it to abort its attack. In practice, however, the idea proved unworkable. The timing required to fire the rockets so that they would successfully destroy an attacker was almost impossible to achieve. The crewman in charge of the rockets had to remain in an exposed position until the attacker was virtually overhead and then fire the rockets with split-second timing. Also, firing the rockets put the Flak gun crews in considerable danger. Experiments with the line-carrying rockets led to the idea being dropped before *U441* actually deployed.[1]

The idea of using 8.6cm high-explosive rockets in place of the line-carrying rockets was also tried out during this period:

> 'The question of using explosive rockets, to be fired from multiple launchers, was investigated thoroughly in October and November 1943. The investigation showed the inferiority of such an arrangement as against a quick-firing Flak gun.'[2]

Another approach was tried in *U986* and one other boat. These boats were fitted with a barrage of 30 rocket-launchers erected completely around the tower. The barrage was divided into sectors, each of which could be fired separately:

> 'The purpose of this was to lay an air burst barrage in the direction of an attacking aircraft, and also possibly as a protection for a submerging U-boat. The chances of a hit are extremely low, but a frightening effect may be expected at least in initial use.'[3]

After completing her trials, *U986* left on her first and only patrol from Kiel on 8 February 1944. She was sunk on 17 April 1944. During the intervening period, she hadn't reported any use of the sector rocket system.[4]

The German experiments with one other class of novel weapons, midget submarines, have direct relation to the story of the Type VII U-boat. The most advanced of the numerous projects developed under the aegis of the *K-Verbände (Kleinkampfmittel-Verbände* – small battle units) was the *Biber* (beaver) one-man sunbmarine, which was deployed in large numbers from the Channel ports Fécamp and Den Helder in late 1944. At the same time, experiments were conducted into the use of Type VIICs to carry the short-ranged *Bibers* to distant targets. Trials held in the Baltic showed that a Type VIIC could carry two *Biber* (1 forward and 1 aft) and launch them in the open ocean. The system was tried operationally only once, in January 1945. Six *Bibers* of K-Flot 265 were loaded on three Type VIICs (*U295, U716* and *739*) which sailed on 5 January for the Kola Inlet with the object of attacking the shipping there, particularly the battleship *Archangelsk* (ex-HMS *Royal Sovereign*) based at Murmansk. The operation was called off on the 8th when it was discovered that the passage to the Kola area had caused multiple structural failures in the *Bibers*, rupturing gasoline lines (the *Bibers* were powered by Opel Blitz truck engines) and opening watertight seals.

1. Ibid. 'The equipment of the boats with line-carrying rockets was given up owing to the unfavourable experiences on *U441* (in-sufficient safety in firing).'
2. Ibid.
3. Ibid.
4. KTB, 29 February 1944. The author has been unable to determine the hull number of the other boat fitted with sector rockets.

▶ **Among the experimental ideas tried out by the Germans late in the war was the use of this Type VIIC to carry *Biber* (beaver) one-man midget submarines forward and aft. The *Biber* was the smallest of the many midget submarine designs the Germans produced at the end of the war. The white band around the tower of the Type VII indicates that this is a training boat. This view shows trials taking place in the Baltic. This set up was tried operationally only once, without success, in Operation 'Caesar'.**

Part Four: Sensor Systems

This chapter covers those systems used to sense the surrounding environment. This includes the various systems used by Type VII U-boats to stay in touch with home and with one another, and to detect the presence and location of the enemy both offensively and defensively. Increasingly, as the war progressed, these systems operated with sophisticated electronics that would have been unthinkable just a few years before.

At the beginning of the war, before the Battle of the Atlantic became dominated by the move and countermove of laboratory scientists tinkering with black boxes filled with tubes, rotors and wires, it was the human eyes on the bridge of a U-boat that were the primary means of finding the enemy. This meant that the world, as seen from a U-boat, was a small one. The lookouts' positions on the bridge were about five metres above the water, meaning that the horizon was at the most 12 kilometres distant in any direction on the clearest day. The only extension of that world was in the form of the constant stream of radio communication from home which brought orders and occasionally news.

At the beginning of the war, the bridge watch would be composed of four crewmen and a watch officer, each crewman watching a quadrant of the horizon and the watch officer keeping an eye on the sky (and on the watch). Rarely, if ever, did the radio watch down below play much of a direct role in finding targets or threats. As the war progressed, the character and composition of these watches changed in reaction to a world that became dominated by dangers that were difficult or impossible to locate with unaided human senses. As the nature of the Battle of the Atlantic changed, the watch became more defensive than offensive, less concerned with finding targets and more concerned with locating the enemy that threatened at any moment to catch them unawares. The radio watch took on a different character, as the *Funkers* manned a variety of receivers that attempted to sense the radars mounted on Allied escorts and aircraft. The increasing dominance of Allied aircraft was such that, by late 1943, even the tower watch had changed in composition to reflect the altered character of the war. Now the watch was officially increased to six men, with four of them scanning the sky in areas known to be patrolled by enemy aircraft and only two watching the sea.[1] The 'horizon' of a U-boat now stretched out visually and electronically for 50 or more nautical miles in search of the airborne enemy.

By 1944, the air threat had effectively forced U-boats to stay submerged in order to survive. The sensor range of a U-boat had again shrunk, now to just the limited world that could be seen from a periscope.

1. KTB, 16 September 1943.

Radios

The new tactics invented by Dönitz to redress the defeat of the First World War were possible only as a result of the advances in radio communications during the years since that war. Radio allowed BdU to maintain tight control over the operations of the far-flung U-boat fleet, at all times, and allowed the boats themselves to report their sightings back to BdU. Dönitz used each report to juggle the alignments of his packs as they swept the North Atlantic for elusive convoys. BdU not only maintained strategic control of operations, but reserved for himself the strict control of the tactical deployment of his boats. The only use of radio not involved with communications to or from BdU was the sending of beacon signals, on BdU's orders, which allowed the first U-boat to sight a convoy to attract the remaining members of a sweep line to the target.

> 'Enormous strides have been made in U-boat communications. It is possible today to operate U-boats over the widest areas accord-

▲ The primary antennae used with the radios carried by Type VII U-boats early in the war were the pair of jumper wires which stretched fore and aft from the tower structure. These were connected to the radios by an antenna lead which ran through the tower structure by means of the insulated connector, seen above the heads of the gun crew on this unidentified boat (not *U807* despite the number in the crest).

▶ This view of the tower of *U377*, a Type VIIC, shows both the antenna connector in the front of the tower structure and the circular DF loop extending above the tower.

ing to plan and to let them operate together. It is thus possible to counter a concentration of merchant ships in convoys with a concentration of U-boats. The convoy becomes the focal point of all U-boats stationed in the area.'[1]

The radio equipment typically carried by Type VII U-boats fell into three main groups, according to the frequency range it covered and the use to which it was put.[2] These were:

Short-Wave (3–30 MHz). The primary means of communication from U-boat Command to individual boats and back again was on short-wave bands. The main receiver unit was the E-437-S, manufactured by Telefunken, which was located in the radio cabin. Broadcasts on these waves were received using the telescopic rod antenna, which largely supplanted the antenna cables which extended fore and aft from the tower structure to the bow and stern. By mid-war, this Telefunken unit was being replaced by a similar set manufactured by Lorenz, known as the Main set, which gave clearer reception.

Transmission of messages back to Germany was carried out by a 200-watt transmitter, the S-400-S,

Radio Frequency Designations

German Designation	English Translation	Frequency Band	Allied Equivalent Designation
Längstwelle	Very-Long-Wave	<100kHz	Very-Low-Frequency (VLF)
Langwelle	Long-Wave	100kHz – 1.5 MHz	Medium-Frequency (MF)
Grenzwelle	Intermediate-Wave	1.5 – 3MHz	–
Kurzwelle	Short-Wave	3 – 30MHz	High-Frequency (HF)
Ultrakurzwelle	Very-Short-Wave	>30MHz	Very-High-Frequency (VHF)

Note: The above table, dated June 1944, gives the state of frequency designations, German and Allied, in use at mid-war. Later in the war, the emergence of radars of ever shorter wavelengths forced the further discrimination of sub-bands within the VHF range. The Germans used a simple system of wavelength designations (shown below); the Allies went in for a more complex system of letter-designated bands that is, with some minor alterations, still in use today (cf., Nav Rad, p. 14). Note that the Allied equivalents given in these tables are approximate, as the Allied and German systems of designating frequency bands didn't exactly match.

German Designation	English Translation	Frequency Band	Allied Equivalent Designation
Meterwelle	Metric-Wave	30 – 300 MHz	P (part) Band
Dezimeterwelle	Decimetric-Wave	300 – 3000 MHz	P (part), L & S (part) Bands
Zentimeterwelle	Centimetric-Wave	>3000 MHz	S (part), X & K Bands

made by Telefunken. In case of failure of the primary short-wave transmitter, a small back-up unit, a 40-watt set (40-K-39a) made by Lorenz, was also carried, usually in the sound room.

Medium-Wave (1.5–3 MHz). Local communications between U-boats was done on the medium-wave band. In general, tactical doctrine discouraged electronic communication between boats in a pack for fear of enemy direction-finding. The sole exception was the use of beacon signals to attract pack members to a convoy. In this case, the risk of enemy DF activity was considered to be smaller than the benefits to be gained from massing U-boats against a convoy. Thus, each boat had to be able to send and receive on the medium-wave band.

A Telefunken all-band receiver, E-381-S, was used to receive medium-wave transmissions. This receiver was sensitive to frequencies between 15 kHz and 20 MHz, allowing it to serve as a back-up to the E-437-S or Main in case it failed. The DF Loop (*Funkpeilrahmen*) was used to receive medium-wave signals and to establish the direction from which they were sent. Beacon signals were sent using a 150-watt transmitter, the Spez-2113-S, also made by Telefunken. The same antennae used for short-wave transmission were also used for medium-wave.

Besides monitoring the medium-wave bands for beacon signals, U-boats also listened on these bands for enemy inter-ship communications and commercial broadcasts of all types. Two receivers were carried specifically for this purpose, the Ela-10.12 made by Telefunken and the R.1 or R.2 receivers made by Radione. The latter served as a back-up to the Ela-10.12, but was primarily used for the entertainment of the crew. It was hooked up to the loudspeaker system in the boat, so that radio broadcasts of music and news from home aimed at U-boatmen could be heard by the crew. The Radione set had a gramophone jack so that the crew could play their own recorded music. A gramophone wasn't part of the official electronics suite of a Type VII U-boat, but virtually every boat procured one. This equipment was also used to pick up the British-operated Atlantiksender, a propaganda broadcast every bit as notorious (and interesting) among the Germans as Tokyo Rose was to the Americans in the Pacific. It mixed enough hard news about the goings on at the French ports and the war in general in with the propaganda to make interesting listening. As was the case with Tokyo Rose, boats were repeatedly ordered not to listen to the Atlantiksender, but often did so anyway.

Very-Long-Wave (>100 kHz). The Germans discovered early on that an effective radio control system, such as Dönitz wished to establish, required the ability to communicate with boats when they were submerged as well as when they were on the surface. The more conventional frequency bands, covered by the short-wave and medium-wave equipment, were the most commonly used because the receiving and transmitting equipment required and the antennae they needed could be easily carried by a small boat, such as a Type VII. They did, however, suffer from the singular disadvantage of being unable to pass through intervening obstructions. Short-wave was the band of choice for long-range communications because it could be bounced off the ionosphere. Medium-wave was used for local communications precisely because it wouldn't bounce and was thus limited to line-of-sight. Neither would penetrate the surface of the water. However, it was discovered that very low frequencies, those below 100 kHz, didn't suffer from these limitations. VLF, if sufficiently powerful, could be received by a submerged U-boat, at periscope depth or deeper, almost anywhere in the world.

To send VLF messages, the Germans built a huge 1,000-kW transmitter, code-named 'Goliath', at Kalbe, near Frankfurt-on-Oder, in the Altmark region of eastern Germany.[3] It was common practice to repeat all messages sent on conventional short-wave bands on VLF as well. These VLF transmissions were received on the Telefunken all-band receiver located in the sound compartment. The DF Loop served as antenna for receiving VLF broadcasts.

Ciphers and Cryptography Equipment

The radio traffic between U-boats and Germany was enciphered to prevent easy access to the contents of the messages by the Allies. Two different approaches were employed. Message content was standardized, codified and compressed into short-form messages which could be used to transmit normal tactical reports, such as sighting reports or fuel status reports, in the minimum number of characters. Any unnecessary words were left out. These standard message forms were then encoded using the Enigma machine using a set of constantly changing keys. This was believed by the Germans to produce unbreakable codes. Additionally, three different levels of encoding were used depending on the sensitivity of the message. Each level of encoding represented a different key setting of the Enigma machine. Normally encoded messages, which made up the vast bulk of incoming traffic, when run through the Enigma using the current standard setting would yield plain language text. In normal practice, the Germans changed this setting every two days. These would simply be entered into the radio log, which would be reviewed and signed off by the watch officer every two hours. Highly important messages were sent using a special key. Only the first word of the message would decode using the standard Enigma key. This word would indicate the special key to be used. These keys were known to the *Funkers* and the boat's officers. When such a message was received, it would be immediately decoded in the presence of the watch officer. If the next word after the key name was 'Kommandant', the rest of the coded message would still fail to decode even using the restricted key. This indicated an 'Eyes Only' message for the CO which could be fully decoded by a key known only to the CO. When one of these rare messages was received, the CO would clear all others from the radio room and proceed with the decoding in privacy.[4]

The Enigma machine on which the Germans depended so completely for signal security was essentially a modified electric typewriter. In its original version, as developed for commercial coding in the 1920s, it used three rotors, each with 26 contacts. Each rotor was wired to connect the 26 contacts in pairs in a different pattern. As the operator typed a letter at the keyboard, an electrical impulse was sent to the appropriate contact in the first rotor and output through the connected contact. This letter was then input into the second rotor and so on to the third rotor. The final output showed up as a light which appeared under one of the letters in a panel of letters in the pattern of a keyboard located above the input keys. As long as the receiver of the message had the same rotors in the reverse order, the message could be decoded at the receiving end. By the time the war began, the machine that was distributed to U-boats (known as the Enigma M) had, in addition to the sockets for three rotors, a sequence of 10 jacks and plugs which introduced further variability to the circuitry. Each boat carried five extra rotors so that the various keys in which messages might be received could be handled. By varying the sequence of rotors and plugs, different keys could be read. A final variant of the Enigma was introduced in February 1942. The Enigma M4 used four rotors, further increasing the complexity of the decoding process. The settings used with the 3-rotor machine had been code-named 'Hydra'; those used with the Enigma M4 were known by the code-name 'Triton'.

The complexity and technical brilliance of the Enigma convinced the Germans that their codes were unbreakable. Nevertheless, the ability that the Allies displayed, particularly after mid-1941, to skirt the waiting U-boat packs often left BdU looking for a traitor, or some other means whereby the British could look over his shoulder.[5] In fact the answer was much simpler and more mundane. The Poles, who had purchased commercial Enigma machines from Germany before the war, helped the British to set up a research group at Bletchley Park which continually worked on breaking the U-boat codes. The capture of the Enigma machine from *U110* on 9 May 1941, together with its rotors and keys, as well as its short signal book, gave the British the tools they needed to read U-boat message traffic. Thereafter, the periodic changes in key setting rarely took more than a week or two to unscramble. From mid-October 1941, until the introduction of the Triton codes, the average recovery time for signals was 48 hours for those sent on the first day of the two-day cycle and just a few hours for those sent on the second, so that the overall average delay in reading U-boat signals was 26 hours.[6] The situation improved temporarily for the Germans in early 1942 with the introduction of the Triton system and a new short signal book. Except for brief breaks, Triton remained unreadable at Bletchley Park until December 1942, and it wasn't until March 1943 that Triton was being read fast enough to be operationally useful to the Allies. Even the introduction of a pair of interchangeable fourth rotors, known as the beta and gamma rotors, in July 1943, failed to slow the decryption times.

The British made regular use of the information gained from the Enigma decodings in re-routing their convoys and positioning their ASW groups. The system they developed for handling the information coming from Bletchley Park was codenamed 'Ultra', after the ultra-secret character of the data. Few ever got to see the Ultra intercepts and fewer still knew where they came from. The Germans never suspected that the Enigma codes had been broken.[7]

◀ When not in use the DF loop retracted into a slot in the tower structure. It was used both for its intended purpose of taking bearings on beacon signals and also as the primary receiving antenna for VLF broadcasts. (Ahme via Schmidt)

HF/DF

At U-boat HQ, various suggestions were put forward to account for the increasing ability of the Allies to defend against U-boat dispositions, none of which seemed satisfactorily to identify the cause.[8] In fact, the ability of the British to decode U-boat radio traffic was only part of the problem faced by the attacking U-boats. Not only were the British increasingly able to avoid the German patrol lines, but when U-boats found and attacked convoys, the defender showed an uncanny ability to find and counter-attack the attackers. Some of this can be explained by successive developments in radar location devices (See Page 122) but, in fact, the most significant technical means employed by convoy escorts in finding U-boats was High Frequency/ Direction Finding (HF/DF). The defenders of the convoys were able to use the continual radio traffic required by *Rüdeltaktik* to pinpoint the U-boat packs.

The technology involved in HF/DF is quite simple. Ever since the invention of radio, it had been known that it was possible, with a directional antenna, to determine the axis along which radio waves were propagated. If two or more such antennae received the same signal, a precise location of the source could be determined by triangulation, at least in theory. DF was in practical use for short-range homing signals on U-boats.

Despite the simplicity of HF/DF and repeated evidence that the British had some means of finding U-boats that defied other explanation, the Germans stubbornly refused to believe that HF/DF was possible. HF/DF was considered to be technically infeasible because of the known fact that DF accuracy is a factor of distance to the source of the transmission. Before the war, DF on a source more than a few tens of miles distant was considered to be valueless due to the inherent inaccuracy of the fix. Given the shortness of U-boat transmissions and the odds against most DF receivers picking up any one transmission, the Germans considered that DF of their many short-wave broadcasts was unlikely.[9]

The technology that overcame these obstacles involved no new inventions, simply the rigorous application of known principles. The inherent inaccuracy of DF fixes at long range was overcome by multiplying the number of fixes to a high enough level. The Allies ringed the Atlantic with HF/DF stations, in Britain, Iceland, Greenland and Newfoundland. To these were later added further nets in the USA, Brazil and Africa. Each land station was equipped with a receiver which scanned the entire short-wave band twenty times a second. The network of land sites was linked by teletype, so that the source of an intercepted message generally could be located within about 50 nautical miles within fifteen minutes. In 1941,

▶ **The retractable rod antenna fitted in a housing on the port side of the bridge of virtually all Type VII U-boats. It is seen retracted, on the left. It is sometimes mistaken in photographs like this for the commander's jackstaff on the right. This was a short temporary staff mounted only when the boat was in port and only for the purpose of flying the boat's commissioning pennant.**

the system was further strengthened by the introduction of shipborne HF/DF. Escorts carrying HF/DF equipment could take high-quality bearings on the short-range 'ground wave' signal. When added to the less precise fixes produced by the land sites, these bearings allowed escorts to close on a U-boat often less than an hour after that boat had made a signal to base.

As late as May 1943, BdU argued that some other means of location must be in use besides HF/DF.

> 'An enemy submarine situation report received on 11 May gave several of our patrols or supply groups in the North Atlantic, and it is becoming increasingly clear that the enemy has excellent radar gear capable of picking up the submarines without their knowing it. In the case of these known dispositions not enough radio messages were sent to provide the enemy with sufficient material for his deductions.'[10]

Nevertheless, U-boats were gradually instructed to use radio less and less frequently. By late 1943, BdU was sending orders to boats that hadn't reported in weeks in the hope, often disappointed, that their silence was causedby their discretion rather than their loss.

1. KTB, 28 September 1939.
2. Inter, p 22. This description is of a typical mid-war radio suite. There were obviously continual variations in the electronics carried by Type VII U-boats.
3. The amount of power and size of antenna required to transmit VLF meant that U-boats couldn't send on VLF bands, but only receive.
4. Together, these keys made up the U-boat code known originally as Hydra and later as Triton.
5. KTB, 18 April 1941. 'The impression is given that the English traffic is being deliberately routed to avoid the attacking disposition. It is therefore suspected that by some means the enemy has obtained information of our attack areas ... I have therefore again given orders within the U-boat arm that the number of persons having knowledge of U-boat operations is to be kept as small as possible.'
6. Atl, vol. 3, pp. 141–143.
7. When Dönitz was told in the 1960s of the Ultra system and the fact that the British were reading his mail from 1941 on, he expressed considerable surprise. He shouldn't have. After all, the German Radio Intercept Service, the B-Dienst, was regularly decoding British radio traffic at all levels from the beginning of the war. He made use of B-Dienst intercepts in planning his convoy battles.
8. KTB, 19 November 1941. This is a long exposition on the causes of the convoys' avoidance of U-boat patrol lines. 'The likely explanation would be that the British, from some source or other, gain knowledge of our concentrated dispositions ... This knowledge could be gained by the enemy:
(1) By disclosure. Everything that can be done has been, by disguise of squares, limitation of radio personnel and our own U-boat codes. The circle of personnel "in the know" is so small that there can be hardly any possibility of disclosure.
(2) By deciphering our radio messages. This matter is being continually examined by the Naval War Staff and is considered as out of the question.
(3) By a combination of radio traffic and reports of sightings. This possibility can, of course, not be investigated as it is not known what information can be gained by the enemy from sighting reports and radio traffic (particularly accuracy in bearing) ...
(4) By radar location and consequent deviation. There is no evidence on this up to now ...'
9. KTB, 27 February 1942. 'I believe that the use of radio on short-waves tends to put the enemy off rather than to attract him; if any fixes are made they cannot be exact enough to permit a submarine chase, even if forces are within attacking distance.'
10. KTB, 12 May 1943.

Radars

The conceptual basis for radar was well known by all the major combatants before the outbreak of the Second World War. The development of the specialized circuitry that would allow the repeated generation of short bursts of very powerful radio waves that made radar possible, however, developed at a very different pace in different countries. The development of radar in Germany lagged somewhat behind that in Britain and the USA, particularly in the development of short-wave radars which permitted the detection of relatively small objects.

Two different kinds of frequencies need to be distinguished in the following discussion: RF (radio frequency) and PRF (pulse repetition frequency). The former is the frequency of the carrier wave, the rate of electromagnetic vibration of the radar signal. The inverse of RF is the wavelength of the signal. Thus a centimetric radar uses a higher-frequency carrier wave than a metric radar. In general, shorter wavelengths are considered desirable because they give greater accuracy of location, can locate smaller objects and require a smaller antenna, but shorter wavelengths had the disadvantage of requiring more complex electronics to develop the needed power at higher frequencies.

PRF is the measure of the number of pulses of radio energy that are transmitted by the radar in a given time period. (Radar is pulsed so that the time from transmission to reception can be measured and the range of the target established.) The inverse of PRF is PRI (pulse repetition interval). PRF controls the effective range of a radar, since the echo must be received before the next pulse is generated in order to establish unambiguously the range of the target. Thus smaller PRF theoretically gives longer range. There are practical limits, both in that power also controls the effective range of a radar and power falls off rapidly with distance, and in that a lower PRF generally leads to a lower signal-noise ratio and a higher chance of false readings.

The technical challenges facing the developers of submarine radars during the Second World War were immense. Radar transmitters, receivers and antennae had to be reduced in size to fit in or on the submarine. (The first operational radars filled entire laboratories.) Submarine radars also had to be made robust enough to survive the rigours of U-boat life. This meant having the ability to survive the jolts of depth-charge attacks as well as the corrosive mixture of sea salt and chlorine which made up the atmosphere within a U-boat. Finally, the antenna had to be strong enough to survive storms on the surface, water pressure of depths below 100 metres and the occasional shock wave of a nearby depth-charge.

The first naval radar developed by Germany robust enough to be installed in U-boats was the FuMO 29,[1] known as the GEMA set after its manufacturer (*Gesellschaft für Elektro-akustische und Mechanische Apparate*). The first experimental FuMO 29 installations were made on a pair of U-boats during the winter of 1938/9. The GEMA set was a reduced size version of the DT-Gerät or Seetakt which operated at a wavelength of 80cm with a PRF of 500. The antenna used in this initial experimental installation was a two by three metre mattress supporting between eight and twelve vertical dipoles. This was mounted in front of the tower, which was cut away in front to allow the antenna to be rotated through a 14° arc. These initial experiments were considered to be something less than successful. The antenna proved to be too bulky, and to effect adversely the underwater performance of the U-boat. The decision was made not to install the GEMA set in further U-boats at that time.

Interest in the GEMA set revived after the war began. As sets became available in limited quan-

▼ The double-row array of dipoles which made up the FuMO 29 GEMA antenna are seen on the tower of *U230*, a Type VIIC. The upper row was for reception and the lower for receiving the return signal. Since the antenna was fixed to the front of the tower, the beam was steered by electronic phase shifting. (MacPherson)

tities after 1940, they were installed in U-boats. Most FuMO 29 sets were installed in the larger Type IX boats, particularly those intended for operations in distant waters, since the GEMA set was seen primarily as a surface search radar. Only a limited number of Type VIIs received the FuMO 29. It had a range of approximately 7.5 kilometres against surface targets and 15 kilometres against aircraft at an altitude of 500 metres. It could give the bearing of the target with an accuracy of two to three degrees.

The antenna used in these installations was quite different from the experimental version. Two rows of eight dipoles were fixed permanently to the curved front face of the tower structure. The upper row was for reception, the lower for transmission. The array was electrically divided into two halves (each two rows of four dipoles), port and starboard, which were energized alternately, giving a crude form of phase shift that covered an arc of 20° across the bow. (Modern fixed-antenna phased array radars use the same basic principle.) In 1942, a new rotating antenna was introduced for the GEMA set. This mounted two rows of four dipoles on a wire mattress frame 1 by 1.5 metres. The 'figure 8' antenna associated with later radar detectors was often mounted on the back of the mattress. The antenna was mounted on the port side of the tower structure, where the rod antenna had formerly been located. When not in use, it retracted into a slot in the tower wall. With this antenna, the GEMA set was designated FuMO 30.

In practice, the GEMA set wasn't very popular with U-boat crews. FuMO 29 was being introduced to the fleet in some numbers at about the same time that the discovery was made of the radiation of the Metox radar detector and other electronic equipment carried by U-boats. The Germans believed that this radiation was the explanation for the increase in air attacks on U-boats without warning from the Metox.[2] Their own scientists maintained that radar at wave engths much shorter than the 80cm band of the GEMA set was a practical impossibility. To many U-boat crews, the idea of adding another electronic device, especially one specifically designed to radiate, seemed nonsensical.

▼ Another of the relatively few Type VIIs fitted with GEMA radar was *U83*, a Type VIIB, seen here transferring supplies at sea. The Olympic Rings in the tower insignia identify the graduating class of the Commanding Officer. (Albrecht)

The acceptance of the GEMA set by U-boat crews wasn't helped by the fact that it didn't work all that well. In its FuMO 29 form, it proved largely incapable of locating surface targets:

> 'We had a FuMO on the side, what we called the mattress. We used it in the Baltic, in the mist, to try to find the harbour entrance at Pillau. It didn't work. I mean, we had some sign on the oscilloscope, but I would never have dared to try bringing the boat in on just that. Out in the Atlantic, we found that it would show targets, but you'd probably see them with the naked eye long before they showed up on the scope.'[3]

Still, the GEMA set did prove useful as an aircraft locator, especially in its FuMO 30 form. This was especially true during the period when the Germans lacked a radar detector capable of sensing the British H2S radar.

> 'Our own radar set is an important and sure means of warning boats of approaching aircraft, especially if radar interception sets are out of order or it is suspected that the enemy has new means of location which cannot be detected. When the GEMA set was used against He 111 and Ju 88, the aircraft were clearly observed in numerous approaches:
> (a) at a flying height of 350 metres at 12km off
> (b) at a flying height of 100 metres at 7km off
>
> Low level aircraft were not reliably observed.'[4]

◀ **This view of the boats of ULD (*Ubootslehrdivision* – U-boat Training Division) Pillau shows four early Type VIIs in the back row. The rest of the boats are all Type IIs. The second and third boats from the left in the back row are fitted with FuMO 29. (Albrecht)**

The failings of the GEMA set were well known to BdU. Already in March 1942, the decision had been made to replace the GEMA set. In its place, BdU suggested the development of a navalized version of the Luftwaffe's FuG 200 *Hohentweil* (Owl) night fighter radar, then entering production. The *Hohentweil-U*, designated FuMO 61, operated at 54cm with a PRF of 50, giving about 30 per cent better resolution than the GEMA. Range against low-flying aircraft was between 15 and 20 kilometres with a bearing accuracy of one to two degrees. The antenna used was nearly identical with that of the FuMO 30. It was also a 1 by 1.5 metre mattress and it was mounted on the tower in the same manner. It differed in having four rows each with six dipoles on the face of the antenna.

The *Hohentweil* was introduced into the fleet in March 1944, the first two boats to be fitted with the new radar being *U311* and *U743*. *Early reports, such as that from U311*, indicated that FuMO 61 was highly effective in locating aircraft:

> 'With reference to the air attack on 12 March [in which *U311* tracked and then shot down an attacking Flying Fortress], *U311* reports: Radar excellent, aircraft located all the time from eight km to one km. Without radar, boat would have been surprised from astern.'[5]

The biggest problem with either standard radar was a general lack of reliability. BdU issued explicit orders for coping with the repeated breakdowns:

> 'The breakdown of radar apparatus is frequently due to bad maintenance. Therefore:
>
> As far as conditions allow, set is to be operated at least half an hour daily in order to test working order and dry out installation. In case of full operation not being feasible (on patrol for example), set to be switched on with lowered antenna, so as to prevent outward radiation. Outside installation to be examined separately with set switched off.'[6]

1. FuMO was a contraction of *Funkmessortungs Gerät* (radio location device).
2. In fact, the British were aware of the radiation of the Metox but never seriously considered using it to locate U-boats. Their radars did a much better job.
3. EvK and WB.
4. KTB, Serial Order No 7, 27 February 1944. The reason why low-level aircraft weren't reliably detected was the same reason why the surface search capabilities of the GEMA set were so poor. The antenna was so low that interference from the water was a major problem.
5. KTB, 16 March 1944.
6. KTB, 1 April 1944.

◀ **Later in the war, Type VIIs typically carried FuMO 30 GEMA or FuMO 61 *Hohentweil-U* equipment, as in this surrendered boat seen at Loch Eriboll after the war. The U-boat's CO leans against the housing for the retracted *Hohentweil* antenna. To make room on the port side of the tower for this, the rod antenna and the DF loop were combined. Note the rod extending out of the slot for the DF loop on the starboard side of the tower. (MacPherson)**

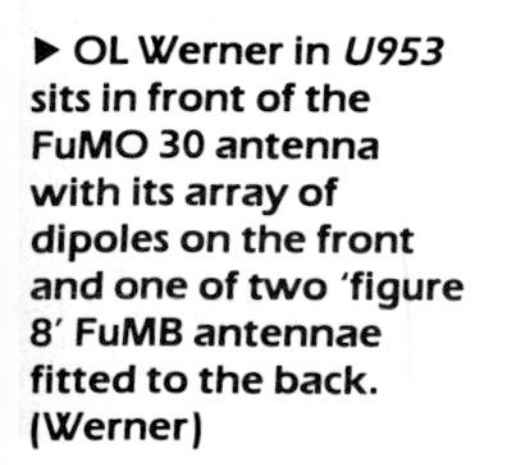

▶ **OL Werner in *U953* sits in front of the FuMO 30 antenna with its array of dipoles on the front and one of two 'figure 8' FuMB antennae fitted to the back. (Werner)**

Radar Detectors

Far more important than radar to the survival of a U-boat in an increasingly hostile environment was the ability to detect enemy radars in sufficient time to allow defensive or evasive action. A series of radar detectors was developed in an attempt to provide U-boats with warning of approaching radar-bearing aircraft in time to dive to safety.

The first encounters between U-boats and British radars came as no real surprise to the Germans. After all, they had had shipborne radar from the beginning of the war and they never doubted that the British would develop the same capability. Nevertheless, it was early 1942 before the presence of enemy radars became a serious enough threat that BdU felt he had to provide a remedy. The presence of surface escort radars was a nuisance but not much more, as long as the number of escorts remained low. It was the appearance of significant numbers of radar-equipped aircraft that finally alarmed BdU.

In fact, the British airborne radar, known as ASV Mk I, had been installed in aircraft since November 1940, but it didn't appear in large numbers until early 1942.[1] The ASV Mk I operated on the 1.4 metre band. Its effects became noticeable to the Germans for the first time in February 1942, when the first of several instances occurred of a U-boat attacking a small, apparently weakly defended, convoy in the Bay of Biscay and never being heard from again.[2] But several more months passed before the suspicion that the British were deploying radar-equipped aircraft seemed sufficiently proven to demand effective countermeasures.

> 'As there is no defence against Sunderlands and heavy bombers, Biscay has become the playground of English aircraft, where, according to GOC Atlantic AF, even the most ancient types of Sunderland can be used. As the English aircraft radar set is developed further, the boats will be more and more endangered, damage will be on a larger scale and the result will be total losses of boats.'[3]

Not until 26 August 1942 did BdU demand that all U-boats be equipped with radar detectors to warn of the approach of enemy aircraft.

The development of an effective means of detecting the ASV Mk I radar had begun months before this directive. In fact, the existence of a French-manufactured device capable of monitoring the 1.4 metre band was brought to BdU's attention as early as January 1942. The first FuMB 1 (*Funkmessbeobachter*) Metox R.600 radar detectors, named after the Paris-based firm which produced them, were experimentally fitted to operational U-boats in July 1942. The results of these initial installations were completely successful.

> '*U107* reports its experiences with radar interception gear: According to it, boat was located four times by day and twice by night. Dived for every location transmission and was not attacked the whole way. A very satisfactory result.'[4]

Based on results like these, the installation of the FuMB 1 in all boats was pushed forward as rapidly as possible. The only major problem with the Metox set was that no adequate antenna existed for immediate installation in Type VII U-boats. (A U-boat's pressure hull made the permanent installation of new sensors difficult. Finding room for the sensor's antenna on the tower was the least of the problems. Installing a new sensor involved making another hole in the pressure hull for the electrical cables, never a matter taken lightly.) The best that could be provided was an improvised antenna constructed out of wooden strips and two lengths of antenna cable. The wood was built up into a two-dimensional cross structure over which were strung the two antenna leads to form vertical and horizontal receivers. This antenna, known as the *Biskayakreuz* (Biscay cross), had to be made small enough to fit easily through the tower hatch since it was stored inside the boat and only brought to the tower when the boat surfaced. It was mounted in a bracket welded to the central periscope stanchion. The *Biskayakreuz* had to be rotated by hand to provide all-around coverage. In the process, a crude directional location capability was obtained. The cables from the antenna ran down through the tower hatch to the Metox receiver in the radio compartment.

The antenna cables proved to be one of the great weaknesses of the initial Metox installations. When the alarm was given, the first act was now to dismount the *Biskayakreuz* and toss it down the hatch before the lookouts headed down into the boat. At best this often resulted in a broken antenna since it would land at the bottom of the tower ladder followed by five or more sets of sea boots intent only on getting down the hatch as quickly as possible. This wasn't too feared an event since the flimsy antenna was as easily repaired as it was broken. More frightening was the real possibility that the antenna cables might get caught on the tower structure and prevent the proper closure of the tower hatch. By the time the hatch was closed the boat was already committed to the dive. If it was discovered then that the antenna cables were caught in the hatchway, it was too late to prevent the boat from submerging. Numerous stories are told by survivors of boats being hurriedly resurfaced with water pouring through a partially open tower

▼In *U230* the *Biskayakreuz* was sited on the periscope stanchion which ran down the centre of the bridge. (Werner)

▶ The *Obersteuermann* in a Type VII U-boat takes a sighting of the sun. In the upper right-hand corner can just be seen part of the *Biskayakreuz* antenna associated with the FuMB 1 Metox set. (Ahme via Schmidt)

hatch, often directly in the path of an approaching aircraft, in order to disentangle the Metox cable. It is impossible to determine how many boats didn't survive the experience.

The Metox set was connected to the boat's loudspeaker system so that the interception of a radar signal sounded an audible alert throughout the boat. The pitch of the alert tone was a direct function of the PRF of the radar. The higher the PRF, the higher the audible alert tone. In similar fashion, the volume of the alarm was a function of the strength of the received signal. This, in turn, was dependent on the orientation of the antenna and the distance of the transmitter. By rotating the antenna, an experienced *Funker* could estimate the bearing and range of the attacker.

The direct relationship between PRF and alert tone pitch was the cause of some problems. Some of the PRFs used by the ASV Mk I translated into sound frequencies beyond the range of human hearing. Only by use of a 'magic eye' detector, an indicator which lit up whenever a signal was intercepted,[5] was this problem partly resolved. Even this wasn't a perfect solution, since the degree to which the 'magic eye' lit up was dependent on signal strength. Aircraft on certain bearings, in relation to the antenna, could be quite close and barely light the 'magic eye'. The problem was only resolved by the introduction of a cathode ray tube oscilloscope (B-Rohr) which showed both the amplitude and PRF of all intercepts visually as perturbations of a line drawn across the screen.[6]

The Metox set covered a broad range of wavelengths, all the way from 1.3 to 2.6 metres. The scanning of these frequencies was done manually by turning a dial on the face of the Metox box. This put a considerable burden on the radio watch, which had constantly to search the range of wavelengths in order to cover all possible threats.[7]

The success of the Metox set was such that a second manufacturer, Grandin, also began producing the FuMB 1. Another French manufacturer, Sadir, joined the programme, beginning production of a slightly modified version of the Metox called R.87, designated FuMB 2 by the Germans. A few examples of another early radar detector, the FuMB 3 Samoa,[8] manufactured by Rohde & Schwarz of Munich, were also used in U-boats, though this set was mainly intended for surface ships.

The introduction of the Metox and its immediate derivatives effectively neutralized the threat of the ASV Mk I radar. At first there weren't enough Metox sets to go round. Boats leaving port with Metox were given the task of providing radar intercept escort for boats not yet fitted with the device.[9] Even after enough Metox sets were available to equip all boats leaving port, there was still the problem of those boats that had left on patrol months before and were now returning through the Bay of Biscay without the benefits of Metox protection. In December, BdU worked out a system of at sea transfer of Metox sets,[10] some boats eventually leaving port with multiple sets.

> '*U176* has been ordered to take over two Metox sets from *U118* and deliver them to *U571* and *U620* on her return passage.'[11]

By the end of 1942, the presence of Metox sets permitted a rapid recovery in the rate of sinkings by U-boats. The number of RAF patrol aircraft was still low enough that diving to avoid air attack was a viable tactic which allowed boats enough time on the surface to attack convoys with effect. This happy state, wasn't to last long. Already in mid-May 1943, BdU was making note of a steady increase in air attacks without warning from the Metox.[12] Not that this should have come as a surprise to the Germans. An RAF Stirling had been shot down over Rotterdam in February 1943. In the wreckage of that aircraft, the Germans had found a damaged black box marked 'Experimental 6'. Upon investigation, it proved to be a prototype of a new ASV radar, the Mk III, which operated at 9.7cm. This radar, known by its code-name H2S, was first introduced in its operational form to the Wellingtons of 172 Squadron in March 1943.

Despite the fact that the BdU knew of the existence of the new ASV Mk III,[13] the Germans nevertheless fell prey to a most extraordinary delusion in an attempt to explain the rash of undetected attacks. The Germans had previously noted that the Metox and Grandin receivers were prone to overheating.[14] Experiments now conducted by Gruppe West showed that the FuMB 1 radiated.

> 'Gruppe West reports, as a result of experiments by Radar Instruction and Experimental Troops, that the Metox radar interceptor produces a radiation of its own, which can be detected by aircraft at the following distances:
>
> 23 km at an altitude of 500 metres
> 33 km at an altitude of 1000 metres
> 50 km at an altitude of 2000 metres
>
> Results exceed considerably the maximum range of the Metox. These results are disturbing in connection with numerous unexplained losses throughout the last weeks. Immediate examination of the situation ... shows the following:
> (1) It appears possible that the enemy utilizes the Metox radiation in order to approach the target, without putting radio location into operation ... The danger of the enemy using the Metox radiation exists above all when the receiver (for example when expecting location or the appearance of further location) remains fixed on a certain tuning and so radiates on a constant frequency. The danger appears to be less if the tuning of the receiver is continually changed (Searching Watch).[15]

Resulting in the following order on 13 August 1943: Radio message at 2315 on all U-boat waves:

> 'The suspicion that the enemy makes use of Metox radiation is further confirmed. Use of Metox and Grandin receivers is now forbidden in all sea areas, as it is thought that the enemy makes use of the receiver radiation to approach the U-boat from a great distance without himself using location gear. All previous orders to the contrary are cancelled.'[16]

The Germans scrambled to find a substitute for the FuMB 1 that didn't radiate and that covered the shorter wavelength of the ASV Mk III. A number of promising developments that were already in the works were rushed to completion. The first of these ready for deployment was the FuMB 9 Zypern, known more often as the Wanz G1 (short for *Wellenanzeiger* – wave indicator) or Hagenuk after its manufacturer. The Wanz G1 was rushed into production in August 1943. The Wanz set covered a somewhat narrower band than the Metox that it replaced, being sensitive between 1.3 and 1.9 metres. More importantly, it

▶ **A conference of U-boat COs was held on the bridge of *U668*, Norway, 17 April 1945. Note the *Runddipol* antenna normally associated with the FuMB 9 Wanz behind the lookout on the left. (via Rumpf)**

introduced automatic frequency search, covering the entire range 24 times a second, stopping whenever a contact was found. Fine tuning was done with B-Rohr and headset.

The Wanz G1 lacked any direction-finding capability because it was used with a new permanent antenna, the *Runddipol* (round dipole). This was a wire mesh frame, a short vertically-oriented cylinder, approximately 20cm in diameter and about 10cm in height. Two rod antennae were fitted to the upper edge of the cylindrical antenna frame, extending upward. Early experience with the Wanz G1 was positive:

> 'While passing through Biscay it is most important that boats remain undetected. They are to surface solely at night and only when the batteries need recharging. Since Hagenuk gear was introduced on our boats, enemy planes often search feverishly for them.'[17]

> The number of planes operating has increased. Despite this, hardly a U-boat has been spotted or attacked since Wanz gear was installed in the place of the Metox. Thus the anti-submarine defence situation has completely changed.'[18]

Despite this success, or perhaps because of it, the major problem with the use of radar detectors came to BdU's attention at this time. Radar detectors were introduced in order to allow U-boats to submerge in time to avoid attack, particularly from the air. This, however, tended to lend official sanction to a defensive frame of mind which BdU felt compelled to counter:

> 'Use of the Hagenuk Wave Indicator should not affect the tactics of boats near the convoy . . . This apparatus is only a means of insuring against surprise attacks near the convoy, but must not induce boats to submerge if the enemy is not in sight.'[19]

The development of the Wanz G1 set was so rushed that it wasn't until it was already in service that it was discovered that this set also radiated. On 5 November 1943, BdU ordered that use of the Wanz G1 be discontinued and that its replacement by the nearly identical, but non-radiating, Wanz G2 take place as soon as possible. As a temporary substitute, a very simple new radar detector, the FuMB 10 Borkum, was rushed out to the fleet. The Borkum set consisted of just the additional circuitry necessary to turn the standard Radione R1 or R2 receiver into a radar detector. The Borkum set plugged into the gramophone jack of the Radione. Borkum covered the band of wavelengths from 3.3 to 0.8 metres. The set was so simple that it provided no tuning over this band, simply covering all bands simultaneously. This made for simple operation, but meant that the *Funker* would be unable to identify what type of radar was being detected. No visual presentation of contacts was provided by the Borkum, loudspeaker presentation being the only means of presenting a contact.

Even had the Wanz G1 set not been found to radiate, enthusiasm for it was bound to wane since it didn't provide coverage of the 9.7cm wavelength of the ASV Mk III radar. This gap was filled by the introduction of the FuMB 7 Naxos (also known as Timor). Naxos provided coverage of just the high-frequency end of the spectrum, in a band between 8 and 12cm wavelengths. Thus it had to be employed in conjunction with the Borkum and/or Wanz sets. Like Borkum, it was composed of just those circuits needed to tune in to the covered wavelengths. Unlike the Borkum, it provided visual presentation of contacts with a B-Rohr. The first Naxos sets were fitted to operational U-boats at the same time as the Borkum, in early November 1943.[20]

Naxos was used with the *Runddipol* antenna and also, quite frequently, with an improvised antenna intended to provide some direction-finding of the intercept. This was a narrow rectangular frame formed into a parabolic section and mounted vertically on a wooden pole. It also had a metal rod about 9cm long which extended out from the pole along the axis of the parabola.[21] Like the *Biskayakreuz*, this antenna was intended only as a stopgap until a permanent installation could be devised. Until then, like the Biskayakreuz, it had to be rotated by hand and, when the boat dived, dismounted and taken inside the pressure hull.

Individually, the Borkum, Wanz G2 (introduced in late November 1943) and Naxos sets were well received by the fleet. In combination they represented, for the first time, full and safe coverage of the entire radar spectrum.

'The installation of detector-receivers Naxos and Borkum (as well as Wanz G2) guaranteed

◄ **The crew of *U-981* lines up on the deck of *U309* after having been rescued on 12 August 1944. Just barely visible on the tower of *U309* is a makeshift Naxos antenna of the type that, when rotated by hand, would give bearing data on the intercepted radar.**

radio interception without the disadvantage of radiation over all hitherto essential wavebands. A watch on wider wavebands was kept by specially equipped boats.'[22]

This last reference was to a number of U-boats fitted with a set of five search receivers covering all bands between 5cm and 3.2 metres. These field watch boats carried a special electronics technician together with its regular radio crew.

The fortuitous combination of Borkum, Wanz G2 and Naxos was replaced during the spring of 1944 by the intentional combination of FuMB 24 *Fliege* (Fly) and FuMB 25 *Mücke* (Gnat). The *Fliege* was first installed in April 1944, together with a permanently mounted rotating antenna similar in shape to the Naxos antenna. This antenna was either mounted inside the DF loop or on its own mast on the tower side. It provided coverage of the 8 to 20cm wavelength band. It was a sensitive receiver capable of detecting an ASV radar at an altitude of 1,000 metres at a distance of 60 kilometres. The first boats reporting on the use of *Fliege* were highly enthusiastic, in part because the rotating antenna allowed bearing data on interceptions with an accuracy of approximately 90°.[23] *Fliege* was often used alone. When it was used in combination with the *Mücke*, which covered the very high-frequency 2 to 4cm band used by the new US Navy AN/APS-4 radar, the combined system was known as the FuMB 26 Tunis. *Mücke* used a conical antenna which was generally mounted just above, and pointing in the opposite direction to the *Fliege* antenna, either within the DF loop or on the separate mast.

The Tunis combination was the last generally deployed radar interception set used by Type VII U-boats. One more system was developed and deployed on a few boats. This was the combination of the FuMB 29 Bali (or Palau) and FuMB 35 Athos, which together were known as FuMB 37 Leros. Ultimately, however, any radar detector was an admission of defeat. As long as the only survival tactic on the approach of an enemy aircraft was to dive, it was only a matter of time before the RAF and US Navy put so many aircraft over the Atlantic that no U-boat could stay on the surface for more than a few minutes.

◄ *U977*, seen after her internment at La Plata, Argentina. Three masts appear to project above the boat's tower. On the right is the rod antenna attached above the DF loop. The middle mast holds the antennae associated with the FuMB 26 Tunis. These were the individual antennae for the FuMB 24 *Fliege* (the aft-facing parabolic antenna) and FuMB 25 *Mücke* (the forward-facing cone). The mast on the left looks like nothing associated with U-boat electronics. It probably belongs to a boat moored behind the U-boat. (Albrecht)

1. NavRad, p 195. The ASV set was first tested in 1940. The first surface escort radar, the Type 286, was developed from the ASV Mk I.
2. KTB, 6 February 1942. 'At 1305 *U82* reported convoy (20 steamers) on southerly course in BE 7429 ... the position compared with previous experiences and the rhythm of the Gibraltar convoys show that it could not be one of these ... Only corvettes had been observed as escort. It was probably a very valuable southbound convoy that was obviously weakly defended and worth attacking by the U-boats intended for the West.'
   KTB, 7 February 1942. 'Despite repeated requests, *U82* has not reported.'
   KTB, 8 February 1942. 'It must be assumed that *U82* was destroyed in attacking convoy.'
   KTB, 26 March 1942. *U587* heard a fast convoy in BE 1970 on course 200 degrees and came in sight of same at 0800 in BE 4612. Course South, speed 13 knots.'
   KTB, 27 March 1942. '*U587* was asked for position report during night. No reply.'
   KTB, 31 March 1942. 'As *U587* has not yet reported, and is overdue in port, boat must be reckoned as lost.'
   KTB, 14 April 1942. '*U252* sighted convoy of 5–10 vessels in BE 5584, 2 escort vessels observed; course South, speed 10 knots. Boat was given freedom of action for attack if conditions are favourable and is to move off before first light.'
   KTB, 15 April 1942. '*U252* has been ordered to make a situation report, has not replied. It is feared that the boat may be lost at the convoy in BE 55. Circumstances here were similar to those in the loss of *U82*; the same sea area, an S-bound convoy with apparently weak escort, favourable weather conditions (new moon) ... I think it possible that, in this area, through which a stream of Westbound U-boats passes, the English sail a dummy convoy of special anti-S/M vessels.' In fact all three convoys were regularly scheduled Gibraltar convoys and the U-boats were lost to the aggressive defence of the convoys' escorts. None was lost to aircraft attack.
3. KTB, 11 June 1942.
4. KTB, 20 August 1942.
5. KTB, 5 March 1943. The magic eye was part of the Telefunken Ela-10.12 all-wave receiver which was removed for use on the Metox. *U185* reported the successful use of the magic eye on 7 April 1943.
6. Ibid.
7. Ibid.
8. The code-name for this set is sometimes given as 'Samos'. This is every bit as likely as 'Samoa'. The Germans used island names as code-names for their FuMB. They used the names of both Mediterranean islands (e.g.: Naxos, Leros) and Pacific islands (e.g.: Bali, Palau, Timor).
9. KTB, 20 October 1942. '*U609* took over radar intercept escort for *U254*.' References like this continued almost daily until mid-November 1942, when the number of Metox sets available was adequate to equip all boats leaving port.
10. KTB, 22 December 1942.
11. KTB, 8 February 1943.
12. KTB, 15 May 1943.
13. KTB, 5 March 1943. 'The enemy is working on carrier frequencies outside the frequency range of present FuMB receivers. The shooting down, over Holland, of an enemy aircraft apparently carrying an apparatus with a frequency of 9.7cm is the only indication at present of this possibility. It is possible that the enemy is attempting to escape from the frequency range of our FuMB, which indicates the knowledge of this and the introduction of countermeasures.'
14. Ibid.
15. KTB, 31 July 1943.
16. KTB, 14 August 1943. Part of a section entitled 'Results of further investigation into the question of Metox radiation.'
17. KTB, 3 September 1943.
18. KTB, 9 September 1943.
19. KTB, 18 September 1943.
20. KTB, 8 November 1943.
21. According to WB, this antenna was known as the 'Naxos Finger'.
22. KTB, 13 November 1943.
23. KTB, 29 April 1944. *U385* reported success with *Fliege*.
    KTB, 2 May 1944. *U473* reported good directional capability of *Fliege*, good enough to allow the aiming of Flak guns. See also KTB, 23 June 1944, Standing Order No. 27.

Hydrophones

Type VII U-boats carried a variety of hydrophonic devices that allowed the location and occasionally the identification of noise sources in the surrounding waters. The basic passive sound location device carried by all Type VII U-boats was the GHG (*Gruppenhorchgerät* – group listening apparatus). This was a cluster of 11 (later 24) circular sound-receiver diaphragms on each side, arranged around the forward dive planes in a semi-circular pattern, open at the bottom. In early-war boats the diaphragms were mounted singly in holes cut in the external hull. As the pace of production increased, they were mounted in pairs (hence the increase in number) set into narrow metal fittings that were welded to the surface of the hull. These individual sound-receivers were linked electrically to a pulse-timer located in the sound room that allowed the crude directional location of sound sources, based on the time difference of arrival of sound impulses. Not only was the quality of direction-finding produced by the GHG moderate at best, but it was very dependent on the direction of the noise source. Because the diaphragms were located on the sides of the bow, they were most effective at locating sounds that were nearly broadside to the U-boat. The farther forward or aft the source, the less accurate the direction-finding produced by the GHG.

Early in the war most Type VIIs were fitted with a rotating hydrophone array intended to overcome the weaknesses of the GHG in sound location. This apparatus, the KDB (*Kristalldrehbasis Gerät*), was a T-shaped form mounted on the forward deckcasing. Within the upper cross-bar of the T were six sound-receivers of the same type used in the GHG. As the KDB was rotated, the operator would be able to determine the direction

◀ *U331*, a Type VIIC, comes into port at La Spezia. The KDB rotating hydrophone array can be seen on the forward deckcasing. (via MacPherson)

▼ The crew of *U89*, a Type VIIC, lines up on deck as the boat pulls into port at the end of a mission. The KDB is visible on the foredeck just aft of the retractable bollards.

from which a sound was coming (or its reciprocal) by listening to the volume of sound through a headset. The bearings obtained from the KDB were far more accurate than was possible with the GHG, particularly towards the bow or stern. However, these bearings could be obtained only when the boat was moving at slow speed. This plus the vulnerability of the KDB, which was easily put out of commission by depth-charging or even deep diving, meant that the use of this device gradually diminished after 1939.

A small number of very late Type VII U-boats carried a sophisticated passive sonar array known as *Balkon Gerät* (balcony device). This was a redesigned GHG in which the sound-receivers were mounted on the outer edge of a circular platform (or balcony) which was faired into the lower bow of the boat. The array of 24 receivers, each with two diaphragms, was able to cover the entire underwater 'horizon' around the boat except for a 60° arc directly aft. Significantly more sophisticated electronics allowed the bearing of sound sources to be determined with considerable accuracy.

Active Sonar

The original inspiration for the evolution of the Type VIIB into the VIIC was to make room for an active sonar system that would allow U-boats to operate effectively in minefields. During the First World War, the British had successfully employed a network of mine barrages to help defeat the German Navy. The Kaiser's U-boats were systematically bottled up by the ever thicker layers of minefields laid across their only access routes to the Atlantic. Minefields laid just off the Flemish port of Zeebrugge in mid-1918 effectively neutralized the Flanders Flotilla which was based there. With this history to look back upon and with no way of foreseeing the swift victory over France that would bestow open access to the Atlantic, the Germans put considerable energy into the development of measures that would give their U-boats better survival odds in a similar environment.

Underwater detection devices in Type VIIC

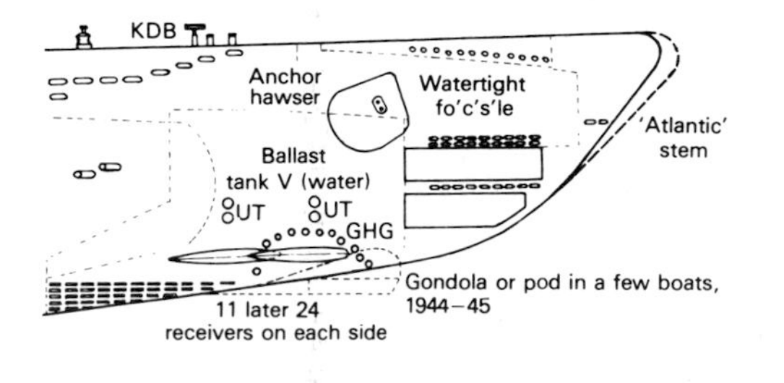

The device that was to provide this active sound location capability was the S-Gerät. The shaft for the sound-generator extended below the control room to the keel. This device generated sound impulses at 15kHz of 20msec duration. In theory it was capable of detecting large objects at a range of 5 to 10 kilometres. Only one S-Gerät was ever actually installed, in *U43*, a Type IXA boat. No S-Geräte were installed in Type VIICs.

Two factors led to the decision not to install the S-Gerät. First, minefields never played an important part in the tactical or strategic disposition of U-boats. At the very beginning of the war, before the dramatic defeat of France opened up the Atlantic, there was considerable fear of a new mine blockade and there was the suspicion that the British were mining the Channel. For several months, BdU re-routed all boats headed for the Atlantic around the north of Scotland.[1] He bitterly bemoaned the loss of time on patrol caused by this wasteful detour. But before this threat seriously affected German plans, the French ports became available and the problem academic.

The more important reason why the S-Gerät was never installed was the U-boatman's traditional reluctance to do anything that would unnecessarily give away his presence. If the S-Gerät could get a usable return signal from 5 or 10 kilometres, then, logically, a listener at twice that distance could hear the S-Gerät. It was much better, in the universal opinion of U-boatmen, to depend on one's own listening capabilities and leave the active sound location to the enemy. (Interestingly, this same discussion reappears regularly in modern naval periodicals. There are many who debate the wisdom of the reliance of modern submarines on active sonar.)

Underwater Telephony

All Type VII U-boats were equipped with a device that allowed the intercommunication between submerged U-boats. The UT (*Unterwasser Telegraphie*) apparatus consisted of a two pairs of diaphragms on each side, one for transmission and the other for receipt of sound-waves, located just aft of the GHG installation low on the bow. The electronics associated with the UT system were located in the sound room. The UT operated at 3.5 kHz and had a range of approximately 10 nautical miles. It was rarely used operationally, both because the sound it emitted could be picked up by the sonar carried by escorts and because the opportunity to use it seldom occurred.

1. KTB, 4 December 1939. 'Letters from captured members of her crew indicate that *U40* struck a mine. This is the first proof of mines in the Channel . . . I must now give up this route into the Atlantic; there must not be losses on passage.'

Infra-red Sensors

In their search to identify the sensor technologies used by the British to locate U-boats in the open ocean, the Germans sometimes grasped at slim evidence. One such narrow thread was the reported use of red searchlights by convoy escorts in March 1943:

> 'Two boats were forced to submerge by destroyers, one boat reported being searched for by an escort vessel with a red searchlight.[1]
>
> One boat was pursued by a U-boat chaser group, and reported the enemy was working with red and white searchlights.[2]
>
> Two boats reported that the enemy was using red searchlights as a defence measure also variously observed to have taken place in the case of previous convoys. It does not appear from the boats' messages that the enemy has had any success as a result of this method.'[3]

These vague reports were taken as evidence that the British had introduced an Infra-red (IR) detection system that allowed for the location of targets at night after illumination with a red searchlight.

> 'Location by enemy destroyers and aircraft by means of IR rays may be considered certain in view of reports by the boats. These were observed up to now without image converter and, therefore, concern only IR rays with visible proportion of light. It is not yet known to what extent IR rays are used without visible proportion of light but this possibility must be considered now or later.'[4]

The Germans responded to the perceived use of IR detection techniques by the British with a high-priority effort to develop their own sensors using light-waves in these long wavelengths. They discovered that active IR illumination, as would be done with red searchlights, was an inefficient use of the technology. Rather, passive IR detection techniques, picking up the non-visible IR radiation from any object hotter than the surrounding ambient temperature, seemed to hold the greatest promise.

The first practical result of this research was an IR detection and signalling device known as *Seehund* (seadog). This system was built around a telescopic IR sensor which received light-waves in the IR range that registered on a readout located in the radio shack. The sensor element was large and hard to handle, making it very unpopular with the bridge watch on boats that carried it. One veteran recalled:

> 'In *U307*, we had a device you had to point like a gun, but it was such a cumbersome thing and had a cable down through the hatchway, so we never used it. It was like one half of a binocular, only larger and with a gun handle, about 60cm long. You could directly locate any heat emissions.'[5]

Another recalled:

> 'We had one like that. We tried it on other boats at home and it worked, but it was so unwieldy, there was no chance out on the high seas to use it.'[6]

The *Seehund* system also included an IR lamp which could be mounted on the bridge so that another boat could use the IR detector for elementary signalling or as a formation light for station-keeping. There is no evidence that the system was ever used in this way.

Another system, that never got beyond the experimental stage, involved a sensor intended to search the horizon and sky continually for heat sources such as ships or aircraft. Known as Flamingo, the system was tested in June 1944 in *U712*:

> 'Later, in the Baltic, we were called on to assist with some experiments. That was when they brought out the Flamingo. It registered IR light. It was a clear bubble, set on a pipe about 50cm high, mounted on the conning tower. The dial indicator down in the wireless room let us see the exhaust from any boats that passed. It ticked over the loudspeaker every time a target came near.'[7]

The irony was that this research, while it resulted in no truly useful detectors, put Germany far in the vanguard of IR sensor development. The British deny ever using red searchlights on convoy escorts and are known to have pursued no serious research into, much less development of, IR detection devices.

1. KTB, 6 March 1943.
2. KTB, 9 March 1943.
3. KTB, 10 March 1943.
4. KTB, 31 May 1943. This is part of an extensive report entitled 'Effects of Radar used by Enemy Forces on U-boat Warfare & Necessary Countermeasures' dated 21 May 1943.
5. WB.
6. EvK.
7. EvK.

Part Five: Countermeasures

As the sophistication of Allied sensor systems increased during the course of the war, the Kriegsmarine was forced to provide its U-boats with countermeasures. These included both those intended to nullify the Allied sensors by reducing the intensity of the return signal (passive countermeasures) and those intended to decoy the sensors by creating false returns (active countermeasures). The Germans developed both passive and active countermeasures against the two primary sensors used by the enemy to detect U-boats: radar and sonar.

Other 'unofficial' countermeasures were occasionally employed by U-boats under attack. The most common was to eject a number of items, including rubbish, oily rags, fragments of wooden fittings, etc., from a torpedo tube to simulate the flotsam left by a sinking U-boat. This was never officially sanctioned because of the risk of damage to the torpedo tube. There is no way of telling whether any pursuers were ever fooled by the ruse.

Anti-Radar Coatings

The Germans reacted strongly to the threat of Allied radars, particularly the airborne radars that so effectively removed the invisibility on which Type VII U-boats depended for their success. The most immediate reaction was the development of radar detectors that would alert a U-boat to the presence of an enemy radar. But this was a purely defensive measure, allowing U-boats to submerge in time and thus survive, but not allowing them to remain on the offensive. To this end, the Germans began active development of anti-radar coatings, designed to absorb enough radar emission to render the U-boat effectively invisible. (The physics of radar are such that a reduction in power of the returned signal by even a small amount can seriously affect the ability of a radar to distinguish a positive return from background noise. A small reduction in returned power translates into a larger reduction in the range at which a target can be detected.) The project began in June 1943 under the code-name *Schornsteinfeger* (chimney-sweep).

While the ideal of complete radar invisibility was never achieved, the Germans did produce and deploy two materials that did significantly reduce the radar signature of a U-boat. The impetus to develop these anti-radar coatings seemed to wane briefly as the introduction of the snorkel in early 1944 allowed U-boats to operate permanently submerged, out of reach of the enemy's airborne radars. However, the H2S radar had resolution sufficient to pick out a snorkel head from among the waves.[1] The experience of early snorkel boats showed that some means of hiding from enemy radar was still needed.[2]

The simpler of the two anti-radar coatings was a material known as *Tarnmatte* (camouflage mat) developed by a Professor Wesch of the *Weltpost-institut* in Heidelberg. *Tarnmatte* was developed to be specifically effective at the 9.7cm wave-length of the H2S radar used by the RAF from 1944 on. It consisted of 2cm-thick sheets of synthetic rubber (*Buna*) with iron oxide powder content. The frequency of radiation which this material absorbed was a direct function of its thickness, requiring critical manufacturing tolerances. Because it was a flexible material and therefore able to cover complex shapes, *Tarnmatte* was adopted exclusively to cover the *Kugel-schwimmer*-type snorkels introduced in 1944.

IG Farben developed an alternative material, known only as the IG-Jaumann Absorber, which had superior absorption characteristics compared to *Tarnmatte* but was much harder with which to work. The IG-Jaumann Absorber was composed of seven layers of thin conductive material separated by layers of a di-electric (non-conductive) material ranging in thickness from 7mm to 9mm. The resulting sheet was a rigid material about 8cm thick. The conductive material was a paper or plastic sheet impregnated with varying amounts of carbon black. The di-electric was a rigid synthetic called Igelit, a polyvinylchloride foam that was approximately 70 per cent air by volume. The amount of carbon in the conductive layers varied in steps from 17 to 41 per cent.

The varying conductivity of the paper layers allowed the IG-Jaumann Absorber to absorb radiation of wavelengths between 2 and 50cm. The radiation absorbed by the paper layers was turned into heat which dissipated into the Igelit layers. It was able to reduce radar reflectance from a snorkel head to between 15 and 30 per cent of that of an untreated snorkel. Because the IG-Jaumann Absorber was rigid, its use was limited to simple surfaces. It was produced by the IG Farben plant at Neustadt in flat sheets and cylindrical sections of varying diameter. Therefore its application was limited to the *Ringschwimmer* snorkel head. The superior performance of the IG-Jaumann Absorber material was part of the impetus behind the late-war decision to standardize on the *Ringschwimmer.*

(It is interesting to note that, after lying dormant for almost 40 years, interest in anti-radar coatings resurfaced in the 1980s. In reaction to the density of modern air-defence environments, aircraft designers have been looking for ways to reduce, or possibly even eliminate, the radar signature of attack aircraft. The whole package of technologies used to reduce aircraft detectability is known today as stealth technology and includes IR signature reduction as well. A major component of stealth technology, at least as has been seen demonstrated on the F-117 attack aircraft and B-2 bomber, is the use of rigid radar absorption panels. No details are known of the composition of these panels, so there is no way of knowing if they are in any way descendents of the IG-Jaumann Absorber.)

1. KTB, 10 September 44. Experiments with the captured H2S (Rotterdam Gerät) radar showed that a snorkel protruding 50cm above the surface gave about 30 per cent the return of a surfaced U-boat and that one raised two or more metres above the surface had 60–70 per cent the radar visibility of a surfaced boat. The KTB's comment: 'It would be better to surface than this.'
2. KTB, 13 June 1944. *U275* reported it had put into St. Peter Port, Guernsey, because its batteries were completely drained. In attempting to attack the Normandy invasion fleet, it had penetrated the Channel but had found that in that heavily patrolled area, its snorkel was typically spotted within ten minutes of being raised.

Anti-Radar Decoys

The Germans developed two active decoy systems in an attempt to counter Allied radars, particularly airborne radars. Unlike the anti-radar coating just described, these didn't try to render a U-boat invisible to radar, rather they attempted to create multiple false returns that would confuse the attacker as to the location of the real target. These two decoys used very similar technology to create the false radar echoes. The differences between them reflected differences in how that technology was to be tactically exploited.

Inevitably, both decoy systems failed in their primary aim of allowing U-boats to continue to operate on the surface in an environment dominated by aircraft. Both systems succeeded, in the short term, in sowing confusion. Numerous instances were recorded of RAF aircraft chasing false echoes. Gradually, the majority of aircraft radar operators learned to distinguish most of the time between the decoys and real returns, due to their different characteristics of movement. Still, the decoys remained effective until mid-1944, when the sheer number of aircraft deployed by the RAF overwhelmed any possible decoy system and the U-boats were finally forced to remain submerged in order to survive.

Aphrodite

The Aphrodite system created false radar echoes by suspending strips of aluminum foil from a hydrogen-filled balloon. The balloon was between 70 and 90cm in diameter when inflated. It floated above the water, attached to a sheet anchor which kept it from sailing away on the wind. The balloon was tethered by a wire rope approximately 50 metres in length. Three aluminium foil strips, each four metres long and spaced at 8-metre intervals along the wire, caused the actual reflections.[1]

Decoys to be launched were brought on deck uninflated and filled from one or two hydrogen cylinders mounted alongside the tower structure. Then, they were launched by simply throwing the anchor overboard. This could be accomplished without undue difficulty in winds up to 25 knots. Once launched, the balloon would remain inflated from two to eight hours. The sheet anchor would limit the windward movement of the decoy to about half the wind speed. Because of the relatively high visibility of the balloon, Aphrodites were intended primarily for use at night or in bad weather.

The use of the Aphrodite decoy was mainly defensive. It was intended that the boat, when able to detect enemy radar emissions, would launch a decoy and submerge, turning to windward. Even before the decoys were deployed, however, it was clear that they could be used to aid the U-boat offensive as well.

> 'The use of the radar decoy device Aphrodite is also most strongly recommended. It gives one boat the opportunity of dissembling a whole group, for instance by letting

several Aphrodites drift past the convoy at night and so make a gap in the escort before it attacks. Or if the boat wishes to attack from a certain quarter and the escort there is too strong, it can precede its attack by a group of scattered decoys so that the escort vessels will occupy themselves with these and thus make things easier for the boat.'[2]

Preparing boats for the use of Aphrodite was straightforward, and the first use of the decoys followed soon after their operational deployment in September 1943.

> 'A submarine operating in the Mediterranean released an Aphrodite off the coast of North Africa, and observed that the place where it was released was illuminated 30 minutes later by shore searchlights. This is probably the first known example of the successful use of Aphrodite.'[3]

And again, in a message sent to all boats:

> 'Two submarines have again used Aphrodite with great success.
>
> (1) Boat was approached by search group, started an Aphrodite and cut across previous course, search group passed astern. One destroyer approached the boat. Boat started Aphrodite, turned away, destroyer passed astern. Searchlights were turned in direction of Aphrodite. Another destroyer was not taken in by the Aphrodite but kept following the submarine, which was proceeding at full speed. It is possible that the destroyer was listening to the boat and thus distinguished it from the Aphrodite.
>
> (2) When cruising in the Bay of Biscay, submarine kept starting Aphrodites during the period when air patrolling was at its strongest. One plane attacked Aphrodite with searchlight and aircraft armament at a distance of 2,000–3,000 metres without picking up the boat.'[4]

The doctrine for employment of Aphrodite was relatively simple. Most boats would simply try to fill the air with as many balloons as possible, hoping that the resulting confusion of radar returns would mask the real boat:

> 'You would have many, many balloons in the air with foil. We had the balloons and a flask on the side of the conning tower, and would fill them and let them go. They were particularly useful if you could then dive and get away. We used them quite a bit in the Bay of Biscay.'[5]

This practice of filling the air with Aphrodite balloons, in fact, proved to be a weakness, leading to orders to be more prudent in the dispersal of the balloons:

> 'Prisoners' statements indicate that the enemy may recognize Aphrodite as a decoy from the appearance of several echoes. Therefore, avoid crowding, start the decoys at greater intervals.'[6]

If Aphrodite had a practical disadvantage, it was that the balloons were notoriously difficult to handle in rough or windy weather. Instances were recorded of the balloons getting caught on the Flak guns or *Wintergarten* railing, but this problem certainly seems not to have dampened the Germans' enthusiasm for the device. As the number and experience of RAF patrol aircraft continued to increase throughout early 1944, however, the major weakness of the Aphrodite system emerged: the fact that a U-boat had to be surfaced in order to use it. Since Aphrodite was a short-term decoy, it could only be practically launched when in the confirmed presence of enemy forces, by which time there often simply wasn't time to deploy the decoy. Further, when the number of enemy air and surface patrols, particularly in the Bay of Biscay, had risen to the point where virtually every U-boat was found by radar within minutes of surfacing, the use of Aphrodite became self-defeating. Instead of one radar echo, a U-boat and its just launched decoys became a cluster of closely spaced radar echoes which simply attracted enemy attention all the faster. Aphrodite simply couldn't succeed in such a densely patrolled environment. Perhaps what was needed was a permanent decoy, one that could be on the surface already, before the U-boat emerged.

Thetis

As soon as a permanent decoy was available, the order went out for its full-scale deployment:

> 'FdU West has been ordered to lay Thetis buoys type 2c in the Bay of Biscay as quickly as possible. These buoys have the same location echo as a submarine, and interfere with location activity by enemy anti-submarine aircraft . . . '[7]

A Thetis 2c buoy was stowed in three pieces in either the forward or after torpedo compartments, and the sections were brought on deck for assembly. The sections were: a 5-metre-long wooden pole to which were attached a cluster of thin metal dipoles at 50cm intervals; a rectangular float of cork or composition material, approximately 65cm on each side and 15cm deep; and a steel tube 5cm in diameter and five metres long. The metal dipoles were effective against the metric frequency of the ASV radar. (Post-war tests by the British showed it to be ineffective against the higher frequency H2S.) Launching a Thetis buoy involved assembling the pieces, the wooden pole and steel tube being attached to opposite sides of the float and throwing the buoy overboard. The buoy would float with the wooden pole held upright by the counterweight of the steel pole. Once launched, the buoy would float indefinitely. It would move very little from the position where it was launched, being relatively uneffected by wind, tide or ocean current. The intent was to seed the Bay of Biscay with enough buoys to confuse Allied radars. Each boat passing through the Bay was to launch buoys each time it surfaced. In general, the quality of radar return from a Thetis buoy was less like a U-boat than that from an Aphrodite, but the long-term advantages of the permanent decoy over the short-lived Aphrodite led to the decision to deploy Thetis buoys in large quantities.[8]

Deployment of Thetis buoys began only three days after BdU's order:

> 'From 11 January, *U267* is laying Thetis 2c decoy buoys in the Bay of Biscay as far as 12°W, in order to interfere with enemy location. Laying will be continued by other U-boats.'[9]

and continued at least until the end of April 1944.[10]

Thetis buoys proved to be effective in operational use:

> ' ... numerous reports of radar locations followed by cancelled position are transmitted from areas where there are no U-boats but possibly Thetis buoys. Confirmation of the effectiveness of Thetis buoys.'[11]

The obvious disadvantage of this approach was the fact that as the enemy learned the position of these permanent radar decoys, they gradually learned which ones to ignore. There was no way the Germans could lay enough buoys to make passage of the Bay of Biscay really safe. Long before enough buoys could be laid to affect seriously the ability of the enemy to find U-boats in the Bay, the dominance of RAF airpower had become so complete in the Bay that U-boats were forced to remain submerged in order to survive.

1. KTB, 15 June 1943.
2. KTB, 5 August 1943.
3. KTB, 5 September 1943.
4. KTB, 15 January 1944.
5. EvK and WB.
6. KTB, 20 March 1944, Admonitory Radio Message No 95.
7. KTB, 8 June 1944. This was part of an additional report to the War Diary detailing enemy ASW activities and BdU's responses.
8. KTB, 11 January 1944.
9. KTB, 11 January 1944.
10. KTB, 22 April 1944. '*U672* on return passage laid remaining Thetis buoys roughly between AL 97 and BE 52, and *U267* between BD 61 and 69.' These map co-ordinates identified areas of the North Atlantic due west of the Bay of Biscay around 20° W (south of Iceland).
11. KTB, 1 May 1945, Appendix 1.

Anti-Sonar Coatings

While radars only became a serious threat to U-boats in 1941, sonar was a clear and present danger from the beginning of the war. Nevertheless, it wasn't until April 1940 that BdU was able to convince his superiors that the search for sonar countermeasures should begin.[1] That search led to experimentation with a coating to be applied to the exterior of U-boats that would, at least partially, defeat the enemy's sound detection systems by absorbing sonar impulses. The Germans began experimenting with a system of textured synthetic rubber (Oppanol) panels known as Alberich. The intent was to cover the entire outer surface of a U-boat with 4mm thick Alberich panels.

The experiments began in 1940 when the tiny *U11* was coated with Alberich panels. Tests on *U11* showed that at best Alberich reduced sonar pulse reflectance by 15 per cent at periscope depth, with the percentage of absorption varying with the depth, temperature and salinity of the water, but generally decreasing with depth. Despite these somewhat disappointing findings, the tests continued in 1941 with the covering of *U67*, a Type IXC assigned to training duties. Tests on this boat had mixed results. Any benefits gained from the Alberich panels were offset by the noise generated by Oppanol panels coming loose as the U-boat moved through the water. In a trial run between Norway and France, *U67* lost 60 per cent of her Alberich panels. (The adhesion of the Alberich panels would remain a problem throughout the programme. Unlike the small area of the snorkel head that was covered by anti-radar coatings, Alberich had to cover the entire boat in order to be effective.) Trials continued on *U67* and on *UD4* (ex-*O26*) but were eventually discontinued due to the inability to overcome the adhesion problems.

The introduction of the snorkel in 1944 revived interest in Alberich, since snorkelling boats were forced to remain at periscope depth, where both sonar and Alberich were most effective. *U480*, a Type VIIC, was the first operational boat to be given a coating of Alberich panels. On its first patrol with Alberich, in August 1944, *U480* reported that the panels seemed to aid in eluding sonar location.[2] Nevertheless, the difficulty in manufacturing and applying Alberich panels was such that few further Type VIIs are known to have been so modified.

One such boat was *U1105*, which surrendered to the British at the end of the war. This boat was tested by the Royal Navy before being scuttled.

They found that adhesion of the Alberich panels remained a problem. Despite the attention of scientists during a nine-day dockyard period, they had no better success bonding the panels to the hull. They found that the textured coating decreased the speed of the boat by about 1½ knots.

1. KTB, 30 April 1940. 'BdU emphasized that the development of a countermeasure to ASDIC, which has already been stated in peacetime to be a most urgent requirement, was essential to the success of future U-boat warfare. BdU again requested that the best sonic technicians, chemists and physicists be set to evolve a countermeasure. CinC issued orders accordingly.'
2. KTB, 11 September 1944. The actual report was cryptic: 'Alberich best method'.

Anti-Sonar Decoys

Easily the most effective of the various countermeasures was the sonar decoy known as Bold (and known to the British as the SBT – submarine bubble target). As the British name for Bold implied, this decoy operated by creating a mass of bubbles underwater which was intended to simulate the sonar echo of a U-boat.

Bold canisters were launched from inside the U-boat from a special ejector tube located in the after torpedo compartment.[1] Like the larger torpedo tubes, the Bold ejector had inner and outer doors allowing the tube to be re-loaded from the inside. Each Bold canister contained 370 grams of a compound of calcium and zinc, designed to break down sea water, producing hydrogen bubbles. This composition was packed into a wire mesh bag which in turn was fitted within a steel or aluminum cup. The cup was covered by a separate waterproof cap. A hydro static valve in the cap controlled the entry of water and permitted the hydrogen gas generated by the interaction of sea water with the chemicals in the cup to escape. As long as the valve stayed open, the gas generation would cause the canister to rise in the water. When the gas pressure inside the cup built up to match the pressure of the water outside, the valve would be forced closed until the canister sank to a deeper depth. By this means the generation of bubbles continued for about 25 minutes at a relatively steady depth.

The size of the bubble mass generated by a Bold canister was very much dependent on the depth at which it was launched. It was discovered that Bold worked better at shallower depths. At depths down to 100 metres, the bubble mass would first appear after about five minutes and reach its maximum after 15 minutes. At greater depths, the bubbles took longer to appear and made a smaller mass. At 200 metres, the bubble mass took more than ten minutes to appear and there was a good chance that the bubble mass would be too small to cause a sonar echo.[2]

The mass of bubbles generated by a Bold canister launched at the correct depth did generate a sonar echo very similar to a U-boat's, and when Bold was first introduced it was extremely successful in deceiving sonar operators. As Allied escorts gained experience with Bold, the stationary character of the bubble mass tended to give away the decoy to experienced sonarmen.[3]

There were two other charges for the Bold system, besides the chemical pill, which are reported to have been used by the Germans. One was a miniature electric torpedo which contained only a battery and an electric motor. It had a 3-bladed propeller at the end to simulate the sounds made by a U-boat travelling on electric drive underwater. It would travel in a small circle until its battery was exhausted and then sink. By British report, it simulated the sounds of a U-boat reasonably well and could be distinguished from the real thing only in calm seas. The other decoy charge was an oil canister which created a slick on the surface intended to simulate that left by a sinking U-boat.

1. The Bold ejector tube was known to U-boatmen on Type VIIs as Rohr 6 (Torpedo Tube 6) or as the *Pillenwerfer* (pill-thrower).
2. KTB, 26 February 1944.
3. Late war Allied sonars had a doppler capability which could not only give the bearing and range of an underwater contact but also its movement relative to the sonar. Such a doppler sonar would discriminate easily between a decoy and a real contact.

Glossary

AK (*Äußerste Kraft*)	Flank Speed. There was also the unofficial *Zweimal AK* (twice flank speed) reserved for emergencies.
Aphrodite	Balloon from which were suspended metal foil strips for the purpose of decoying radar. Called RDB (Radar Decoy Balloon) by the British.
ASDIC (Sonar)	British WWI Allied Submarine Detection and Investigation Committee, and the sound location device developed by that organization.
ASV (Anti-Surface Vessel)	Radar carried by British aircraft for detection of surface targets, originally in the 1.4 metre band, later, as Mk III model, in 9.7cm band.
AZ (*Aufschlagzündung*)	Contact detonation (of torpedoes or mines).
B-Dienst	Radio Intelligence Service.
Balkon-Gerät	Late-war echo location (passive sonar) device.
Bold	Sonar deception decoy. Called SBT (Submarine Bubble Target) by the British.
Borkum	Code-name for FuMB 10.
BdU (*Befehlshabers der Uboote*)	Commander in Chief, Submarines/Flag Officer, U-boats.
DT-*Gerät (Dezimeter-Teknik*)	Original series of German naval radars, generally in 80cm band.
Eel (Ger: *Aal*)	Slang for torpedoes.
Falke (Eng: falcon)	Early acoustic torpedo (T4).
FaT (*Flächenabsuchender Torpedo*)	Early anti-convoy torpedo (T1 FaT I, T3 FaT II & T3a FaT II).
FdU (*Führer der Uboote*)	Commanding Officer, Submarines. C-in-C Submarines prior to creation of BdU position in 1939. After that, regional COs reporting to BdU.
Flak (*Flugzeug-abwehrkanone*)	Anti-aircraft gun.
Fliege (Eng: fly)	Code-name of FuMB 24.
FuMB (*Funkmessbeobachter*)	Radar detector.
FuMO (*Funkmessortungs Gerät*)	Radar.
GEMA (*Gesellschaft für Elektro-akustische und Mechanische Apparate*)	Manufacturer of the FuMO 29 & 30 radars.
GHG (*Gruppenhörchgerät*)	Fixed hydrophone array, set in semi-circle around forward dive plane.
Grandin (cf. Metox)	Alternate name for Metox (actually name of one of the manufacturers, in Paris, of FuMB 1).
GW (Germania Werft)	Shipyard and diesel manufacturer, owned by Krupp.
Hagenuk (cf. *Wanz*)	Alternate name for *Wanz* (actually name of manufacturer, in Kiel, of *Wanz*).
IWO	First Officer.
IIWO	Second Officer.
KDB (*Kristalldrehbasis Gerät*)	Rotating hydrophone array.
KL (*Kapitänleutnant*)	Rank equivalent to LT (US). Generally shortened to 'Kaleu' or 'Kaleunt' in daily use. The most common rank for COs of Type VII U-boats.
KK (*Korvettenkapitän*)	Rank equivalent to LCDR (US).
KTB (*Kriegstagebuch*)	War diary, log.
LI (*Leitender Ingenieur*)	Engineering Officer.

Lords, see Pairs	
LuT (*Lagenunabhängiger Torpedo*)	Later anti-convoy torpedo (T1 LuT I, T1 LuT II, T3a LuT I & T3a LuT II).
MAN (*Maschinenfabrik Augsburg Nürnburg*)	Diesel manufacturer.
Metox (cf. Grandin)	Manufacturer of FuMB 1.
Mücke (Eng: gnat)	Code-name of FuMB 25.
MZ (*Magnetischerzündung*)	Magnetic detonation (of torpedoes or mines).
Naxos	Code-name for FuMB 7 radar detector.
Obersteuermann	Quartermaster of the boat. Ranking CPO in a U-boat.
OKM (*Oberkommando der Marine*)	Naval command.
OL z.S. (*Oberleutnant zur See*)	Rank equivalent to LTjg (US). Occasionally given command of Type VII U-boats.
Pairs (Eng: Lords)	Slang for U-boat ratings.
Pi	Abbreviation of *Pistole*, the detonator of a torpedo.
S-Gerät (*Such Gerät*)	Active sonar apparatus.
SKL (*Seekriegsleitung*)	Naval high command.
SMA (*Schachtmine A*)	Shaft Mine A.
Smut (also: *Smutje* or *Kombüse*)	Ship's cook.
Snort	Slang for snorkel.
Thetis	Radar decoy buoy.
TM (*Torpedomine*)	Torpedo tube mine. Came in TMA, TMB & TMC models.
Tunis	Code-name for FuMB 26.
TVA (*Torpedoversuchsanstalt*)	Torpedo Experimental Establishment. These were located at Gotenhafen and Eckernförde.
UZO (*Überwasserzieloptik*)	Surface torpedo and gun attack sight.
Wabo (*Wasserbomb*)	Depth-charge.
Wanz (cf. *Hagenuk*)	Contraction of *Wellenanzeiger*. Popular name of FuMB 9.
Zaunkönig (Eng: wren)	Later acoustic torpedo (T5 & T5a – also T11 Zaunkönig II).

Appendices

▲ *U29*, a Type VIIA, is painted in the earliest of U-boat camouflage schemes, dark grey hull and light grey tower. The individual boat number is painted in dark grey. This was the boat with which Schuhart sank the aircraft carrier HMS *Courageous* in the early days of the war. (SFL)

▶ Another Type VIIA, this time *U33*, in the overall dark grey scheme adopted shortly before the war. Note the netcutter on the bow, a very rare feature seen only on a few boats during the pre-war period. (SFL)

▶ **An unidentified Type VIIC in the Atlantic. A dark grey diamond shape has been outlined on the light grey background of the tower. Most of the hull is painted dark grey, with the lower point of the light grey interior of the diamond carried down on to the hull. (NARA)**

Appendix A: General Appearance

For the most part, Type VII U-boats were grey. The official wartime colour for Kriegsmarine warships was standard naval light grey (*schiffstarnfarbe hellgrau* – 31_1). All external vertical surfaces of U-boats down to the normal trim waterline were to be painted this colour, in reality a medium grey of very neutral tone. The upper surfaces of the saddle tanks and the band on the boat's side between normal trim waterline and lightest trim waterline were painted dark grey (*schiffstarnfarbe dunkelgrau* – 31_2). Those horizontal deck surfaces that were intended to be walked on were made of wood which was painted a dark grey deck compound (*deckfarbe dunkelgrau für außen* – 51). The extreme forward and after sections of the deck were painted standard light grey. The underbody was supposed to have been painted with a red antifouling compound (*schiffsbodenfarbe* S. B. I *rot* – 22a) but seems just as often to have been covered with the dark grey waterline colour.

This basic colour scheme had gone through several evolutions before the war. The first U-boats to be launched in 1935 were painted overall dark grey on their hull, with the sides of the conning tower painted light grey. The U-boat's number was painted on the side of the tower in dark grey in numerals approximately 1.5 metres tall. This scheme evolved over the next few years to one of overall light grey and then, in about 1938, to one of overall dark grey. U-boats painted in this scheme carried their hull number in white on the tower side. This was the standard scheme at the outbreak of war. The only concession to the hostilities was the painting over of the large white hull number. The standard wartime scheme of light and dark grey was gradually implemented as boats were repainted and new ones joined the fleet during the winter of 1939 and the spring of 1940.

In general, after the beginning of the war, U-boats rarely sported an evenly applied fresh coat of paint. Unlike the Kriegsmarine's surface fleet, which spent the bulk of its time in harbour, the U-boat fleet was heavily employed. Boats spent the minimal time in port necessary for repairs, reprovisioning and resting the crew, and there was little time for any but the most needed repainting. Unless they were fresh from refit, operational U-boats were usually streaked with soot and rust, and patchy with paint applied at various times in the past.

Camouflage

U-boats, of all boats, seemed to require nothing more than the basic wartime coat of paint, and the regulations never called for anything more than this. The reasons were simple. U-boats had neither the space to store paint nor the spare time and crew labour to maintain camouflage. Further, a U-boat's best visual protection was diving. In the North Atlantic, the Type VII U-boat's primary theatre of operations, a boat at any depth much below periscope depth could not be spotted, even from the air. Nevertheless the Kriegsmarine loved to invent elaborate camouflage patterns for its ships and U-boats were no exception. While by far the bulk of Type VII U-boats were never painted anything but the basic colours and pattern;[1] a sufficient number were camouflaged to merit mention.

Camouflage could be seen on a few boats at the outbreak of war. The most famous was that carried by *U25*. This involved at least two additional colours in jagged stripes and panels and a large bright red-and-white shark's mouth on the front of the tower. This early flamboyance died down quickly and camouflage schemes disappeared during the hard winter of 1939–40, only to re-appear on a small number of boats operating from the French Atlantic ports during 1940. These schemes were generally composed of various patterns of dark grey bands or shapes painted over the basic light grey. On very rare occasions, white stripes were used as well. In general the camouflage was restricted to the tower area, though there were instances of patterns extending over the whole boat.

Camouflage schemes for Type VII U-boats showed up in some seas far more than others. There were even standard patterns for some theatres of operation. The schemes found on the Atlantic boats were generally dazzle-type schemes that used large shapes or stripes in the hope of disrupting visual rangefinding. In the Mediterranean, a pattern of grey 'splotches', sometimes smoothly contoured, some times jagged in shape, applied at regular intervals over the entire boat, was nearly standard. This scheme was intended more as protection from identification by aircraft after the boat had submerged. The waters of the Mediterranean, being far clearer than the Atlantic, allowed boats to be seen from the air at a much greater depth. A U-boat at periscope depth could be clearly seen from the air in daylight. The pattern of splotches of dark paint was supposed to break up the boat's shape sufficiently to prevent detection from the air when at periscope depth. Boats operating out of Norway frequently had the upper half of the tower, above the lower spray deflector, painted white. This was intended to allow the boat to blend in better with the sea mists and fogs which often hang close to the surface of the water in high latitudes.

Whatever the intent, the use of camouflage gradually died out during 1943, as boats increasingly found themselves forced to spend most of a patrol submerged.

Below left: A closeup of the tower of *U136* (Kapitänleutnant Zimmermann) passing through the entrance channel of St-Nazaire harbour on return from patrol. The CO, in his typically beaten-up white cap, rests his arm on the brace for the jumper cables. An angular stripe of dark grey rises up to the edge of the tower. The boat's insignia, a lobster, is painted on the front of the tower. (NARA)

▼ A crewman of *U136* holds three large bouquets. Greenery of all kinds was a traditional part of the greetings ceremony for a returning boat. Note the lobster pin on his cap, reproducing the ship's insignia. (NARA)

▶ **Having passed through the entrance, *U136* manoeuvres into Berth 11 in the reinforced concrete U-boat shelter at St-Nazaire. The angular dark grey stripe seen on the boat's tower clearly extends down the side of the hull to the waterline. (NARA)**

▼ **A Type VII U-boat manoeuvres near a pair of docked U-boats at an unidentified port. The boats in the foreground, a Type VII and a Type IX, are painted strictly according to regulations. Note the two-tone appearance of the deck. The Type VII in the background has a camouflage stripe of dark grey across its tower.**

◀ One of the best-known U-boat commanders to survive the war was Adalbert Schnee. Before he went on to serve on Dönitz's staff and marry one of his daughters, he cut his teeth as CO of *U201*, seen here at Brest, 21 May 1942. The camouflage of wavy grey stripes is unusual in being evenly applied along the length of the boat and in being sprayed on with feathered edges, rather than in the more normal hard-edge, straight-line style. The snowman was a play on Schnee's name, which in English is 'snow'. (NARA)

▼ *U660* sinking in the Atlantic on 12 November 1942. The crew is standing calmly on deck prior to abandoning ship. The camouflage is unusual in employing a white stripe on the tower. The use of colours other than grey was very rare. (via Ken MacPherson)

▲ An even more unusual variant on the same theme. *U458* sports a white stripe bordered in dark grey or, possibly, black. The stripe seems to mimic the angular nature of the seagull insignia. (SFL)

Above right: *U596*, seen coming into port at La Spezia, clearly displays the even pattern of dark grey splotches typical of boats serving in the Mediterranean.

▶ *U83*, a late Type VIIB, docks at La Spezia in February 1942. She too shows an even pattern of dark grey splotches. These have ragged edges in a further attempt to break up the boat's shape.

◄ **Commanded by Oberleutnant zur See Lührs, *U453* is greeted at Pola later in the war. She carries a variant on the Mediterranean camouflage scheme, large, irregular, but smoothly outlined patches of dark grey. This photograph must date from mid-1943 or later, judging by the presence of a 2cm *Flakvierling* on the extended *Wintergarten*.**

◄ **After participating in the successful attack on convoy PQ17, *U251* returns to Narvik. Like many boats that operated out of Norwegian bases, she has the upper section of her tower painted white to blend in better with the pale horizon common in Arctic waters.**

Insignia

While most Type VII U-boats were painted to look alike, they were almost universally emblazoned with boat's insignia (*Bootswappen*) on the side of the tower. These were never officially authorized, but were universally tolerated by the U-boat command. In general, they were considered desirable because they served as a source of pride and self-identification for crews. They frequently gave some individuality to boats that otherwise looked almost identical. So popular were these insignia that many crews had metal replicas made and fastened them to their field caps. So pervasive were the insignia that a boat without one was considered odd. One veteran recalled:

> 'We didn't have an insignia on our boat. That had something to do with our commander. He was very low in the estimation of our crew. He was a kind of dapper man and he didn't extend himself in the slightest. He didn't want an insignia. We had all kinds of tries. Our crew had some very nice guys. They came up with a few ideas. I don't know why, but he always turned them down. After all, it was the commander's prerogative.
>
> If he had been a smart man, he would have put an insignia on. It gives so much spirit and morale. The whole U-boat spirit was made up of little things which came together to support that spirit.'[2]

U-boat flotillas also had insignia and these were occasionally painted on boats. This was sometimes carried in the place of an individual boat's insignia; more often, it was in addition to the individual insignia. Individual boat's insignia were inspired by a variety of sources. These included:

Civic heraldry. A large number of German cities or towns sponsored U-boats, contributing monies to their construction and taking up periodic collections of food and clothing for the crew. These boats often had the town's crest painted or mounted on the tower. It was not unusual for these boats to have another, more personal, insignia applied as well.

Class symbols. Graduating classes from the *Kriegsmarine*'s Naval Academy would chose insignia representing the class. If a boat's commander was such a graduate, it was common for his class insignia to become the boat's. Examples included: 1936 – Olympic Rings; 1937a – crossed daggers; 1937b – upright dagger through a wedding ring; 1939b – a shield with a wheel, gallows and shark, etc. Graduates of the merchant marine academy often used a compass rose as an insignia.

Patriotic imagery. Any number of patriotic graffiti became boats' insignia. They generally showed Churchill or the British bulldog getting the chop in one way or another.

Folklore. German folklore provided some of the better-known insignia, including the famous wooden-eyed pastor

▶ **Four Type VII U-boats of 7. Ubootsflotille are docked at St-Nazaire in the entrance channel. All four boats carry the snorting bull flotilla insignia on their tower sides. (SFL)**

◀ **The first and most famous of personal insignia, which later became the first and most famous of flotilla insignia, was the snorting bull adopted by Günther Prien's *U47*. This closeup of *U47*'s tower shows the insignia painted just under the edge of the tower. Kapitäuleutnant Prien stands to the right. His IWO, Oberleutnant zur See Endrass, who went on to become an ace in his own right, stands to the left. It was Endrass who thought up the snorting bull emblem. (NARA)**

who was ever on the lookout for his unfaithful wife's lovers.

Good luck signs. Horseshoes and other signs supposed to bring good luck were a natural choice for boat's insignia. Otto Kretschmer's *U99* went so far as to weld horseshoes to the tower. The element of luck in a boat's survival was much on the mind of some commanders. However, *U48*, the most successful boat of the war, used exactly the opposite approach. Its insignia was a black cat 'times three'.

Personal. All sorts of personal references, play on words, etc., formed the basis of a large number of insignia. Typical of these was the snowman insignia of Schnee's *U201*.

In addition to insignia, boats in the training flotillas carried tactical signs. These were a variety of geometric symbols, often in combination. This symbol set included squares, rhomboids, parallelograms and triangles. They were most often painted on in white, but sometimes included other colours. Boats permanently assigned to the training flotillas, as opposed to new boats just working-up on their way to the front, often had a 1m-high yellow band painted around the tower. As these training boats were mainly combat veterans, they often retained the insignia that had been painted on during their time at the front, making them very colourful indeed.

1. The U-boat survivors interviewed by this author all agreed that their boats were painted nothing but standard grey.
2. WB. He was describing *U534*.

◀ This combination of insignia could be confusing without some explanation, because along with the snorting bull of 7th Flotilla is the sawfish insignia of the 9th Flotilla based at Brest. The answer lies in the identity of the boat. This is *U96*, seen in the entrance channel at St-Nazaire. She was part of 7th Flotilla and thus wears the snorting bull. She was commanded at this time by Lehmann-Willenbrock, who went on to take over the 9th Flotilla, taking his personal sign, the sawfish, with him. Buchheim, in his novel *The Boat*, fictionalizes two patrols he observed in *U96*. (NARA)

◀ Another view of *U201*, 'Adi' Schnee's boat. On the forward part of the tower is the crest of Remscheid, indicating that this boat was sponsored by that city. Schnee himself sits on the edge of the tower at the right. This photograph predates the photographs of *U201* on pages 142 and 150, as can be determined by the early style spray deflector without the extended flange that became standard. Note the considerable verbiage painted on the tower in dark grey. (NARA)

▶ Another boat from the same series of early Type VIICs built at Germania Werft, *U203*, has the crest of Essen attached to its tower. Most of the boats in the series of twelve boats following *U201* were sponsored by cities. The crew of *U203* enjoys a rare moment of good weather and relaxation, except for the lookouts who still must scan the horizon. (NARA)

▶ *U203* flies a home-made pennant from the commander's jackstaff. The same crest seen in the previous view is shown along with the letters MÜBU, which are a contraction of the commander's name, Mützelburg. The commissioning pennant hangs in front of Mützelburg's.

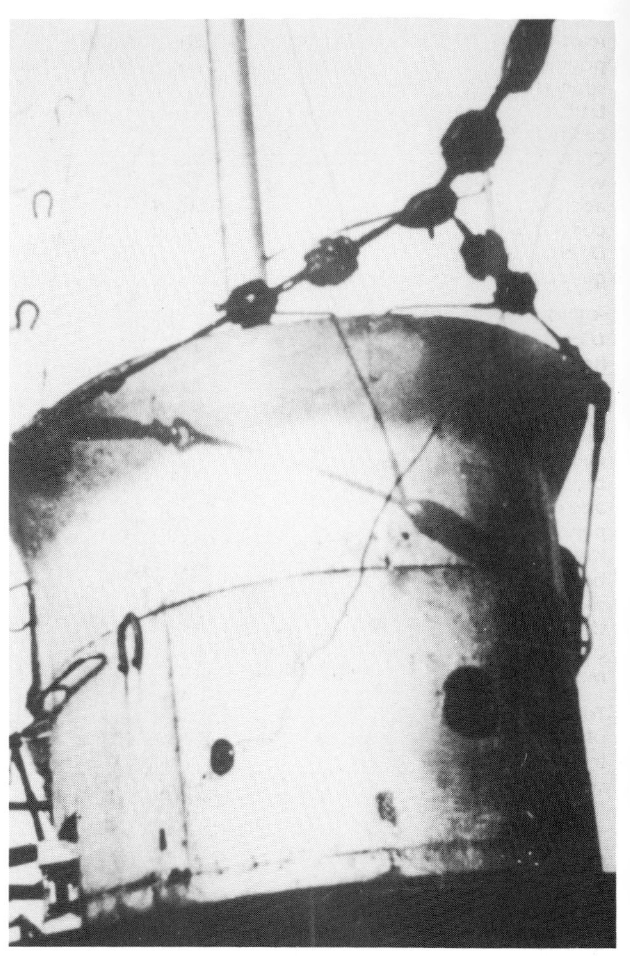

Above left: The insignia of *U52* was the Naval Academy class symbol of its commander, Kapitänleutnant Barten. His class was 37b. Its symbol was the upright dagger through a wedding ring. The swastika was part of the class symbol. Its presence here is one of the very rare instances of such iconography showing up on a U-boat. (SFL)

◀ Another famous boat, *U333*, pulls into La Rochelle after a close encounter with a target off Florida. The insignia of three small white fish, certainly must have something to do with the boat's number. It was probably inspired, at

least in part, by a popular American song of the day, 'Three Little Fishes'. *U333*'s commander, 'Ali' Cremer, ended the war, almost by accident, as the commander of Dönitz's headquarters guard unit. (NARA)

◀ Otto Kretschmer's *U99* was known as the horseshoe boat. At Kretschmer's insistence, that good luck symbol was used everywhere it could be, on the tower side and on the victory pennants. Kretschmer's luck held, but his boat's didn't. He lived out the war in a POW camp. *U99* was sunk in March 1941. (SFL)

Top right: The tower of *U34* shows another interesting combination of insignia. *U34* was a Type VIIA which was relegated to training duties late in 1940. While still a combat boat, she acquired the patriotic insignia still seen on the tower, a snorting elephant stomping on the head of Winston Churchill. As a training boat, it acquired the black-and-white checkerboard tactical sign.

▶ *U333*, in the photograph opposite flies triangular pennants from its attack periscope, one for each ship it sank. This was the traditional way to show off a U-boat's successes. Each pennant bore the estimated tonnage of the victim. Here, a crewman in an unidentified boat paints the numbers on a string of pennants as his boat returns from a successful patrol. (NARA)

◄ *U201* again, on yet a third occasion. This view shows Schnee's boat bedecked with oakleaves upon return from another successful patrol, sometime in 1942. The number of pennants is one indication of the success enjoyed by this boat. The life-preserver from one of its victims (HMS *Laertes*) hanging in front of the tower is another. For his cumulative successes, Schnee was awarded the Oakleaves to the Knight's Cross upon his return. The snowman also received the same honour. (NARA)

◄ One of the most elaborate of boat insignias was the Nordic dragon motif painted on the tower of Von Bülow's *U404*, seen at St-Nazaire on 14 July 1942. The insignia has obviously been recently painted. It shows only minor wear. The undercoat of light grey shows more signs of the wear on paint caused by the North Atlantic. (NARA)

Appendix B: Admiral Dönitz

No story of German U-boats in the Second World War would be complete without an account of the life of *Grossadmiral* Karl Dönitz. He was, after all, the driving force behind the development of the U-boat arm prior to and during the war. The Type VII U-boat was the boat he wanted in order to fight that war. The U-boats' successes were the direct result of his tactical concepts. The U-boats' defeat was equally due to failures on his part.

In 1918, Karl Dönitz was a 27-year-old *Oberleutnant zur See.* He had joined the Imperial Navy as a cadet in 1910 and, as a *Leutnant zur See*, was assigned duty in the light cruiser *Breslau* in 1913. He served in that ship until her internment in Turkey. SMS *Breslau* became the Turkish *Midilli* and Dönitz, with the rest of the original German crew, served on, nominally in the Turkish Navy. Distinguishing himself during a number of Black Sea operations, he was promoted to *Oberleutnant zur See* in 1915. In December of the following year he requested transfer back to Germany and to the U-boat arm. He served his apprenticeship as watch officer in *U39* under the second highest-rated commander in the war. *Kapitänleutnant* Walter Forstmann. (Forstmann was the second most successful of U-boat commanders in either world war, second only to the legendary Lothar von Arnauld de la Perrière, and Forstmann's *U39* was the second most successful U-boat of either war, after von Arnauld's *U35*, in terms of both number of ships sunk and tonnage.) Dönitz's first command was the small minelayer *UC25*, which he took over in the Mediterranean on 1 March 1918. Later, he took command of *UB68*, a UBIII-type sea-going U-boat operating out of Pola.

At 0100 on 4 October 1918, off the southern coast of Sicily, he nosed *UB68* in towards a Malta-bound convoy and sank a straggling freighter before he was forced to dive by the escort. He resurfaced later and managed to catch up with the convoy again at dawn. He had just taken the boat to periscope depth in order to attack once more, when the boat took a sudden uncontrolled plunge which was only halted at 100 metres, well beyond the UBIII's rated depth of 75 metres. *UB68* popped to the surface in the midst of the convoy and came under fire from all sides. With no more compressed air in his tanks, he couldn't dive again. With no chance of fighting his way free, Dönitz took the only remaining course of action, ordering his crew to abandon ship after opening the seacocks. He was taken into captivity barely a month before his country followed his example and surrendered to the inevitable.

Oberleutnant zur See Dönitz spent the next eight months in captivity, returning to a devastated, defeated Germany in July 1919. He was at a loss as to what to do. The Navy had been his life and U-boats his main passion. So, when he was offered a commission in the tiny post-war Reichsmarine by his former commander in the Mediterranean, he jumped at the chance. His only condition was that, when the Germans were again permitted to possess U-boats, he would be given one to command.

Dönitz stayed in the *Reichsmarine* and thrived. By 1935, he had risen to the rank of *Fregattenkapitän* and was in command of the light cruiser *Emden*. When he brought her back home from her annual overseas cruise in June of that year, he requested that he be continued in that command for another year. Instead, Admiral Raeder selected Dönitz to take over direction of the newly revealed U-boat arm of the *Reichsmarine.* Dönitz had had nothing to do with the convoluted history of clandestine U-boat development dating back to the early 1920s. But the passing years had been spent thinking long and hard about why the promise of victory had slipped away in 1918 and what could be done differently or better should the opportunity ever come again. Now it seemed, he would get a chance to try out his ideas.

▶ Vizeadmiral Dönitz receives a report from his son-in-law, Adalbert 'Adi' Schnee. Dönitz held this rank between 1940 and 1942, while still BdU.

Dönitz was promoted to Kapitän z.S. and, on 27 September 1935, he formally commissioned the First U-boat Flotilla (Flottille Weddigen). His official position, besides being CO of Flottille Weddigen, was FdU (*Führer der Uboote*), giving him effective command of U-boat training and tactical development. His position and rank, however, gave him very little influence in the decision-making of the Kriegsmarine and no control over U-boat design or construction. Nevertheless, he used his persuasive powers to best advantage and won as many battles as he lost. He wanted fewer Type II boats than were actually built and more Type VIIs. Most of all, he wanted more U-boats of any kind. But, he was able to control the desire of the surface ship oriented leadership of the Kriegsmarine to bind U-boats operationally to fleet movements and to build large fleet-type U-boats designed solely to support the surface fleet. By the time war broke out, in September 1939, he had built a U-boat force that was smaller than he knew he needed, but was one that reflected his thinking, trained to a fine edge of perfection and ready to wage a war by his precepts.

Dönitz was promoted to the rank of Konteradmiral soon after the outbreak of war and, more significantly, given the title of BdU (Befehishabers der Uboote – C-in-C, U-boats). The change in title represented a recognition by Raeder and the leadership of the Kriegsmarine that U-boat represented the only credible naval weapon Germany possessed. While Dönitz often failed to get his way in the early days of the war, his power and influence could only increase as the weapon he had forged moved from success to success. In September 1940 he was made Vizeadmiral and in March 1942 Admiral. On 30 January 1943, Raeder resigned after Hitler had ordered him to scrap the remaining capital ships the Kriegsmarine possessed in order to build more U-boats. Not too surprisingly, Dönitz succeeded him as Grossadmiral in command of the Kriegsmarine. Dönitz retained that position until, in the waning days of the war, he was named Hitler's successor as head of the German State. Virtually his only official act in that position was to accomplish the orderly surrender of the now utterly defeated German forces. At the end of the war, he is reported to have said to his

◀ Dönitz was promoted to Admiral's rank in 1942, retaining this rank and his position as BdU for less than a year before replacing Raeder as Grossadmiral. Here he is performing the duty he enjoyed he most, decorating his most successful commanders. In this case, he has just given the Knight's Cross to *U556*'s CO, Herbert 'Parsifal' Wohlfarth.

long-time friend and confidant Eberhard Godt, 'Now, I wish to hear no longer of the death of heroes.'[1]

Dönitz was attracted to the Nazi Party in 1930, together with many other young officers, because he saw the strong nationalism of the Nazis as a way back from the reduced circumstances in which Germany and, in particular her Navy, found herself. Nevertheless, he had no patience with doctrinaire thinking of any kind and resisted the Nazis' efforts to politicize the U-boat service.[2] This was known to the Allies, who included him in their list of major was criminals because of his obvious importance to the German war effort, but gave him by far the mildest sentence at Nuremberg because of the way he had conducted himself throughout the war.[3]

He had two sons. Both served in the Kriegsmarine during the war. Both were killed in action. Peter was lost in *U954*; Klaus in the S-boat *S141*.

After spending ten years in Spandau prison, Dönitz was released, still unrepentant, having twice fought wars which were lost for reasons that he believed were beyond his control. If the loyalty of the men who served under him is any measure of his worth, it must be said that he was revered by those whom he commanded, despite their appalling losses, until his death as an old man in a nation and world at peace.

1. 10th, p 360. Godt was Dönitz's 'God of Operations', the man responsible for putting his ideas into action.
2. Conduct, p iii. The Kriegsmarine was always the least political of the armed services of Nazi Germany. Unlike the Luftwaffe, which was created and led by the party, the Navy saw itself only as the legitimate successor to the Imperial Navy. In U-boats the standard naval salute was much more common than the Nazi salute, if any saluting was done at all. U-boat insignia almost never displayed Nazi iconography.
3. Dönitz was convicted of two war crimes: failure to rescind the 'Commando Order' which mandated that all enemies captured behind German lines were to be killed out of hand, and failure to prevent the employment of slave labour in shipyards.

▶ As the last head of state of the Third Reich, Dönitz presided over the collapse of Germany. Here, he is being taken into British custody at Flensburg on 23 May 1945. Behind him comes Albert Speer, Germany's resourceful Minister of Armaments. Speer and Dönitz were friends and mutual admirers; collectively they presented themselves as the voice of reason in a country descending into madness.

Appendix C: Hull Number Table

The following table lists the series of hull numbers (U-numbers) of Type VII U-boats that were known to have been contracted for by the Kriegsmarine. For each series of consecutive hull numbers, the following information is provided: the sub-type, the start and end numbers of the series, the number of boats from that series that were planned, started (for which materials were actually ordered), laid down (on which assembly had begun on a building slip) and completed (were turned over to the Kriegsmarine), the shipyard at which that series was to be built and any appropriate comments. At the end, the totals for each building stage are given and then broken down by sub-type.

Type	Start-#	End-#	Planned	Started	Laid Down	Completed	Yard	Notes
A	27	32	6	6	6	6	AG Weser	
A	33	36	4	4	4	4	GW	
B	45	55	11	11	11	11	GW	
C	69	72	4	4	4	4	GW	
B	73	76	4	4	4	4	Br-Vulkan	
C	77	82	6	6	6	6	Br-Vulkan	
B	83	87	5	5	5	5	Flender-werft	
C	88	92	5	5	5	5	Flender-werft	
C	93	98	6	6	6	6	GW	
B	99	102	4	4	4	4	GW	
C	132	136	5	5	5	5	Br-Vulkan	
C	201	212	12	12	12	12	GW	
D	213	218	6	6	6	6	GW	
C	221	232	12	12	12	12	GW	
C	235	250	16	16	16	16	GW	
C	251	291	41	41	41	41	Br-Vulkan	
C/41	292	300	9	9	9	9	Br-Vulkan	
C	301	316	16	16	16	16	Flender-werft	
C/41	317	330	14	14	13	13	Flender-werft	330 cancelled
C	331	349	19	19	19	19	Nordsee	
C	350	370	21	21	21	21	Flens-burger	
C	371	400	30	30	29	29	Howaldts	395 cancelled
C	401	430	30	30	30	30	Danziger	
C	431	450	20	20	20	20	Schichau	
C	451	458	8	8	8	8	DW Kiel	
C	465	486	22	22	22	21	DW Kiel	474 bombed after launch & never completed
C	551	650	100	100	100	100	B&V	
C	651	686	36	36	33	33	Howaldts	684–686 cancelled
C/41	687	698	12	0	0	0	Howaldts	Projected
C/42	699	700	2	0	0	0	Howaldts	Projected
C	701	722	22	22	22	22	Stülken Sohn	
C/41	723	730	8	8	0	0	Stülken Sohn	
C	731	750	20	20	20	20	Schichau	
C	751	782	32	32	29	27	ND W'haven	780–782 cancelled; 769–770 abandoned
C/41	783	790	8	8	1	1	ND W'haven	785 completed
C	821	824	4	4	2	2	Oder-werke	823 & 824 cancelled
C	825	828	4	4	4	4	Schichau	
C/41	829	840	12	12	2	2	Schichau	835 & 836 completed
C	901	902	2	2	1	1	Vulkan Stettin	902 cancelled
C	903	904	2	2	2	2	Flender-werft	
C	905	908	4	4	4	2	Stülken Sohn	906 & 908 abandoned
C/41	909	912	4	4	0	0	Stülken Sohn	All cancelled
C/42	913	920	8	6	0	0	Stülken Sohn	Projected & cancelled
C	921	930	10	10	10	10	Neptun	
C/41	931	936	6	6	0	0	Neptun	All cancelled
C/42	937	950	14	6	0	0	Neptun	Projected & cancelled
C	951	994	44	44	44	44	B&V	
C/41	995	1050	56	56	32	29	B&V	1026–1046 & 1048–1050 cancelled; 996, 1011 & 1012 abandoned
C	1051	1058	8	8	8	8	GW	
F	1059	1062	4	4	4	4	GW	
C	1063	1066	4	4	3	3	GW	1066 cancelled
C/42	1067	1080	14	14	0	0	GW	All cancelled
C/42	1093	1100	8	8	0	0	GW	All cancelled
C	1101	1106	6	6	6	6	Nordsee	
C/41	1107	1114	8	8	4	4	Nordsee	1111–1114 cancelled
C/42	1115	1130	16	9	0	0	Nordsee	Projected & cancelled
C	1131	1132	2	2	2	2	Howaldt	
C/41	1133	1146	14	14	0	0	Howaldt	All cancelled
C/42	1147	1160	14	8	0	0	Howaldt	Projected & cancelled
C	1161	1161	1	1	1	1	Danziger	
C/41	1162	1190	29	29	11	11	Danziger	1174 & 1176–1177 cancelled but completed as Russian
C	1191	1210	20	20	20	20	Schichau	
C/41	1211	1220	10	10	1	1	Schichau	1217 completed
C/41	1271	1285	15	15	9	9	Br-Vulkan	1280–1285 cancelled

Type	Start-#	End-#	Planned	Started	Laid Down	Completed	Yard	Notes
C/42	1286	1300	15	12	0	0	Br-Vulkan	Projected & cancelled
C/41	1301	1312	12	12	8	8	Flensburger	1309–1312 cancelled
C/42	1313	1330	18	6	0	0	Flensburger	Projected & cancelled
C/41	1331	1338	8	8	0	0	Flenderwerft	All cancelled
C/42	1339	1350	12	12	0	0	Flenderwerft	All cancelled
C	1351	1400	50	0	0	0	B&V	All projected
C/41	1401	1404	4	4	0	0	B&V	All cancelled
C/41	1417	1422	6	6	0	0	B&V	All cancelled
C/42	1423	1434	12	12	0	0	B&V	All cancelled
C/41	1435	1439	5	5	0	0	B&V	All cancelled
C/42	1440	1500	61	24	0	0	B&V	Projected & cancelled
C/41	1801	1804	4	4	0	0	AG Weser	All cancelled
C/42	1805	1822	18	18	0	0	AG Weser	All cancelled
C/41	1823	1900	78	6	0	0	AG Weser	Projected & cancelled
C/42	1901	2000	100	4	0	0	AG Weser	Projected & cancelled
C/42	2001	2100	100	4	0	0	AG Weser	Projected & cancelled
C/42	2101	2110	10	4	0	0	GW	Projected & cancelled
C/42	2301	2320	20	18	0	0	Schichau	Projected & cancelled; some maybe completed as Russian
Totals			1452	1041	717	709		
A			10	10	10	10		
B			24	24	24	24		
C			643	593	582	577		
C/41			323	239	91	88		
C/42			442	165	0	0		
D			6	6	6	6		
F			4	4	4	4		
Totals			1452	1041	717	709		

References

Primary Sources

The information in this book is based almost entirely on the study of primary records. Fortunately for a researcher into the history of U-boats, most of the official records of the Kriegsmarine survived the war. This may be largely attributed to the fact that Admiral Dönitz and his subordinates believed that they had fought an honourable war and therefore had no need or desire to hide their actions. Dönitz acted to preserve the records of the Kriegsmarine in general and of the U-boat service in particular, believing that history would judge him fairly. These records fell into British hands at the end of the war, because Dönitz and his staff had retreated to Flensburg in the far north of Germany, in the British sector of the front. Taken to London, the U-boat records were translated into English. There they were microfilmed by the US Navy between 1945 and 1947. After their analysis by ONI, the microfilms were declassified and handed over to the National Archives (now called NARA – National Archives & Records Administration) where they can be found today.

In 1985, the staff of the Modern Military Headquarters Branch, Military Archives Division at NARA produced a useful volume entitled *Records Relating to U-Boat Warfare, 1939–1945* (Library of Congress Cat. No. 58–9982), a partial subject index of the microfilmed U-boat records. These records are composed entirely of KTBs, including those of BdU, of regional and flotilla commands and of nearly all individual U-boats. This is the second in their series *Guides to the Microfilmed Records of the German Navy, 1850–1945*. As well as being an indispensable reference to the U-boat records held in the USA, this book serves as a handy synopsis of the careers of those U-boats for which records have survived.

Kriegstagebuch des BdU, Record Items PG 30247–30362, National Archives Microfilm Publication T1022, Record Group 242, NARA.

Dönitz, Karl, *The Conduct of the War at Sea*, Division of Naval Intelligence, Office of CNO, US Navy, Washington, DC, 15 January 1946.

US Naval Technical Mission in Europe, *The German Schnorchel*, Letter Report No. 113–45(S), 22 June 1945.

US Naval Technical Mission in Europe, *Anti-Radar Coatings*, Letter Report No. 10–45, 1 May 1945.

The U-Boat War in the Atlantic 1939–1945, Ministry of Defence, HMSO, London, 1989. This is a reproduction of the originally classified history of the U-boat war written by KK a.D. Günther Hessler immediately after the war at the Admiralty's request. Hessler was assisted in these efforts by Jürgen Rohwer.

Secondary Sources

Arena, Nino, *Il Radar: la guerra sui mari*, S.T.E.M.–MUCCHI, Modena, Italy, October 1976.

Crémer, Peter, *U-Boat Commander: A Periscope View of The Battle of the Atlantic*, Naval Institute Press, Annapolis, MD, 1984. Original English publication as *U333* by The Bodley Head Ltd. in 1984. Original German publication by Verlag Ullstein GmbH, Berlin, W. Germany in 1982.

Dönitz, Karl, *Memoirs: Ten Years and Twenty Days*, Greenhill Books, London, 1990. Originally published as *Zehn Jahre und Swanzig Tage* by Athenäum Verlag in 1958. The new edition has an Introduction and Afterword by Jürgen Rohwer.

Farago, Ladislas, *The Tenth Fleet*, Drum Books, New York, 1986. An excellent rendering of the Battle of the Atlantic from the American side.

Herzog, Bodo, *U-boote im Einsatz 1939–1945: Eine Bilddokumentation*, Podzun-Verlag, Dorheim, Germany, 1970.

Jung, Dieter, et al, *Anstriche und Tarnanstriche der deutschen Kriegsmarine*, Bernard & Graefe Verlag, Munich, Germany, 1977.

Frank, Wolfgang, *The Sea Wolves*, Holt, Rinehart & Winston, Inc., New York, 1955.

Friedman, Norman, *Naval Radar*, Naval Institute Press, Annapolis, MD, 1981.

Lenton, H.T., *German Submarines 1* and *German Submarines 2*, Doubleday & Co., In., Garden City, NY, 1967. Originally published in England by Macdonald & Co., Ltd., in 1965.

Preston, Anthony, *U-boats*, Arms & Armour Press, Ltd., London, England, 1978

Rohwer, Jürgen, *Axis Submarine Successes: 1939–1945*, Naval Institute Press, Annapolis, MD, 1983. Originally published as *Die U-Boote-Erfolge der Achsenmacht 1939–1945* by J. F. Lehmanns Verlag, Munich, Germany in 1958.

Rössler, Eberhard, *The U-boat: The evolution and technical history of German submarines*, Naval Institute Press, Annapolis, MD, 1989. Original English edition with the same title published by Arms & Armour Press, Ltd., London, England in 1981. Original publication as *Geschichte des deutschen Ubootbaus* by J. F. lehmanns Verlag, Munich,

Germany in 1975. This is the definitive technical history of U-boat development.
—*Die deutschen U-Boote und ihre Werften*, Bernard & Graefe Verlag, Munich, Germany, 1979.
—*Die Torpedos der deutschen U-Boote*, Koehlers Verlag, Herford, Germany, 1984.
Tarrant, V. E. *The U-Boat Offensive 1914–1945*, Arms & Armour Press, London, 1989.
United States Submarine Losses, World War II, Naval History Division, Office of CNO, US Navy, Washington, DC, 1963. Despite the title, this publication actually contains probably the most comprehensive list of U-boat losses available.
Watts, Anthony J., *Axis Submarines*, Arco Publishing Co., In., New York, NY, 1977. A volume in the Wrld War 2 Fact File series.

Index

Page numbers in italics refer to an illustration or caption on the indicated page.